MAKING SPACES

MAKING SPACES

Putting Psychoanalytic Thinking to Work

Edited by

Kate Cullen, Liz Bondi, Judith Fewell, Eileen Francis, and Molly Ludlam

Routledge
Taylor & Francis Group
LONDON AND NEW YORK

First published 2014 by Karnac Books Ltd.

Published 2019 by Routledge
2 Park Square, Milton Park, Abingdon, Oxon OX14 4RN
52 Vanderbilt Avenue, New York, NY 10017

First issued in hardback 2019

Routledge is an imprint of the Taylor & Francis Group, an informa business

British Library Cataloguing in Publication Data

A C.I.P. for this book is available from the British Library

ISBN 13: 978-0-367-10173-2 (hbk)
ISBN 13: 978-1-78049-165-3 (pbk)

Edited, designed and produced by The Studio Publishing Services Ltd
www.publishingservicesuk.co.uk
e-mail: studio@publishingservicesuk.co.uk

CONTENTS

PART II
MAKING SPACE TO LOVE

PART III
MAKING SPACE TO WORK

ACKNOWLEDGEMENTS

This volume grew out of work initiated in and by the Scottish Institute of Human Relations (SIHR). Our thanks go to Amanda Cornish and the Board of SIHR for enabling an initial idea to become a tangible reality. Special thanks are also due to Oliver Rathbone, Constance Govindin, and Rod Tweedy of Karnac Books for their unfailing helpfulness along the route to publication.

Many of this book's chapters draw on their authors' professional practice in clinical or other settings. We wish to express our appreciation to all those involved, including patients, clients, students, supervisees, course participants, members of SIHR, and other colleagues; each of them has made an indispensable contribution.

All the material illustrating professional practice accords with ethical requirements. A variety of different means have been used to protect sources. In some cases, permission to describe the work has been sought and granted, with presentations based directly on work with individuals or groups, with or without disguise, according to the basis of permission. In other cases, the material presented is based indirectly on professional experience, perhaps using composites in which elements of different cases are combined, or forms of distillation and fictionalisation. Whatever methods have been used to protect the identities of patients, clients, students, colleagues, and others, the intention is to draw on their stories respectfully, and with gratitude for the learning they have made possible.

The editors would also like to thank all the contributors, whose engagement and commitment brought this book to fruition. We owe particular thanks to Monica Lanyado for her generosity in providing the book's Foreword, to Antony Gormley for his kind permission to reproduce the image of *Exposure, 2010*, and to Richard Calvocoressi for his artistic advice and support.

ABOUT THE EDITORS AND CONTRIBUTORS

Lindy Barbour is a teaching fellow in counselling and psychotherapy at the University of Edinburgh. She trained as a psychodynamic counsellor at the Scottish Institute of Human Relations (SIHR) and has worked as a student counsellor in higher education. She is a published poet and is currently developing a course in creative practices, exploring the connections between poetry and psychotherapeutic practices.

Liz Bondi is Professor of Social Geography at the University of Edinburgh, where she contributes to professional education in counselling and psychotherapy, primarily at doctoral level. Liz began her academic career in human geography, which she continued while training part-time in counselling. After completing her training, she joined SIHR. Combining her academic background in human geography (and the social sciences more generally) with her interest in counselling and psychotherapy, she has led or contributed to a series of research projects about the cultural shaping of counselling and psychotherapy in Scotland. She also applies ideas from counselling and psychotherapy to the developing field of "emotional geographies". She is founding editor of the journal *Emotion, Space and Society* and author of numerous academic papers, as well as co-editor or co-author of several books. She is a COSCA-accredited counsellor who maintains a small practice in the voluntary sector.

Nicola Chadd is a psychoanalytic psychotherapist and consultant clinical psychologist in the Specialist Psychotherapy Service of the Tees, Esk and Wear Valleys NHS Foundation Trust. She trained with the North of England Association of Psychoanalytic Psychotherapists. After completing her training, she also joined the SIHR and the associated adult psychotherapy service. She has, for many years, been involved in teaching, training, and supervision, and currently contributes to the teaching on the Tavistock/Leeds Foundation Course in Psychoanalytic Psychotherapy, the Teesside Doctorate in Clinical Psychology, and the psychoanalytic psychotherapy trainings in Scotland and the North of England.

Kate Cullen is a psychoanalytic psychotherapist in private practice. Kate trained initially as a teacher and worked in secondary schools in the UK and in West Africa. Her work as a pastoral care teacher led her to train as a counselling psychologist and, later, as a psychoanalytic psychotherapist at the London Centre for Psychotherapy, now part of the British Psychotherapy Foundation. On returning to Scotland in 2006, Kate joined SIHR and worked in the adult psychoanalytic psychotherapy service. She has a private practice in Fife.

Judith Fewell is a psychoanalytic psychotherapist in private practice in Edinburgh and an Honorary Fellow at the University of Edinburgh. For many years, she worked as a freelance trainer within the statutory and voluntary sectors in Scotland, delivering workshops and courses based on psychodynamic thinking for professionals and volunteers while training as a psychoanalytic psychotherapist at the SIHR. She took up a post at the University of Edinburgh in counselling and psychotherapy, during the course of which she contributed to the development and delivery of the postgraduate Diploma in Counselling, supervised masters and doctoral students, and participated in the research programme. Judith has held a long-term interest in, and commitment to, the single case study as a legitimate form of research into psychotherapeutic practices and understandings. This has led her to explore and write about how personal and professional narratives of the psychotherapist can help illustrate and illuminate psychoanalytic theory and practice.

Eileen Francis worked as a speech and language therapist in health and education settings before becoming a lecturer in the Speech Unit at Moray House Institute of Education, Edinburgh. She later became a member of the department of professional and curriculum support studies and was appointed senior lecturer: enterprise. She is a former President of the Scottish Educational Research Association and chaired the Board of SIHR 2005–2010.

Joan Herrmann is a child and adolescent psychotherapist. Until her retirement in 2011, she was Head of Service for Adolescent Psychotherapy in the Glasgow NHS. Joan is currently the Lead for the Children and Young Persons Service (CYPS) in Human Development Scotland, and has a private practice. She was an active member of SIHR as a teacher and as a therapist. Joan began her career as an ethologist, and has a PhD from Rutgers University (USA). Her post-graduate research was in child development at Cambridge University and the Bethel Hospital in Norwich. She was a lecturer in Napier College for nine years, before her interest in clinical work led to her training in child psychotherapy at SIHR. She is a member of the Association of Child Psychotherapists, the British Psychoanalytic Council, the Scottish Association of Psychoanalytic Psychotherapists, and the Association for Psychodynamic Practice and Counselling in Organisational Settings (APPCIOS).

Debbie Hindle is a consultant child and adolescent psychotherapist. She trained at the Tavistock Clinic, where she received her doctorate through the University of East London in 2000. For over twenty years, she worked in a child and adolescent mental health service in Nottinghamshire, before moving to Scotland to head the Clinical Training in Child Psychotherapy at SIHR in Edinburgh. During this time, she also did clinical work in a specialist CAMHS service in Glasgow for children who were fostered or adopted. She has written extensively about her work with children, young people, and their families, including two co-edited books: *Personality Development: A Psychoanalytic Perspective*, and *The Emotional Experience of Adoption: A Psychoanalytic Perspective.* Currently, she supervises students in training, is co-editing a book, *Sibling Matters: A Psychoanalytic and Developmental Perspective,* and is dedicated to continuing to disseminate psychoanalytic thinking to a wide range of professionals through co-ordinating and running a series of ten-week courses for Human Development Scotland.

Sue Jervis was a staff welfare officer employed by the civil service when she began her training as a psychodynamic counsellor at SIHR in 1989. She then changed careers and worked as a counselling service manager, supervisor, and independent practitioner at various locations around the UK. In between doing these jobs, she accompanied her husband to two overseas postings. Returning to Scotland in 2003, she became a member of SIHR. However, her renewed career in the counselling field was quickly disrupted again when her husband was assigned to successive foreign jobs. While abroad, Sue completed postgraduate studies that led her into psychosocial research. She has since written several papers and presented workshops on the process of using psychoanalytically informed research methods and also on her research into the emotional experiences of servicemen's wives. Her publications include the book *Relocation, Gender and Emotion: A Psycho-Social Perspective on the Experiences of Military Wives* (2011).

Marie Kane set up the first local government equality unit in Scotland, an experience that instilled an abiding interest in organisational change. She is an organisational consultant (Marie Kane & Associates), an Associate of Real World Group (the internationally known centre for excellence in leadership research and development), an Associate of Tavistock Consulting, and an Associate of OPUS (the Organisation for Promoting Understanding of Society). A longstanding member of SIHR, she was elected a Board Member from 1999–2005. She also undertakes work as a member of Human Development Scotland's organisational consultancy group, and has been a staff member, and Director, of SIHR Group Relations Conferences. She has a particular interest in expanding work with organisations in Scotland to incorporate a psychodynamic perspective. She established the SIHR Working Below the Surface project, designed to explore organisational themes from a "below surface" perspective, which has involved almost 400 professional staff in three national conferences and a seminar series.

Monica Lanyado was the founding course organiser of the Child and Adolescent Psychotherapy Training at SIHR, Edinburgh. She is a training supervisor at the British Psychotherapy Foundation, formerly the British Association of Psychotherapists, and is joint Series Editor, with Ann Horne, of the Independent Psychoanalytic Approaches with Children and Adolescents (IPACA) Series. Her publications include *The Presence of the Therapist: Treating Childhood Trauma* (2004) and, co-edited with Ann Horne, *The Handbook of Child and Adolescent Psychotherapy: Psychoanalytic Approaches* (1999, 2009), *A Question of Technique* (2006), *Through Assessment to Consultation* (2009), and *Winnicott's Children* (2012). She has retired from clinical practice but continues to supervise colleagues and trainees, to teach, and to write.

Murray Leishman was a Church of Scotland minister, working in a parish when he became interested in psychoanalytic thinking and went into analysis. He later became a chaplain at the Royal Edinburgh Hospital. When Jock Sutherland returned to Scotland, Murray became involved with him in setting up SIHR and was one of the early trainees, initially in a group analytic setting, and then training as a psychoanalytic psychotherapist. He set up the clergy groups in the Royal Edinburgh hospital to work with other chaplains to understand what was happening in the patients, and in those who worked with them, to increase the effectiveness of the pastoral care they were trying to provide. Murray also worked for many years in private practice. He has recently retired from this work, but remains interested and available for consultation. Murray contributed to the Introduction to *The Autonomous Self*, the collected writings of Jock Sutherland.

Susan Lendrum trained initially as a teacher and worked in secondary schools, colleges, and a university in Germany. Her interest in psychoanalysis led her to train as a psychoanalytic psychotherapist at the University of Sheffield. She co-conducted Balint-type groups for GPs and other health professionals while working as a student counsellor, and was involved in counselling and psychotherapy training. While working as an adult psychotherapist in hospital settings, she trained as a psychodynamic supervisor, developing her supervisory work with both individuals and groups in a range of settings. On returning to Scotland, Susan joined SIHR and became involved in developing supervisory training within the Institute and beyond. She has recently returned from developing non-violent communication training with school pupils, supervising teachers and educational advisers in South Africa. She has published a number of articles, chapters, and books, including *Gift of Tears: A Practical Approach to Loss and Bereavement Counselling and Psychotherapy* (1992 and 2004) with Gabrielle Syme.

Molly Ludlam trained as a psychoanalytic psychotherapist at SIHR. Her interest in couple, family, and parent–child relationships stems from experience as a secondary schoolteacher and a social worker in an NHS Child and Family Mental Health service. She served on the council of SIHR from 1999–2005, becoming its chair in 2003. She is a member of the British Psychoanalytic Council, a Full Member of the British Society of Couple Psychotherapists and Counsellors, and is Editor of its international journal, *Couple and Family Psychoanalysis*. She has written widely about couple and parental couple relationships, including *Couple Attachments: Theoretical and Clinical Studies*, (2007) co-edited with Viveka Nyberg, and two chapters, one co-authored with Francesca Calvocoressi, in Hindle and Shulman's *The Emotional Experience of Adoption* (2008).

Susan Maciver is a psychodynamic counsellor with a specialist training in working with children and young people. She is a member of the Association for Psychodynamic Practice and Counselling in Organisational Settings and of the British Psychoanalytic Council. Most of her training was at SIHR and she became a member in the late 1980s. Since then she has contributed to courses and services in SIHR, for many years combining this with her career as a secondary school teacher and school counsellor. At present she has a private practice and contributes to Human Development Scotland services and short courses.

Tom C. Russ is a clinical research fellow at the Alzheimer Scotland Dementia Research Centre at the University of Edinburgh and an honorary specialty registrar in old age psychiatry in NHS Lothian. Noting the parallels between adolescence and later life while working in the adolescent department of the Tavistock Clinic, he approached SIHR on returning to Edinburgh. This resulted in the founding of the Working with Older People group, which has been running now for five years. His research interests mainly relate to the epidemiology of dementia, particularly geographical variation in dementia rates and early life environmental risk or protective factors.

Jill Savege Scharff is a supervising psychoanalyst and past chair, International Institute for Psychoanalytic Training at the International Psychotherapy Institute in Chevy Chase, Maryland, teaching analyst,

Washington Center for Psychoanalysis, and Clinical Professor of Psychiatry, Georgetown University, Washington DC. Having trained at the Royal Edinburgh Hospital, SIHR, the Tavistock Clinic, and the Washington Center for Psychoanalysis, she was certified in psychiatry by the Royal College of Psychiatrists, the American Board of Psychiatry and Neurology, and in adult and child psychoanalysis by the American Psychoanalytic Association. She is the author of *Projective and Introjective Identification and the Use of the Therapist's Self* (1992), co-author of *Tuning the Therapeutic Instrument: Affective Learning of Psychotherapy* (2000) and *The Interpersonal Unconscious* (2011), and editor of *The Psychodynamic Image: John D. Sutherland on Self and Society* (2007), and *Psychoanalysis Online* (2013). Dr Scharff is in private practice with adults, children, couples, and families in Chevy Chase, Maryland.

Alexandra Scott trained as a child and adolescent psychotherapist at the SIHR from 2000–2005. She currently works as a child and adolescent psychotherapist for Barnardo's Scotland Fostering, specialising in work with childhood abuse and trauma and children looked after away from home. Alexandra teaches on a range of topics and has a particular interest in infant mental health. Her research interests are on the effect of disability on the early parent–infant relationship, and on the effects of trauma on infant development. Her doctoral research was on the care and treatment of pre-school children who had been severely traumatised in infancy. Alexandra has developed a number of courses for a variety of professions that highlight the importance of observation and the development of observation skills, which are central to child psychotherapy training and practice.

Grant Wilkie is a Consultant Psychiatrist in Psychotherapy based in Lanarkshire. He completed his medical and basic psychiatric training in Edinburgh before moving to Glasgow to specialise in psychotherapy. Over this period he trained as a psychoanalytic psychotherapist at SIHR. In 1996, he was appointed as the first consultant psychiatrist in psychotherapy for Lanarkshire and has spent his consultant career developing a service for this area. His main interests are in the application of psychoanalytic ideas to the work of mainstream mental health services, working with families, and the application of psychoanalytic and systemic ideas to the understanding of organisations.

FOREWORD

Monica Lanyado

True to its title, this collection of papers from psychodynamic clinicians and thinkers in Scotland demonstrates just how useful psychoanalytic ideas can be when put to work outside the consulting room. The reader is invited to think about work in such varied settings as social research groups working with army wives, the clergy trying to offer pastoral care within a religious context, supporting patients and staff in care homes for the elderly, facilitating the training of psychiatrists, organisational consultancy to large companies—to name just a few. Plus, there is discussion of training and further professional development for a range of caring professions. The ways in which the observational skills, examination of the transference relationship within the many settings, and the supervisory process, all of which are intrinsic to psychodynamic training, can be usefully adapted for these different professions are creatively described.

The need for the caring professions to work with and within a sound understanding of group and organisational processes and defences shines through in chapter after chapter, regardless of the setting for the work itself. This is psychoanalysis in a different kind of "practice"—deeply practical/pragmatic and engaged with the complexities of human relationships in the external world of groups and organisations, as well as the intricacies of the internal world. This powerful influence comes from Jock Sutherland and the co-founders of the Scottish Institute of Human Relations (SIHR) in the 1970s, which was, presumably, a name carefully chosen and not just echoing the name of its sister Institute (Tavistock Institute of Human Relations), south of the Border. Indeed, at that time, the primary need to create an environment in which psychoanalytic training might grow was a key concept in creating the climate in which psychoanalytic trainings of several kinds could then take root, as indeed happened. Times have moved on, and this book emerges at a watershed, when change had to take place and be accepted, and a new organisation, Human Development Scotland, has emerged as a phoenix from the ashes, to take the collective thinking contained in this book further into the twenty-first century.

It is helpful to be able to place current thinking within a historical context, and a number of the contributors provide us with this. Understanding the roots, issues, and controversies of this work, and hearing about them first hand from some of the well-seasoned contributors, is heartening as well as grounding for those who continue what can often feel like "the fight" to ensure a reflective space for professionals who work in emotionally demanding, caring professions. Finding ways to try to think about and make some sense of bewildering and often painful and anxiety-provoking communications from patients and other professionals continues to be essential for good practice. Without this kind of space, it is all too easy for professional defensiveness to become established, which is not only ultimately unhelpful to those we are trying to help, but also puts the well-being and humanity of the professional him or herself at risk.

This is good, solid, but, sadly, increasingly supposedly "old-fashioned" thinking in a culture where speed and number crunching statistics have lost sight of the investment of time that is required for lasting change to take place. A number of quick fixes can ultimately take much longer and be less effective than one more solid and insightful piece of work. This imbalance towards "short-termism" will, one hopes, in time be redressed when it becomes clearer which "baby" has been thrown out with the "bathwater" of cuts to services. One also hopes that the work described in this book will give an indication of the continuing need to support the helping professions to do their work adequately, so that valued social structures within health, education, and social care do not unravel.

The overriding impression on finishing reading the book is the impressive and helpful spread of psychoanalytic thought within the helping professions in Scotland. It is good to know that, despite the difficulties that all professions are facing in this area, the kind of applied psychoanalytic thinking described is very much alive, well, and valued.

PART I

OPENING UP SPACES FOR PSYCHOANALYTIC THINKING

CHAPTER ONE

The development of psychoanalytic spaces in Scotland: historical overview and introduction

Liz Bondi and Molly Ludlam

J. D. Sutherland, one of the founders of the Scottish Institute of Human Relations (SIHR), was fond of quoting Kurt Lewin's aphorism, "There is nothing more practical than a good theory" (Lewin, 1952, p. 169). The title of this book, *Making Spaces: Putting Psychoanalytic Thinking to Work,* describes not only the process of applying psychoanalytic ideas, but also speaks to a human anxiety evoked by the struggle to find one's place in the world, and by the need for spaces in which to love, to work, and to grow. Psychoanalytically speaking, human responses to this anxiety are understood to be ambivalent. So, externally, they are expressed in a tension between, for example, a search for wilderness *vs. a* need for city dwelling, whereas internally, they might be found in a conflict between seeking individuality and solitude *vs.* a compulsion to bond together as a defence against the fear of abandonment and isolation. Psychoanalytic thinking provides resources to help us make and explore spaces in which this anxiety can be contained and worked with, both within the consulting room and, as this book illustrates, in a wide variety of other settings. These spaces shape our inner and outer worlds, and create conditions in which to develop our capacities for loving, working, and growing.

Psychoanalysis studies and works with relationships. Through making a relationship, a space is opened up in which to create and develop the self as well as the potential of another person. The urge to discover would appear to be an innate human drive through which we, as a species, can explore and realise the full wealth of our human, or internal, and our environmental, or external, experience. This book provides examples of the various ways in which that urge has been thought about and applied in a wide range of contexts by people influenced and inspired by psychoanalytic thought and practice, especially as it has been developed in Scotland. In so doing, we aim to contribute to a growing body of work that emphasises links between psychoanalysis, as practised traditionally in the consulting room, and its applications in a variety of other domains, that are also committed to working with the complex interaction of inner and outer worlds through person-to-person relating (Lemma & Patrick, 2010).

A recurrent tension arising from such applications is that between holding to core tenets of a solely psychoanalytic approach and engaging with other practitioners who bring beliefs and principles from different fields. Put another way, how do we navigate a path between keeping the "true faith" to which a small cohesive group might adhere without risk of dilution and providing a broad church that is able to accommodate divergent and sometimes incompatible beliefs between which disagreement is inevitable? This tension has existed since the early days of psychoanalysis, being expressed in splits, famously between Freud and Jung, as well as in accommodations achieved in the 1940s within the British Psychoanalytic Society when different training traditions were accorded recognition. It is a tension given particular expression in the meeting between psychoanalysis and Scottish culture in the early twentieth century. This meeting shaped the subsequent unfolding of psychoanalytic thinking and practice in Scotland and, in this chapter, we explore that unfolding in order to contextualise the accounts offered by subsequent contributors. We give particular emphasis to the legacy of both W. R. D. Fairbairn (1889–1964) and J. D. Sutherland (1905–1991) because it was their thinking and writing that most powerfully shaped Scotland's psychoanalytic spaces. There is nothing parochial in the contribution of either of these men. On the contrary, their work ensured that influences traceable to their formative Scottish context have found their way into the rich conversations that enable psychoanalysis to adapt and evolve all over the world. This book offers examples of this influence in the activities of members of the SIHR, whether taking place in Scotland or elsewhere.

For some forty years, the SIHR provided an organisational home for a wide variety of activities informed and inspired by psychoanalysis. In this chapter, we discuss the development of psychoanalysis in Scotland and the ancestry of the SIHR. During the preparation of this volume, the SIHR closed. However, many of the ideas and activities it fostered survive and thrive, and much of what the SIHR represented lives on through the many people it has influenced. This book seeks to make more widely available aspects of the unique thinking and practice that it fostered.

Psychoanalysis took root in Scotland quite slowly. Freud's ideas reached the UK around the turn of the twentieth century, cited, for example, in scientific papers concerned with the paranormal (Alexander, 1998). London and Cambridge swiftly became the key centres for early British psychoanalysis, early enthusiasts finding a variety of ways in which to assimilate them into the existing intellectual and relational environment (Forrester, 2008). During the First World War, attempts to treat shell-shock prompted the adaptation of elements of psychoanalytic technique much more widely, fostering new applications that were adopted in new places. In the novel *Regeneration*, Pat Barker (1991) famously portrayed W. H. R. Rivers' (1864–1922) efforts to listen to, and make sense of, the trauma suffered by British officers sent to Craiglockhart War Hospital in Edinburgh. Rivers, who, before the war, had been based in Cambridge, may not have used Freud's ideas about the sexual origin of neuroses, but, nevertheless, his methods owed much else to psychoanalysis, including Freud's idea of transference. Moreover, while Rivers was at Craiglockhart, he was visited by a second lieutenant of the Royal Garrison Artillery by the name of W. R. D. Fairbairn, who was much impressed by his work (Sutherland, 1989). We shall return to Fairbairn shortly.

As well as bringing doctors such as Rivers from London and Cambridge to Scotland, the First World War influenced many Scottish-born and Scottish-educated men to take an interest in psychoanalytic thinking and practice. One example is that of Hugh Crichton-Miller (1877–1959), the son of a Scottish minister based in Italy, who was educated in Scotland before training as a doctor. During the First World War, he drew on ideas garnered from both Freud and Jung to develop psychotherapeutic methods for treating shell-shock, and, after the war, he continued this work by establishing the Tavistock Clinic as an outpatient psychotherapy clinic for traumatised and neurotic children and adults (Dicks, 1970). Although sited in London, this institution played a key role in the development of psychoanalysis in Scotland.

The Tavistock Clinic had a strained relationship with the emerging psychoanalytic establishment in London, becoming a place associated with "independent minded" psychoanalytic practitioners of the interwar years (Rayner, 1990). One such was Ian Suttie (1889–1935), who was born and educated in Scotland, where he trained as a doctor before joining Crichton-Miller at the Tavistock Clinic. In the 1920s and early 1930s, Suttie presented a series of papers, later assembled into a volume entitled *The Origins of Love and Hate*, which challenged and recast several of Freud's ideas (Suttie, 1935). According to Cassullo (2010) Suttie's book was one of the "secret books" (p. 5) of psychoanalysis, "its very existence ignored" (p. 6), if not denied, but quietly exerting such a profound and lasting influence on many of the most well known British psychoanalysts of the mid-twentieth century that its core ideas "are likely to appear rather commonplace to contemporary analysts" (p. 9).

That Scottish ideas might be an important strand of the independent-mindedness associated with Tavistock Clinic is suggested by Miller (2008), who observes that "when psychoanalytic ideas arrive[d] in Scotland, they enter[ed] into a quite distinct cultural inheritance" (2008, p. 42). In Miller's account, central to this distinctiveness was a theological tradition that was very different from both Freud's and Klein's Jewish heritage, as well as from the forms of Christianity dominant in London and Cambridge. Indeed, one of Suttie's principal challenges to Freud was a critique of his prejudice against religion. For Suttie, making space for love was vital, and he viewed non-authoritarian features of Christianity that are exemplified in Scottish Presbyterianism as powerful models and allies for psychoanalysis.

While Crichton-Miller and Suttie drew on their Scottish heritage to influence the development of psychoanalysis in and beyond the UK (Miller, 2008), it fell to others to begin the process of developing psychoanalytic thinking and practice within Scotland. In this, Fairbairn played a crucial role. Having decided to abandon his initial plan to enter the ministry and to train instead as a psychoanalyst, in 1919 he enrolled as a medical student at the University of Edinburgh (Sutherland, 1989). After graduating, he spent a period working as a general practitioner near London, during which time he advanced his psychoanalytic training, in part through an analysis with Ernest Jones. (A close colleague of Freud, Jones was a major figure in the promotion of psychoanalysis in the Anglophone world.) Fairbairn soon returned to Scotland and, in 1925, after spending two years working as a psychiatric assistant at the Royal Edinburgh Hospital, he established a private psychoanalytic practice in Edinburgh. He also began to contribute teaching on psychoanalysis for the University of Edinburgh's Department of Psychology.

Fairbairn was deeply committed to psychoanalysis. Alongside his sustained psychoanalytic practice, he was soon writing and presenting clinical papers. By the early 1940s, his ideas were developing in highly original ways. Unlike Suttie, he did not see himself as challenging Freud's theory, but, in retrospect, we can see that the body of work brought together in his book *Psychoanalytic Studies of the Personality* (Fairbairn, 1952) amounted to a significant reframing of psychoanalytic theory, from which "drive theory" and the "death instinct" has disappeared, to be replaced by a coherently elaborated theory of internal object relations. Like Suttie, Fairbairn grew up and was immersed in a Scottish Presbyterian religious sensibility, which was deeply woven into the fabric of Scottish cultural life. In both men's thinking, the need for love is of primary importance. In Fairbairn's theory, the infant's need for maternal love inevitably generates anxieties and frustrations, against which the infant must defend him- or herself unconsciously by splitting off parts of the psyche from the central ego. There is a close parallel between this concept and the Christian narrative of a fall from grace: both narrate an expulsion from a deeply loving relationship, and in which to be human means suffering the consequences of exile from it (Hoffman, 2004).

In Ogden's words, "Fairbairn's theory of internal object relations constitutes one of the most important contributions to the development of analytic theory in its first century" (Ogden, 2010, p. 102). And yet, his work has attracted far less attention than that of several of his contemporaries, who included Klein, Bion, and Winnicott. This neglect might be due to Fairbairn's relative isolation in Edinburgh, far away from the centre of British psychoanalytic activity in London. He was also embedded in the Scottish cultural context with its particular version of Protestantism that, until after the Second World War, was relatively resistant to the forces of secularisation with which psychoanalysis in Vienna, London, and Cambridge had been associated. His relative isolation might also have contributed to his writing style, in relation to which an exclusionary cycle appears to have developed. Because he elaborated a distinctive and original theory, he coined and used terms that other psychoanalytic theorists had not used, including, for example, the "endopsychic structure", the "central ego", the "exciting object", the "rejecting object", the "libidinal ego", and the "internal saboteur". Moreover, because his work has been neglected, these terms remain unfamiliar and have not been widely incorporated into a UK-based psychoanalytic lexicon. Fairbairn's unique terminology served, thus, to express his separateness from his London contemporaries, as well as something of his personality. Perhaps he needed a space that was separate from the London *mêlée*, and to be on native soil, in order to leave the "parental" Freudian home and develop his own psychoanalytic self.

The consequence of his isolation and criticism of Freud was, however, that he was largely ignored, even by the independents, such as Winnicott, whose approach, paradoxically, is not dissimilar. Despite this overt neglect of Fairbairn, however, a number of commentators have argued that, like Suttie's work, Fairbairn's has been deeply, albeit implicitly, influential, slowly and quietly seeping into psychoanalysis through the work of interpreters, including Greenberg and Mitchell (1983), Guntrip (1971), and Scharff and Scharff (1987), as well as that of Sutherland (1989) himself.

Another possible reason for the limited explicit engagement with Fairbairn's ideas is that he appears to have been something of a loner, no doubt influencing many of his patients and immediate colleagues, but not gathering a significant group of psychoanalysts around him. Importantly, he did not create or inspire the creation of psychoanalytic training in Scotland. Neither did he develop or facilitate the development of Scottish institutions through which psychoanalysis could put down secure roots. When he died, there was no organisational base for psychoanalysis in Scotland ready for others to take forward.

During Fairbairn's lifetime, others had taken initiatives that gestured towards something like a community of psychoanalytic practitioners in Scotland. For example, from the late 1930s onwards, Winifred Rushforth (1885–1983) spearheaded a series of activities that blended psychoanalysis with other approaches to healing, around which a substantial network of practitioners developed. Through the Davidson Clinic for Medical Psychotherapy (1940–1973), Rushforth pioneered the provision of psychotherapy for ordinary people at a cost they could afford, which, in some cases, meant no cost at all (Rushforth, 1984). She developed an annual Summer School for doctors and other professionals interested in the Clinic's approach to psychotherapy and healing, and, for many years, ran psychoanalytically informed dream groups. Nevertheless, she was something of a maverick, eventually becoming known more as a New Age guru than a psychoanalyst (Rushforth, 1981). Like Fairbairn, but for different reasons, she had no interest in creating or fostering a specifically psychoanalytic institutional base in Scotland, or in developing psychoanalytic training on a model comparable with that which was becoming available in London.

By the 1960s, psychotherapeutic ideas were being taken up much more widely in a variety of settings in Scotland (Bondi, 2013). For example, marriage (later relationship) counselling was being offered to more and more people, drawing on a variety of ideas, including psychoanalytic ones, but still there was no coherent network of psychoanalytic practitioners based in Scotland and nowhere to turn for immersion in psychoanalytic training. Then Sutherland, Medical Director at the Tavistock Clinic in London (1947–1968), returned to Scotland. Murray Leishman's account, in Chapter Fourteen of this volume, of the eager welcome his homecoming received speaks to the idea that if the words of the prophet are to be received in his (or her) own country, not only should there be a receptive, hungry audience, but also that he (or she) must speak in words which can be readily understood and repeated. Sutherland hypothesised that Fairbairn's work had been ignored largely because of the "hard intellectual work required" (Sutherland, 1989, p. 144). Sutherland's own style, in contrast, was to simplify his language as much as possible, so as to reach out relationally and to foster engagement with others. It won him listeners and loyal followers, as both Leishman and Jill Scharff (Chapter Two) attest.

Born in Edinburgh, Sutherland had studied psychology at the University of Edinburgh, which is where he first encountered Fairbairn. Inspired by him, Sutherland went on to complete a medical degree at the University of Glasgow, before embarking on his own psychoanalysis with Fairbairn. The Second World War took him to London to work, first as a psychiatrist, and then as Medical Director at the Tavistock Clinic. On his retirement, in 1968, he returned to Edinburgh. Although Fairbairn and Sutherland differed in character and style, as an intellectual giant in his own right, Sutherland embraced the task of explicating Fairbairn and of demonstrating the practical application of both his and Fairbairn's theories. Fairbairn had, after all, been Sutherland's analyst for five years before he went south. He contemplated having a further analysis at that point and told his new colleagues that he wanted "somebody like Fairbairn. They said, 'That's no good. You've got to go to a *real* analyst'" (Scharff, 1994, p. 402). Yet, although he admired his new analyst, Sylvia Payne, Sutherland never forgot Fairbairn's continual concern for people's suffering, and his prioritisation of the alleviation of their despair over any supposed analytical "success". These were the values which informed the training programmes developed by the Scottish Institute of Human Relations, the organisation which Sutherland and several colleagues established in 1971, and which became familiarly known by some as the MacTavy.

If making Edinburgh the "secure base" from which to work served an important psychological function for Fairbairn, we might wonder about the impact on the relatively gregarious Sutherland of spending twenty years at what had become the centre of psychoanalytic and psychological enquiry in the UK: the Tavistock Clinic. In doing so, he made a journey replicated throughout history by people drawn to test their mettle or find their fortune in the big cities. Human beings—or, at least, many of us—predominantly thrive where they can join together to channel rivalrous feelings into competitive striving to attain excellence. It would seem that Sutherland used the larger arena that London offered to develop his authority and sense of what he might achieve politically. Although he kept in touch with Fairbairn, who regularly sent him his manuscripts, he later confessed that, excited by his work at the Tavistock, an experience so different from his earlier Scottish one, "I avoided the implications of what Fairbairn was thinking for most of my life" (Scharff, 1994, p. 423). It was only after he had returned home (Fairbairn having died in 1964) that Sutherland felt ready to undertake a self-analysis and "began to really think about his ideas on the self and the subselves" (p. 423).

Thus, at the ripe age of seventy, Sutherland discovered even greater self-potential as a reflective thinker, energetically taking in and applying ideas. He also devoted more time to writing. The compendium of twenty-four of his papers, *The Autonomous Self* (Scharff, 1994) presents his contribution to four spheres of work: object relations theory; group relations; community mental health, and the self. Their breadth describes and maps his field of vision, and the whole *oeuvre* is greater than the sum of its parts. Near the end of his life, he was able to complete one of his greatest tributes to Fairbairn, in *Fairbairn's Journey into the Interior*, published in 1989 for the centenary of Fairbairn's birth. All the while, Sutherland had himself been conducting an important journey of his own, searching his internal, previously unanalysed spaces to make sense of the role of the self in relationships. Sutherland had found in his private papers Fairbairn's notes testifying to the latter's own self-analysis; he had some anxiety about whether to make these available, but decided to do so, having considered that Fairbairn could have chosen to destroy them. It is characteristic of him that he also made his own self-discoveries available to be shared. This fits powerfully with his belief in the significance of open systems in the configuration of the self and also with his desire to ensure that the institute he had co-founded was an open learning system.

In his crucial role as co-founder of the SIHR, Jock Sutherland had created a home in Scotland for psychoanalysis such as had not existed previously. The time and the climate were clearly propitious. The vision Sutherland described in his seminal Malcolm Miller memorial lecture of 1979, "The psychodynamic image of man", found ready application in the community, as Jill Scharff describes in Chapter Two of this volume. This series of lectures had been set up by Douglas Haldane (1926–2012) a child and adolescent psychiatrist, inspired by the work of Winnicott, Bowlby, Emery, and Trist. Haldane had initiated the first child and family clinic in Cupar in the 1960s and, in turn, played a vital role in helping to develop the links between the growing SIHR and the community.

Sutherland's broad range of interests and the open learning system the organisation propounded drew many others in, and, over twenty years, training courses in adult and child and adolescent psychoanalytic psychotherapy were joined by a renowned Human Relations and Counselling Course, Family Therapy Training, Analytical Groups and

Associated Applications, Group Relations conferences, and a full range of clinical services. As several of the chapters in this book reflect, the cross-fertilisation between these activities led to further creativity in their application, examples being new reflections on infant observation illustrated by Nicola Chadd (Chapter Four), the development of bespoke courses in child and infant observation described by Debbie Hindle and Alexandra Scott (Chapter Five), the supervision groups, which Susan Lendrum writes about (Chapter Twelve), innovations in conceptualising couple relationships, discussed by Molly Ludlam (Chapter Seven), and insights from organisational consultancy explored by Marie Kane (Chapter Eleven). In an organisational map of the late 1990s, there were fifteen separate "projects" sheltering under the Institute's umbrella. The fact that participants valued its courses and services and took their skills into work in the NHS, universities, social work, and education is illustrated in this book in contributions by Joan Herrmann (Chapter Six), Sue Jervis (Chapter Nine), Grant Wilkie (Chapter Fourteen), and Susan Maciver and Tom Russ (Chapter Fifteen). While this outward-facing engagement can and should be seen as a measure of the Institute's success, it left unanswered the Institute's perennial questions about how to continue to sustain itself.

Like other psychoanalytic institutions, the SIHR had to create a space capable of fostering the inherent outsiderness of psychoanalysis. For all such bodies, authenticity lies in being subversive; that subversiveness is exemplified by their need to make space for hate: empathy for another's suffering might be an essential component of effective therapy, but psychoanalytic practitioners also hold as equally important for the therapist's survival the recognition of what Winnicott so powerfully identified as "hate in the countertransference" (Winnicott, 1975). If psychoanalysis were to become part of the establishment, it might forfeit its imperative to question, to look beyond superficial comfort and, as Fairbairn did in challenging Freud, give voice to an "inconvenient truth". Hence, it finds itself continually trying to maintain a place on the fringes, in the liminal spaces, the potential of which Liz Bondi (Chapter Three), Lindy Barbour (Chapter Eight) and Eileen Francis (Chapter Ten) discuss.

The book's first part, "Opening Up Spaces For Psychoanalytic Thinking", explores the growth of spaces for psychoanalytic thinking. In Chapter Two, Jill Scharff reflects on the changing ways in which she has worked with the dynamic interplay between inner and outer worlds to which she was introduced by Sutherland. Looking back to the early 1970s, she recalls and evokes the flavour of psychoanalytic practice in the clinic and the community, as well as the psychoanalytic education fostered by the SIHR. All this was framed and enlivened by object relations theory in a broadly Fairbairnian tradition. However, this was no narrow church in which the "true faith" was to be protected against other influences. For Scharff, the creative consequences of the translation of Fairbairn's ideas into a South American context helped to enrich psychoanalytic theory in ways that echo, but also differ from, a British object relations tradition, which she illustrates using a case study from her own practice. In Chapter Three, Liz Bondi also looks back, this time to Freud's discussion of "The question of lay analysis", in which, she argues, he set out an unambiguously interdisciplinary vision for psychoanalysis in which the humanities and social sciences figure prominently. She brings this vision into dialogue with her own background in human geography to introduce the idea that psychoanalysis has its own geographies. Pointing to the central importance accorded to spatial concepts and metaphors like boundaries and spaces, she describes psychoanalysis as a liminal practice that necessarily occupies and works across boundaries and thresholds.

Against the background of these chapters concerned with the creation of spaces for psychoanalytic thinking, the rest of the volume consists of three further sections which explore the making of spaces: spaces in which to love, in which to work, and in which to grow. There are many overlaps and connections between loving, working, and growing, and, therefore, many connections to be made across these sections. However, the groupings also enable us to illustrate how the broad themes of loving, working, and growing can be enriched through the creation of spaces that are enabled by psychoanalytic perspectives.

This second part part of the book, "Making space to love", opens with Chapter Four, in which Nicola Chadd discusses infant observation in theory and practice. Observing infants and their carers in the early months of life illuminates not only what it is to love and to hate, but also the life-and-death terrors that are so close to the surface at this time. In such circumstances, making space to love is often about nurturing the capacity to withstand our deepest anxieties. In Chapter Five, Debbie Hindle and Alexandra Scott note that relationship-based practice is at last poised to make a comeback in the field of social work practice. In this context, they show how the principles of psychoanalytic infant observations have been made available through a range of SIHR short courses designed for social workers working with children and their families. They describe how these courses enable participants to develop their observational skills and deepen their understanding of children's perspectives, all the while drawing actively on their own emotional experience to help understand the unconscious dynamics that interfere with, or foster the availability of, spaces in which to love. Chapter Six continues the focus on working with children and families under pressure. Inspired by Sutherland's outward-looking engagement with psychoanalysis, Joan Herrmann reveals how psychoanalytic thinking can play a very valuable role in multi-disciplinary settings, especially if brought out from the clinic into staff teams. Here, it has the potential to make spaces available to think and reflect in new ways. As she illustrates, psychoanalysis can be put to work to enable recognition of some of the subtle and powerful ways the inner lives of troubled children may be made manifest in their outward relating, so, almost uncannily, reproducing the environments in which their development has already been imperilled. This insight provides a foundation upon which new spaces to love might begin to be imagined and brought into being. In Chapter Seven, which concludes the section, Molly Ludlam draws attention to the perinatal couple whose relationship frames their newborn infant's world. The perinatal period is a fragile time for the parents as individuals and for their relationship. Rather than locating depression uniquely in the mother, she argues that it might be helpful to think of the relationship itself as subject to depression. In this context, couple therapy might be a valuable intervention that, by supporting the capacity to mourn, has the potential to foster space in which to love.

The third part, "Making space to work", turns to settings beyond the clinic in which psychoanalytic thinking might be used in the service of a variety of forms of work. In Chapter Eight, Lindy Barbour considers the work of teaching in higher education. She explores potentially productive parallels between psychoanalytic ideas and contributions to research about teaching and learning in higher education. Remaining tentative about the reach of psychodynamic thinking, she invites instead a partnership in which different perspectives enrich one another. Turning to another domain within the world of higher education and beyond, in Chapter Nine, Sue Jervis asks what psychoanalysis might offer to social research. Drawing on her own experience as a psychosocial researcher, she shows how the conduct and analysis of research interviews is usefully informed by psychoanalytic thinking. Like Lindy Barbour, she is tentative, recognising the challenges and inviting dialogue with other perspectives, but also offering resources to assist social researchers to reflect upon what they do. In Chapter Ten, Eileen Francis also draws on her own experience, this time as a speech and language therapist who, across her career, has moved between professional practice and professional education. Using psychoanalytic ideas, she narrates how her position evolved alongside a process of building within her mind the institutional spaces in which she has worked. In so doing, she provides an illustration of how this process works individually and collectively. Chapter Eleven turns directly to organisational life, and Marie Kane focuses on the powerful themes of envy and shame to explore how we come to know—or not—our place within the organisations to which we belong. She shows how easily space to work can be squeezed, to the detriment of individuals and organisations, and how psychoanalytic thinking can be put to work to open up spaces anew.

The fourth and final section of the volume, "Making space to grow", explores the making of spaces for growth in work settings and in life. In Chapter Twelve, Susan Lendrum discusses how she used psychoanalytic thinking to foster the growth of a group of experienced clinical psychologists working in NHS settings. She draws on relational psychoanalysis to describe her supervision practice and she illustrates how she used the relational resources of the group to foster a space in which these clinicians could grow. Chapter Thirteen stays within NHS settings, but moves into the front-line work of the trainee psychiatrist. Grant Wilkie draws on his experience of running psychoanalytic Balint groups for these doctors. With this kind of support to develop capacities for psychoanalytically informed associative ways of thinking that are very different from their well-established exercise of scientific reasoning, doctors are enabled to make spaces for professional growth. Wilkie argues that applied psychoanalytic thinking of this kind is relevant to all those working in mental health services, where the unconscious dynamics of psychotic illness inevitably "get into" all the staff who work with these patients and into the organisational structures designed to support them. In Chapter Fourteen, the focus shifts to religious ministers, with whom Murray Leishman worked in the early days of the SIHR. Indeed, he himself trained as a minister before becoming a chaplain at a psychiatric hospital where he was based when Sutherland returned to Scotland. Leishman swiftly developed his psychoanalytic experience under Sutherland's tutelage and proceeded to work at the interface between psychoanalysis and ministry. He describes how the clergy group-work project made psychoanalytic thinking available to ministers and how it provided a space in which they could grow. Growing into old age is a privilege of a long life, and it presents challenges to ageing individuals, those close to them, and those charged with their care. Until recently, these challenges were relatively neglected by psychoanalysis, but that is beginning to change, as Susan Maciver and Tom Russ explain in Chapter Fifteen, which concludes this book. Drawing on both clinical practice and literature, they offer psychoanalytic insights into the stresses of growing old. Against this background they show how psychoanalytic ideas—especially about projective processes—can be used to support care work in institutional settings. In so doing, psychoanalysis can help to make space in which people can "grow into" their old age, and those who support them can grow, too, in their caring skills and their capacity for compassion. With the theme of compassionate care rising on the political agenda, the importance of making available insights from psychoanalysis becomes increasingly significant.

This book illustrates that the coming together of human beings into a shared space fosters opportunities to create loving, collaborative relationships from which to grow. Yet, as Winnicott observed, without separation, there can be no dependency. Unlike Freud, Fairbairn saw the infant as innately relationship-seeking. Furthermore, he envisaged dependency as a life-long process of personal growth, beginning with the baby's total dependence on others and completed by mature dependence in the adult. Thus, throughout this developmental journey, dependence on relationships with others becomes a vital resource. In Fairbairn's vision, early total dependence gradually extends, ultimately coming to rest in culture and society. Following Sutherland, it might be said that one of the purposes of making relationships, as well as to seek physical care, is so that we can more fully discover ourselves *and* the potential of others through mutual relationships. We see, then, human lives, in their inner and external spaces, as involving a tidal ebb and flow between coming together and separating, between periods of growth and of lying fallow, sometimes just surviving traumatic change and at others able to learn from experience, being at one and the same time aware of the earth's continual evolution and of our own ultimate inevitable death. As Freud wrote to Jung on 17 February 1908, "one must try to learn something from every experience" (McGuire, 1974, pp. 119–121). The psychoanalytic task, therefore, is to make space for learning from experience, and for continuing learning from life's possibilities as well as from its vicissitudes.

References

Alexander, S. (1998). Psychoanalysis in Britain in the early twentieth century: an introductory note. *History Workshop Journal, 45*: 135–143.

Barker, P. (1991). *Regeneration*. New York: Viking.

Bondi, L. (2013). Between Christianity and secularity: counselling and psychotherapy provision in Scotland. *Social and Cultural Geography* doi:10.1080/14649365.2013.802369.

Cassullo, G. (2010). Back to the roots: the influence of Ian D. Suttie on British psychoanalysis. *American Imago, 67*: 5–22.

Dicks, H. V. (1970). *Fifty Years of the Tavistock Clinic*. London: Routledge & Kegan Paul.

Fairbairn, W. R. D. (1952). *Psychoanalytic Studies of the Personality*. London: Tavistock.

Forrester, J. (2008). 1919: psychology and psychoanalysis, Cambridge and London – Myers, Jones and MacCurdy. *Psychoanalysis and History, 10*: 37–94.

Greenberg, J. R., & Mitchell, S. (1983). *Object Relations in Psychoanalytic Theory*. Cambridge MA: Harvard University Press.

Guntrip, H. J. S. (1971). *Psychoanalytic Theory, Therapy and the Self.* New York: Basic Books.

Hoffman, M. (2004). From enemy combatant to strange bedfellow. The role of religious narratives in the work of W. R. D. Fairbairn and D. W. Winnicott. *Psychoanalytic Dialogues, 14*: 769–804.

Lemma, A., & Patrick, M. (2010). *Off the Couch: Contemporary Psychoanalytic Applications*. London: Karnac.

Lewin, K. (1952). *Field Theory in Social Science*. London: Tavistock.

McGuire, W. (Ed.) (1974). *The Freud/Jung Letters: The Correspondence between Sigmund Freud and C. G. Jung*. Princeton, NJ: Princeton University Press.

Miller, G. (2008). Scottish psychoanalysis: a rational religion. *Journal of the History of the Behavioural Sciences, 44*: 38–58.

Ogden, T. (2010). Why read Fairbairn? *International Journal of Psychoanalysis, 91*: 101–118.

Rayner, E. (1990). *The Independent Mind in British Psychoanalysis*. London: Free Association Books.

Rushforth, W. (1981). *Something is Happening: Spiritual Awareness and Depth Psychology in the New Age*. Winnipeg, Canada: Turnstone.

Rushforth, W. (1984). *Ten Decades of Happenings*. London: Gateway Books.

Scharff, D. E., & Scharff, J. S. (1987). *Object Relations Family Therapy*. Northvale, NJ: Jason Aronson.

Scharff, J. S. (Ed.) (1994). *The Autonomous Self: The Work of John D. Sutherland*. Northvale, NJ: Jason Aronson.

Sutherland, J. D. (1989). *Fairbairn's Journey into the Interior*. London: Free Association Books.

Suttie, I. D. (1935). *The Origins of Love and Hate*. London: Kegan Paul, Trench, & Trubner.

Winnicott, D. W. (1975). Hate in the countertransference. In: *Through Paediatrics to Psychoanalysis* (pp. 194–203). London: Hogarth Press.

CHAPTER TWO

Inner and outer worlds: then and now*

Jill Savege Scharff

"Let me gi'e thanks noo fur ma lot
I micht no ha'e been born a Scot"

(Kate Bone, Prayer to Saint Andrew)

Introduction

Of all the psychodynamic theories, object relations theory is outstanding in having the explanatory power for comprehending the inner world and the outer world; self, family, and society. I first came upon object relations in 1969 as a young registrar at Dingleton Hospital when, attending the University of Edinburgh Department of Psychiatry course in psychological medicine, I heard John Sutherland lecture on human development. I had already studied Freud's psychosexual stages and found his theory too linear, too biological for me (Freud, 1905d). I had found that Erikson's (1950)

* This chapter is modified from "Inner and outer worlds: Then and now, the practical application of psychodynamic theories", a presentation given by the author in celebration of the fortieth anniversary of the Scottish Institute of Human Relations, Edinburgh, 2011.

theory of psychological challenges to be solved at each developmental stage went some way towards connecting Freud to the real world of parents and children, but it still was not enough. Then, thanks to Sutherland, I found Fairbairn (Birtles & Scharff, 1994; Fairbairn, 1952, 1963; Grotstein & Rinsley, 1994, Scharff & Birtles, 1994; Sutherland, 1989).

Then: object relations theory, the bridge between inner and outer worlds

Sutherland's lecture on human development, illustrated with now familiar diagrams, introduced me to object relations theory. Sutherland featured Fairbairn's concept of a pristine self at birth experiencing inevitable frustrations, taking in experience, protecting itself by splitting and repression, and organising into conscious and unconscious internal object relationships that continue to modify perception and experience and to grow and learn from experience (Fairbairn, 1963; Sutherland, 1963). It made so much sense. I remember the feeling of "Aha!" This was what I had been waiting for—a theory that was truly cybernetic, a theory that could account for growth and development, a theory that could understand couples and families as well as the infants that they cared for, and a theory that could, therefore, apply across the various modalities of individual, couple, family, and group therapy (Scharff & Scharff, 2005).

So, that is how I first found Fairbairn, upon whose theories I have built the foundation for my professional contributions. Equally important, I had also found John Sutherland. He, it turned out, was not only Fairbairn's main expositor (1963) and later biographer (1989), but also a highly creative thinker about the self and an advocate for individual and community mental health (Scharff, 1994, 2007; Sutherland, 1966, 1993). In 1970, I was fortunate to be appointed to an innovative position in community psychiatry, a joint post of the Royal Edinburgh Hospitals group and the City of Edinburgh, in which I would be registrar (and later senior registrar) to John Sutherland. I would be supervised by him in individual psychotherapy, group therapy, and community psychiatry, and I would quickly learn that everyone called him Jock.

It was when I was being supervised by Jock that I became totally convinced of the beauty and flexibility of object relations theory, enriched by open systems theory, as an overarching explanatory model for the dynamics of the inner world and its expression in the outer world. Jock was equally comfortable in the clinic or the community. Alongside his supervision of my work, he brought the same analytic sensibility to his supervision of my community work in a disadvantaged area of the city of Edinburgh, a recently constructed neighbourhood in the outskirts called Craigmillar. In our work together, the dual focus on individual and community development let me see the correspondence between the two situations. In 2011, I added link theory to further extend the grasp of object relations theory.

Then: object relations in the internal world

With the support of Jock's supervision, I learnt to work in twice-a-week psychotherapy with a woman who, beleaguered by the demands of children and a busy husband, presented with depression and a phobia of her son's mouth. Unable to bear the sight of his open mouth and his protruding tongue, she avoided looking at him. Feeling rejected, he responded by anxiously attaching to her and stimulating further rejection. Our hypothesis was that she was projecting her own neediness in him and rejecting it there, and he was pleading for it to be acknowledged. In object relations terms (explicated in greater detail below), the individual's central ego was splitting off and repressing the libidinal object, and the split-off rejecting object was further attacking it. In relation to her son, the woman had split off the repressed libidinal object and located it in him, where she attacked him vigorously to keep the experience of painful longing at bay. In attacking the boy, she was also displacing rage at her husband for putting her in a difficult family situation with messy children in a charming but decrepit house that was hard to keep clean.

Then: object relations in the outer world of community psychiatry

Meanwhile, I was visiting Craigmillar twice a week, too (Savege, 1975). The city had relocated the trouble-making poor people who lived in the crumbling inner city tenement buildings and placed them all in modern, high-rise buildings in Craigmillar so as to give them a more spacious environment and concentrate the distress, supposedly for ease of management. However, the people who had lived on top of each other in the old tenements were unhappy in their new high-rises with more green space around. They did not feel safe; they did not feel close; they did not feel respected. They were upset that a coffin could not lie flat in the new lifts. They worried that, because local violence had destroyed the phone booths, which were essential since they could not afford a telephone, communication in an emergency was unreliable. Unemployed youths were getting into trouble.

In object relations terms, the central ego of the city had split off a needy part of itself and tried to push it out of consciousness. Then the repressed returned to push for reintegration into the whole via gangs bringing terror to the centre of the city, illness to the hospitals, and social needs for medical and welfare services. The Craigmillar Health and Welfare Centre would address those needs. An integrated response to the split-off pieces would be fundamental to getting the whole picture and devising a comprehensive system of help, but the workers were too busy to collaborate. It was my job to consult to all of them—the social workers, marriage guidance counsellors, the Citizens Advice Bureau workers there, and the lay neighbourhood advisory workers—but I quickly realised that I could not do so piecemeal. To be effective in the community, the groups needed to work together. Like a therapist analysing resistance to treatment, I had to analyse the resistance to collaboration before we could move ahead. Fear of the other, role confusion, distrust, territorial disputes, and feelings of helplessness in the face of huge demand required patience and understanding. Most problematic for me were the non-professional neighbourhood workers in the mix—highly articulate, effective local people who fought well for the community. Social workers were afraid that the neighbourhood workers would dilute their professionalism. Doctors trained in the medical model were not used to listening to the opinions of social workers.

I was idealistic and a bit naïve. I went into a Town Council meeting to report on my work. Unknown to me, the press was in attendance. My far too frank and vivid account was reported in the evening paper. I called Jock in a panic. He called the head of the hospital to alert him, and called me back. "Dr Affleck says nobody reads the evening paper. You don't need to worry unless it comes out in *The Scotsman*." I spent a sleepless night. Next morning, I was relieved to find no mention of my gaffe in *The Scotsman*. Later that week, I was with the small therapy group I led with Paul O'Farrell. One of the group members, who happened to work at the newspaper, was angry with me. He said to the group, "A piece about her [meaning me] came across my desk, and I said, 'I don't want her here', so I put it on the bottom of the spike." We worked on his wish to destroy me, and he never knew that he had rescued me.

Back at the Health Centre, the various disciplines and the neighbourhood workers had to learn to live in balance and harmony, an effect that would filter through to the community. As a person must be encouraged to be an autonomous self, the community must be allowed to express itself, to take action, to relate to other parts of the city. It must devise its own shape and grow into it. Like a person, it needs space for reflection to conceive of itself and plan for its future. So, it needs meeting places and centres for education and culture. It needs community autonomy and mature interdependence with other parts of the city. Sutherland brought object relations theory to the community task. The community brought something else: a belief in creativity as the route to community power and change. Craigmillar had a Festival Society that put on a yearly pageant. The committee that ran the Festival developed expertise in management and became capable of social action on behalf of youth and old people particularly. Having become adept at political action, the Craigmillar Festival Society earned the right to advise the city corporation on the use of government funds for community development.

Outside the care of patients, supervision of junior psychotherapists, and consultation to the Craigmillar community that was part of his job, Jock also volunteered his time, often working with his colleague, Max Paterson. With them, I was invited to consult to Marriage Guidance and Pastoral Counselling Associations, Youth Agencies, and a sex counselling programme at the Church of Scotland. Echo Mackenzie, a drama specialist from Glasgow, and I worked with a group of drama teachers to found the Scottish Centre for Creativity and Communication.

Then: object relations in teaching at the Scottish Institute of Human Relations

These outreach activities are typical of the partnerships that characterised the Scottish Institute of Human Relations. Since 1971, when

Jock Sutherland led a group of colleagues to found the Scottish Institute of Human Relations, his dual focus on person and society has continued to guide the work at the Scottish Institute (Harrow, Leishman, Macdonald, & Scott, 1994). Looking back on the occasion of the twentieth anniversary of the Scottish Institute of Human Relations, Harrow, Leishman, and Brearley (1989) described the importance of always listening to the needs of the health professionals in the field so as to design an institution that is relevant to those needs and remains relevant by staying in partnership with them. They also noted that the health of the institution depended on each of its internal components staying aware of their interdependence, each playing its part in the whole. In other words, the institution grows on the same principle as the individual mind, and must recognise that it is a product of its relationships and that it needs a culture of meaningful relationships in order to survive and function well.

That year, 1971, saw the first offering of the Scottish Institute, a weekly course for mental health professionals called "The Caring Contract"—to this day an excellent title. I was in the first class to take that course. We began the evening in a case discussion group with others from our own disciplinary background, and, after a short break, we reconvened in randomly assigned multi-disciplinary groups. I was in the psychiatrists' case discussion group led by Willie McIntyre and in the multi-disciplinary process group run by Janet Hassan and, I think, Max Paterson. Willie McIntyre was also my analyst, but in those days we did not have the luxury of avoiding extra-analytic contact. Paul O'Farrell and Alan Cooklin were in Jock's group therapy supervision group with me, and both of them were in analysis with Jock. When the negative transference was active, the atmosphere could be a bit tense, but Jock handled it with aplomb and a glass of sherry as we approached six o'clock. Willie McIntyre maintained his role as my teacher in the Scottish Institute setting. I found him to be a reliable, well-modulated person in his analytic role, but, as a teacher, he could become furious with a student who annoyed him. That was rather frightening, but I never saw that side of him in the consulting room.

The Scottish Institute had to survive beyond the time of Jock's leadership, and, after a rocky time, it grew in stability and relevance. In the decades after I took that early course, it offered an increasingly diverse range of opportunities, including individual, group, and child psychotherapy training and consultative teaching programmes and clinical services at clinics in Edinburgh and in Glasgow.

Now: object relations theory expanded by link theory

I have learnt from colleagues in South America, where the extended family is of great importance, about the work of Pichon-Rivière. Sutherland had not alerted me to Pichon-Rivière, which is not surprising, given that his writing had not yet been translated into English. Yet, Pichon-Rivière's thinking had many similarities to his own, which is also not surprising, given that Pichon-Rivière had been reading Fairbairn on the endopsychic situation and Klein on the internal world and its interaction with the mothering figure. In another sense, it is a shock to find that Fairbairn's influence has spread to South America when it is less well known in neighbouring England.

Until now, I have been referring to object relations theory, a cybernetic theory of interacting systems, rather like the theory of relativity current in the 1940s, but a theory of the individual that Fairbairn drew from the study of dyadic interaction between patient and analyst. Fairbairn described the endopsychic situation as one in which the central ego relates to an ideal object shorn of the painful need-stimulating aspects of early experience that led to feelings of painful longing, and of the need-rejecting aspects that led to angry abandonment: traces of experience that were too overwhelming for the infant mind to retain in consciousness. The central ego splits off from itself and represses two parts of the ego: the libidinal ego to deal with the exciting object, and the antilibidinal ego to deal with the rejecting object. The antilibidinal ego further represses the libidinal object. All the repressed internal object relationships seek to return to consciousness so that the central ego can reintegrate. When two personalities combine in marriage, the internal object relationships seek to return to consciousness through the agency of the mind of the spouse, who is then treated according to his or her valency to resonate with projected parts of the other spouse's internal objects or parts of the ego (Dicks, 1967).

Like Henry Dicks, who looked beyond the individual patient to the marital joint personality, Pichon-Rivière looked beyond the dyadic focus to the nature of the link created by the combination of their personalities and the organising effect of that link on the internal world of each of them (Pichon-Rivière, 1971). He called it the theory of *el vinculó*, translated as link theory. Not to be confused with the usage of the term *link* in object relations, where it refers to linking of thought and feeling, attacks on linking, and linking of genital elements as a representative of the oedipal couple, link theory refers to the construction of internal and object relations through the interaction of the twin pillars of individual influence and social interaction. Link theory has echoes of object relations: for instance, in Bion's concept of containment, or Winnicott's focus on transitional space, but the theory also takes us into the realm of chaos theory, where we are looking at an overarching organisation of the internal and external world into which the infant arrives.

The baby is delivered into the link of internal object relations and social influences, and grows and develops to adulthood within those parameters. Through the link, the individual mind forms, is shaped, and manages the unconscious of the individual, and the groups of which the individual is a part. On the vertical axis lies the link to the good experiences and traumatic losses of the previous generation. On the horizontal access lies the link among individuals and groups, families, and the wider society. The link is accessed by the infant's need for love, nurture, safety, and knowing. The link is expressed at the individual level in dreams, individual actions, symptoms, and bodily experiences. You can hear the similarity to earliest Freud. To join this to object relations theory, we can expand this definition to say that the person expresses the link in manner of speech, in dreams, in physical and mental symptoms, in attitude to work, and in quality of relationships.

Now: the internal and the outer world: object relations and the link

I describe a case to illustrate these issues, interspersing the material with commentary.

Mercy is a twenty-seven-year-old American attorney with a government department (see also Scharff & Scharff, 2011). When she was eight years old, Mercy immigrated to the USA from Romania with her mother, who had agreed with her husband to come ahead to prospect for economic opportunity that would sustain their family, so that they could get out of Romania. Mercy's father and brother joined them a year later. Life in the USA was more secure than in Romania, but the parents had to work in menial jobs beneath their qualifications. They did not speak much about their feelings or their family life in Romania, and Mercy was left with a sense of sadness and mystery about them. When she was twenty-six, she married Harry, a "wonderful" international businessman who is the dominant one in their relationship. She admires his strength of character and adores his highly functional family, but she feels inferior to them.

Mercy married Harry as her ideal object about whom she felt no ambivalence. Harry is a worthy container for this projection. However, she projected her libidinal ego into him and cherished it there, leaving her central ego depleted and devoid of sexual energy. She is unable to escape the attack from her internal saboteur, leaving her feeling less ideal than he is. Part of her is in a schizoid retreat to avoid discovery, and this part is in resonance with a sense of secrecy about her parents' history.

Mercy is a tall, blonde woman whose pleasant looks are overcast by a depressed expression. Mercy and Harry are devoted to their careers, each involving occasional travel. After each of them had travelled separately on business, Mercy to a country she had not previously worked in, they met up in a small town in Romania where her grandparents live near her uncles and cousins. When she got there, Mercy immediately became surprisingly remote and listless. Harry thought that she was upset to see her grandparents getting older. Mercy felt so awful about being unable to connect to her family that she pushed to return early to the USA, where, however, she did not feel any better. Mercy became even more withdrawn, physically slowed down, and clinically depressed. Her depression deepened until she seemed to be in a trance. It was some months before Mercy revealed the trigger for her depression: she had had an affair during her trip. Betrayed, Harry left the house and Mercy's individual therapist referred Mercy to me for psychoanalysis.

Mercy was deeply remorseful. She could not understand what had happened to her, infidelity being completely out of character for her. This alerted me to the possibility of a dissociated state having taken over when she was out of her usual milieu. I thought that something associated with that country might have upset her intrapsychic economy and led to uncharacteristic behaviour and poor judgement. However, it was not specific to the particular country. The significant factor was that, away from her own milieu where she subordinated herself to Harry and his family, Mercy, on her own for two weeks in a totally new environment, felt free to be herself again. She felt acknowledged and appreciated by a colleague. She felt as if something was happening to her outside of her control as their relationship became incredibly close and she herself felt inspired and powerful to the extent that she took the initiative to have sex the night before she left. As soon as she saw Harry, she was filled with remorse and hated herself for feeling so much less than Harry before the affair and even less after it, her only remaining power being that of keeping the secret that would explain her withdrawn, sad state of mind.

Mercy's parents always felt inferior to others. Then Mercy carried forward those feelings in relation to her husband and his family. Associating with him, she hoped to build her sense of self as an American woman, but then she felt she had lost her self. She used her sexuality to reassert her sense of herself as a free and powerful individual.

In the foreign atmosphere, the repression directed at Mercy's libidinal ego lifted, and it was gratified by the sexual excitement of an affair. The rejecting object directed its hostility at Harry instead. Back home, the rejecting object reasserted its hostile repression and attacked the libidinal ego and the central ego, which now became depleted of vitality and filled with guilt.

Mercy recognised her subservience in the marriage prior to, and after, the affair, and connected it with her bending herself to suit her parents' need for her to thrive in the USA and fulfil their hopes of a better life. She also recognised that the guilt about the pain she has caused Harry is similar to the guilt and excessive concern she feels about how downtrodden her parents are and how out of touch they are with their families in Romania. So, Mercy keeps telephone contact with her grandparents, even though she dreads the calls because she feels constantly drawn into their unexplained sadness. She calls, but she withdraws from the impact of the atmosphere that is inexplicably sad by going into a kind of trance.

In terms of link theory, Mercy was born into a link in which the vertical axis connected to a culture of torture, repression, and secrecy for survival in the grandparent generation, and cultural dislocation and separation in the parents' generation. On the horizontal axis, she was connected through her education and her life in the USA to a middle-class life of learning and opportunity, a life of greater security and fulfilment than her parents enjoyed.

When Mercy's mother heard about the affair, she told Mercy that she had had an affair the year that she and Mercy were in America before being joined by her father and brother. This affair had hurt Mercy's father deeply and might explain some of the parents' depression. Coincidentally, Harry's mother told them of an affair she had had. Harry was furious at his parents' apparently ideal marriage having this hidden flaw. Harry stuck by Mercy loyally, but every so often he broke down in fear and anger, mirroring his parents' marriage, which had seemed strong, but had broken down.

On the horizontal axis of the link, Mercy was affected by hidden infidelity, shame, and guilt, augmented by her husband being on a similar link, which affected the integrity of the link they created as a couple.

Mercy spoke of going into a trance in response to the mystery of her grandparents' sadness. I had seen for myself that her affair had left her in a trance-like state. These two trance-like features gave me the idea that the affair had occurred in a trance. In a moment outside her reality in the USA, Mercy had experienced a direct unconscious, unverbalisable intergenerational transmission from her parents' fracturing experience between two countries. Her affair burst open one element of a family secret she had been searching to unravel, and exploded her husband's apparent security.

To put it in terms of link theory, the couple relationship lay at the crosshairs of a link on the vertical axis, connecting Mercy to her grandparents' unexplained sadness, and on the horizontal axis connecting both members of the couple to their parents' marital histories.

Mercy had a dream of being in a room looking at a door. She said,

> "Something was happening behind that door that I couldn't understand. I pushed the door, but it wouldn't open. I saw that there was a slit under the door that I could look through, and when I bent down to look under the door, I saw another room and I could almost see another door. I looked under the first door at the second door many times, but I couldn't quite see because the second door was too far away, the slit was too small, and the angle not quite right. But whatever was happening behind the

> second door was the explanation for a big discovery. A whole lot of spiders kept heading for the first door and going in under it to the space beyond. Then the angle changed, and I saw them all go in behind the second door, and that was like, 'Aha, that explains it!'"

Fairbairn saw a dream as a short film of the endopsychic situation. In this dream, we can imagine that the doors represent the levels of repression affecting her internal object relationships. I also look in the dream for evidence of the transference. I saw myself in the spiders, as many versions of me scurrying around the doors of her unconscious mind. I thought that the first door represented the problem of unconscious communication with her parents, especially her mother, a door which she had begun to open in analysis, and the second door would lead to exploring with me the impact of the previous generation, for which she was now preparing the way.

Mercy continued telling the dream:

> "Grandma came in to the room, and so did Harry. I had all the things I was holding—candy, a book, many random items. I found it hard to hold on to them all, and I kept dropping some of them and would have to pick them up. Grandma was trying to take some of them, and I really didn't want her to. So I reorganised them to hold on to them. I hid two candies in the pages of the book. She really wanted them, and I shouted, 'No you can't have them; this is the one thing you can't have.'"

Two candies are hidden in a book. The candies represent a pair of exciting objects that are desired by the grandmother, but denied to her. The libidinal ego is projected into the grandmother and the antilibidinal ego rejects it and this rejection also protects the exciting internal object represented by the candies. I thought that the two candies as "one thing" represented the fragile internal couple (based on Mercy's experience of her parents' and her in-laws' marriage) and the actual couple with her husband that she is fighting to save from the onslaught of the link to the past. I also saw Mercy's transference to me as the grandmother who must be kept at bay.

Mercy continued,

> "For instance, when I answered her about the two candies and said, 'No you can't have them,' it was so hard to say it, but I only had to say it once about this one thing, these two candies. I was adamant. I said to myself, 'No, you can't let her have them, and you can't feel bad about it.' I don't

know if I should bother calling my grandparents because I can't talk to them about how I feel about what they are not saying. I can't tell them that they make me feel bad and guilty. I feel blocked. I can't get through to what it is that they aren't saying. If I don't call them I feel bad, and I don't want to do it, but I feel I have to."

I said, "You know there is a block, but you aren't sure you want to get beyond it, just like in the dream you find a way to see past the first blocked door to the second blocked door, but not what's behind it."

Mercy responded, "It feels as if there is a secret that would explain me. Am I just making it up? This secret?"

I said, "It is a powerful hidden thing you don't feel entitled to see yet, but have to deal with, whether you alone made it up or not."

"This is my life now. But why did I have to shout at her?"

I said, "You were urgently trying to protect yourself and Harry from the effects of the past."

She said, "I'm not sure what I'm protecting us from. How can the past affect Harry and me?"

I said, "It already did. Your parents and Harry's parents both had a painful problem with affairs, and that pattern re-emerged in your marriage. Even though you had no conscious knowledge of it, the need to solve an emotional problem was transmitted from both families to you as a couple having to deal with infidelity and the hurt it caused."

She said, "That's possible, given how much sense some of this has made, and how I've felt."

The dream had done its work of revealing to Mercy the transgenerational transmission of trauma and marking her wish to transform its effects on her. The dreamwork enabled her to confront the troubling uncertainties of the previous generation, and leave them in the past.

This recalls the link for me. I, too, had a grandmother with a secret hurt that I wanted to know all about, and, like Mercy, I had to figure it out for myself and then let it go. Like Mercy, I, too, am Americanised and felt distant from my Scottish mother, whose discomfort with my American ways I did not fully appreciate. She thought I was becoming soft. But, as time went on, central heating came to Aberdeen, too. Now I have lost the comforts of a mother in Scotland to return to. Still, my Scottish roots are evident in me, and I am evidence of them, born as I was into a culture rich in expressing and exporting ideas.

Now: object relations in teaching with the group affective model

Sutherland appreciated Fairbairn's object relations concepts and applied them to community mental health and psychotherapy education. David Scharff and I applied them to couple and family therapy (Scharff & Scharff, 1987). Combining Fairbairn's views on personality formation with Bion's (1961) findings on the unconscious life of groups, we arrived at the design of training programmes using the group affective model at the International Psychotherapy Institute in Washington, DC, and reaching out to China, Russia, and Central America (Scharff & Scharff, 2000; Scharff & Varvin, 2014; Setton, Varela, Scharff, & Scharff, 2005).

Students who come to learn psychoanalytic concepts often feel disturbed by what they have come to learn. It is one thing to recognise the function of exciting and rejecting objects in a patient or a family in treatment, and quite another thing to recognise the craving and longing, the feelings of rage and abandonment, arising from them in oneself. Learning itself is an exciting object. Students come eager to be enlightened, but the shame of ignorance and the difficulty of learning can make them hate the learning task, the teacher, and the institution. In education, transference and countertransference abound and are usually ignored. In the group affective model, we focus in small groups on the students' emotional responses, as well as on their cognitive appreciation of the concepts and their clinical application. Individual reactions combine with others to create observable processes that illustrate the very concepts under discussion. At the institutional level, we note that one small group might proceed with enthusiasm and with so much delight in their group leader that they create envy in another group, while that group is filled with resistance and complaints about its leader: one group functions as an exciting object, the other as a rejecting object. In this split, each individual can avoid recognising ambivalence about the learning task and mourning the object that is neither perfectly good and loveable nor perfectly bad and hateable. In plenary meetings, we contemplate the institution itself as a whole, comprising all its small groups, each one of which represents one aspect of the total endeavour. Again, we apply object relations concepts to understanding the institution, the reciprocal process of teaching and learning, and the individual and group unconscious life.

In my personal life and in my professional work, object relations theory supplemented by link theory propels my thinking about the inner world and its correspondence in the outer world. Object relations theory and link theory apply across the therapeutic modalities, across class distinctions, and across nations. They are equally useful in individual therapy with private patients and community work with underserved areas. They give us a way of working with individual unconscious patterns and their interaction with the unconscious of others in couples, in families, and in countries on the world stage. We teach object relations and link theory to psychotherapists, and those same theories apply to the design of the teaching programme. The theory being taught provides the theory with which to study the processes of unconscious communication in the learning process itself.

The University of Edinburgh's Department of Psychiatry and the Scottish Institute of Human Relations were the settings for my appreciation of the value of object relations theory. When I went on to train in adolescent and family therapy at the Tavistock Centre in the early 1970s, and when I became a trainer at the Washington School of Psychiatry in the 1980s, I applied object relations theory to understanding family dynamics. In the 2000s, learning about link theory has added a dimension to object relations theory for me by including earlier generational experiences and wider socio-politico-cultural influences. David Scharff and I have melded concepts from chaos theory, attachment theory, neuroscience, object relations, and link theory to elaborate our understanding of inner and outer worlds and arrive at our concept of the interpersonal unconscious (Scharff & Scharff, 2011).

From then to now, object relations theory from Edinburgh, via London and Washington, remains relevant, flexible, and accommodating to new ideas. It continues to inspire the development of psychoanalytic theory and its teaching through training programmes in psychoanalysis and psychodynamic psychotherapy around the world. Object relations theory holds its place as the bridge between inner and outer worlds.

References

Bion, W. R. (1961). *Experiences in Groups and Other Papers*. London: Tavistock.

Birtles, E. F., & Scharff, D. E. (Eds.) (1994). *From Instinct to Self*, Vol. 2. Northvale, NJ: Jason Aronson.

Bone, K. (n.k.). Prayer to Saint Andrew, from privately produced pamphlet, reprinted by the Scottish Poetry Library. Accessed November 2012 at: http://www.scotslanguage.com/books/view/15/1089.

Dicks, H. V. (1967). *Marital Tensions*. London: Routledge.

Erikson, E. (1950). *Childhood and Society* (revised paperback edn). New York: Norton, 1963.

Fairbairn, W. R. D. (1952). *Psychoanalytic Studies of the Personality*. London: Routledge & Kegan Paul.

Fairbairn, W. R. D. (1963). A synopsis of object relations theory. *International Journal of Psycho-Analysis*, *44*: 224–225.

Freud, S. (1905d). *Three Essays on the Theory of Sexuality*. *S.E.*, *7*: 135–243. London: Hogarth.

Grotstein, J. S., & Rinsley, D. B. (Eds.) (1994). *Fairbairn and the Origin of Object Relations*. London: Free Association Books.

Harrow, A., Leishman, M., & Brearley, J. (1989). The development of an institute for the caring professions. *Psychoanalytic Psychotherapy*, *4*(2): 183–196.

Harrow, A., Leishman, M., Macdonald, M., & Scott, D. (1994). Introduction. In: J. S. Scharff (Ed.), *The Autonomous Self: The Work of John D. Sutherland*, (pp. xv–xxv.) Northvale, NJ: Jason Aronson.

Pichon-Rivière, E. (1971). *La Psiquiatría, una Nueva Problemática. Del Psicoanálisis a la Psicología Social*. Buenos Aires: Nueva Vision.

Savege, J. (1975). Psychodynamic understanding in community psychiatry. *Psychotherapy and Psychosomatics*, *25*: 272–278.

Scharff, D. E., & Birtles, E. F. (Eds.) (1994). *From Instinct to Self, Vol 1. Selected Papers of W. R. D. Fairbairn*. Northvale, NJ: Jason Aronson.

Scharff, D. E., & Scharff, J. S. (1987). *Object Relations Family Therapy*. Northvale, NJ: Jason Aronson.

Scharff, D. E., & Scharff, J. S. (2011). *The Interpersonal Unconscious*. Lanham, MD: Jason Aronson.

Scharff, D. E., & Varvin, S. (Eds.) (2014). *Psychoanalysis in China*. London: Karnac (in press).

Scharff, J. (Ed.) (1994). *The Autonomous Self. The Work of John D. Sutherland*. Northvale, NJ: Jason Aronson.

Scharff, J. (Ed.) (2007). *The Psychodynamic Image: John D. Sutherland on Self and Society*. London: Routledge.

Scharff, J. S., & Scharff, D. E. (2000). *Tuning the Therapeutic Instrument*. Northvale, NJ: Jason Aronson.

Scharff, J. S., & Scharff, D. E. (Eds.) (2005). *The Legacy of Fairbairn and Sutherland*. London: Routledge.

Setton, L., Varela, Y., Scharff, D. E., & Scharff, J. S. (2005). Teaching object relations theory with the Group Affective Model. In: J. Scharff & D. Scharff (Eds.), *The Legacy of Fairbairn and Sutherland* (pp. 271–282). London: Routledge.

Sutherland, J. D. (1963). Object relations theory and the conceptual model of psychoanalysis. *British Journal of Medical Psychology, 36*: 109–124.

Sutherland, J. D. (1966). The psychotherapeutic clinic and community psychiatry. *Bulletin of the Menninger Clinic, 30*: 338–350.

Sutherland, J. D. (1989). *Fairbairn's Journey to the Interior*. London: Free Association Books.

Sutherland, J. D. (1993). The autonomous self. *Bulletin of the Menninger Clinic, 57*(1): 3–32.

CHAPTER THREE

A liminal practice? Making interdisciplinary spaces for psychoanalysis

Liz Bondi

Introduction

Like many counsellors and psychotherapists in the UK, I trained on a part-time basis in the middle of an apparently quite unrelated career. In my case, I was an academic based in human geography, interested in feminist debates about gender, knowledge, and everyday life. When I began my training, I was familiar with a variety of feminist engagements with psychoanalytic ideas. However, my knowledge was largely theoretical and I looked forward to understanding what psychoanalytic ideas might mean in practice. I did, indeed, learn about that, but much else in my training surprised me. It had not occurred to me, for example, that I would find the language of counselling and psychotherapy to be so resonantly spatial in its talk of such themes as "boundaries", "interior worlds", and the configuration of consulting rooms. The distance between my original discipline of human geography and the new field I was entering did not seem as great as I had anticipated, and the area of overlap held out great promise.

In the years since then, I have "migrated" from an academic post in human geography to one in counselling and psychotherapy, but my position is intrinsically hybrid in that I am a Professor of Social Geography who is based in a department of counselling and psychotherapy, and I contribute to conferences and scholarly activities in both fields.

Although I have found the interface between human geography and psychotherapy to be a rich one, it remains unusual, and my hybrid position can cause confusion and bemusement. People ask me how on earth can geography and psychotherapy be combined? In this chapter, I aim to shed some light on this combination, and, in so doing, to reflect on the title of this book. What does it mean to "make spaces" in which psychoanalytic thinking can be put to work? I argue for the relevance—implicitly as much as explicitly—of geographical ideas to psychoanalytic thinking and practice in the context of a wider commitment to the value of disciplinary openness and porosity that this volume elaborates. I begin by revisiting Freud's essay "The question of lay analysis" (1926e), drawing attention to the way in which his defence of lay analysis articulates an interdisciplinary vision for psychoanalysis. Then, still focusing on "The question of lay analysis", I turn to what I call "Freud's geographies". I draw out two distinct dimensions of these geographies, one concerned with geographical variation and the other with spatial concepts. With respect to the former, I point to geographical critiques of the kind of position Freud took, which assumed that psychoanalysis could develop into a universally invariant theory and practice unaffected by local circumstances. Contrary to this, and disagreeing with Freud, I offer examples of how psychoanalysis has been shaped by the contexts in which they have developed, generating different schools and a dynamic pattern of geographical variation.

Turning to spatial concepts, I again locate Freud's position in relation to geographical debates and illustrate the continuing influence of spatial thinking. Just as psychoanalysis inhabits geographically variable external environments, so, too, it invokes interior realms of extraordinary complexity and diversity. Agreeing with, and seeking to take forward, this aspect of Freud's geographies, I argue that, in a variety of ways, psychoanalytic thinking appeals to and explores liminal spaces located at the interface between interior and exterior worlds. In so doing, I hope to illustrate something of the interdisciplinary potential that lies between psychoanalysis and geography (Kingsbury & Pile, 2014).

Freud on the question of lay analysis

In "The question of lay analysis" (Freud, 1926e), and the postscript published a year later (Freud, 1927a), Freud argued that educated lay people, by whom he meant people other than qualified medical doctors, should be able to train and practise as psychoanalysts. He noted that "lay analysts who practise analysis today [are not] any chance collection of riff-raff, but people of academic education, doctors of philosophy, educationalists, together with a few women of great experience in life and outstanding personality" (Freud, 1926e, p. 245). On Freud's account (1926e, p. 228), at this time in its history, psychoanalytic training institutes were still in their infancy, existing only in Vienna and Berlin, with plans afoot for a third institute in London. However, Freud allowed himself to imagine what a university education in psychoanalysis might look like and argued that it would need to include

> branches of knowledge which are remote from medicine and which the doctor does not come across in his practice: the history of civilization, mythology, the psychology of religion and the science of literature. (Freud, 1926e, p. 246)

Freud also emphasised the potential for collaboration between psychoanalysis and other disciplines and professions. For example, he envisioned psychoanalysts and educationalists working together in support of child development, and speculated about the possibility of "spending a little to get the 'social workers' . . . trained analytically and to turn them into a band of helpers for combating cultural neuroses" (Freud, 1926e, p. 250). His interest in the psychological expression and meaning of myths, creative arts, and historical events underlay his view that psychoanalysis "cannot do without the cooperation of people who have had a preliminary training in the *mental* sciences" (Freud, 1927a, p. 257, original emphasis). A new translation of some of Freud's essays by Alan Bance (Freud, 2002) uses the much more familiar term "the humanities" to describe what the translators of *The Standard Edition* refer to as "the mental sciences".

Although Freud argued for the superiority of psychoanalysis relative to other forms of psychological healing, he also recognised that the blending of psychoanalytic insights with other ideas was inevitable. He noted how psychoanalytically trained clergy "are often able to relieve their parishioners of the inhibitions of their daily life by confirming their faith – after offering them a little analytical information about the nature of their conflicts" (Freud, 1927a, p. 256). In this context, he suggested that "the words 'secular pastoral worker' might well serve as a general formula for describing the function which the analyst, whether he is a doctor or a layman, has to perform in his relation to the public" (Freud, 1927a, pp. 256–257). Expressing his commitment to a psychoanalytic theory firmly grounded in practice, he emphasised the "inseparable bond between cure and research", and he argued that "only by carrying on our analytical pastoral work [can] we deepen our dawning comprehension of the human mind" (Freud, 1927a, p. 256).

By framing psychoanalysis as "analytical pastoral work" or "secular pastoral" care, Freud simultaneously put distance between psychoanalysis and medicine, and positioned psychoanalysis as a successor to religiously based pastoral care. Elsewhere, of course, he articulated an antireligious stance more fiercely, but the key point to which I wish to draw attention is that Freud's discussion and defence of lay analysis was not simply about the relationship between psychoanalysis and medicine. Crucially, Freud also articulated an interdisciplinary and multi-disciplinary vision for psychoanalysis in which both the theory (for Freud, the "science") and the practice have the potential to enrich and to be enriched by a diverse range of other academic fields and professional practices. The explorations in this volume of a variety of applications of psychoanalytic thinking in the context of other professions and practices might, therefore, be thought of as expressing something of Freud's vision from nearly a century ago.

In promoting his interdisciplinary vision in "The question of lay analysis", Freud made no direct reference to geography as an academic discipline or field of study. This is not particularly surprising. While geographers, perhaps most notably Glacken (1967), have traced geographical thinking to and through the ancient world and subsequent eras, geography did not find a distinct place within university education until the late nineteenth century. Its ensuing disciplinary institutionalisation was messy, contested, and uneven (Livingstone, 1992). It did not fit easily within the developing academic division of labour, straddling the physical and human sciences. It has not always held together across this academic fault-line, and struggled for recognition in some places, notably the USA, as well as with the general public (Johnston & Williams, 2003; Smith, 1987). However, although Freud did not refer explicitly to geography as a discipline, in two rather different ways he did, nevertheless, engage with geographical concerns. First, he situated his argument for lay analysis in relation to geographical variations in the circumstances in which psychoanalysts then practised, and secondly, he emphasised the value of spatial concepts to psychoanalytic theory. I elaborate each of these features of his account in turn and use them to reflect further on the relevance of geography to psychoanalysis and its various psychotherapeutic offspring.

Geographical variations in and beyond the question of lay analysis

Freud's original essay drew attention to differences between Austria, where, in the mid-1920s, the right to treat the sick was legally restricted to medical doctors, and both Germany and America, where "every patient can have himself treated how and by whom he chooses" (Freud, 1926e, p. 183). As Freud explained, his essay was prompted by "a charge of quackery [i.e., fraudulent medical practice] brought against a non-medical member of our Society, Dr Theodor Reik, in the Vienna Courts" (Freud, 1927a, p. 251). The 1927 postscript closes with reference to the very different context of psychoanalysis in America, where, he acknowledged, "lay analysts put analysis to all kinds of mischievous and illegitimate purposes and in consequence cause injury to their patients and to the good name of analysis" (Freud, 1927a, p. 258).

Freud was, thus, clearly at pains to acknowledge that local circumstances matter. However, while he expressed sympathy with American colleagues in relation to the specific problems they faced, he was also insistent that "the question of lay analysis must not be decided on practical considerations alone and local conditions in America cannot be the sole determining influence on our views" (Freud, 1927a, p. 258). For Freud, it was imperative that principles—in this case concerning who should be eligible to train as an analyst—be considered and established separately from what might be pragmatic locally. He assumed that the new profession of psychoanalysis, like that of medicine, had the potential to rise above the specificity of time and place.

In so doing, Freud deployed a commonplace way of understanding the difference that place makes, which is as a more or less idiosyncratic local context from which universal and implicitly placeless ideas and practices need to be abstracted. So, while geographical variations may have borne upon the science and profession of psychoanalysis in the 1920s, Freud's vision and aspiration appears to have been that local anomalies would, in due course, be transcended, so that a singular psychoanalysis could achieve something akin to global reach.

That progress might expunge significant aspects of local variability is a widespread trope of twentieth century thought (Harvey, 1989). It is closely linked to the aspirations of scientific theories and practices of many kinds, in which fundamental principles are formulated without reference to context. This kind of universalism has been subject to criticism from a range of perspectives. For example, feminist historian of science Donna Haraway, who initially trained as a biologist, argued that knowledge is necessarily "situated", in the sense of arising from a particular perspective or location, and, therefore, as bearing the impress of its originating context (Haraway, 1988). In another register, professor of planning Bent Flyvbjerg, inspired by his research on the Danish planning system, has argued that a key characteristic of the social sciences is that they address concerns that lose their meaning if abstracted from real, context-specific examples (Flyvbjerg, 2001). This makes a great deal of sense in relation to psychoanalysis, where the value of theoretical ideas is much less in their capacity for unvarying universality than in the scope they offer to be adapted and worked with in specific contexts. Picking up more specifically on Freud's view that geographical variations are contingent anomalies, geographers have long contested this position, arguing instead that spatial variations are intrinsic to the nature of an enormous range of phenomena in the human world (and, indeed, the non-human world) (Massey, 2005). On this account, *where* psychoanalytic work takes place shapes what it is. In what follows, I illustrate this claim with brief reference to geographical variations in the disciplinary location of training, in the legal parameters of practice, and in relation to psychoanalytic theory.

For Freud, the discipline of psychology had failed to engage adequately with ordinary mental life by ignoring unconscious processes and assuming "that all mental acts are conscious to us" (Freud, 1926e, p. 196). Freud argued that psychoanalysis constituted a new kind of psychology, which had the potential to become "not the whole of psychology but its substructure and perhaps even its entire foundation" (Freud, 1927a, p. 252). Freud's ambition for psychoanalysis has not been realised: as far as I am aware, nowhere is it regarded as the basis or foundation of psychology more generally. Rather, in the decades since the establishment of psychoanalysis, its relationship to psychology has varied temporally and geographically, in some times and places becoming rather fraught. Referring to the UK and North America, Erica Burman has described psychoanalysis as "the repressed other of psychology", but in other parts of the world, such as Latin America, "psychoanalysis has been allied with psychology, and is even a dominant form of psychology" (Burman, 2008, p. 5). In many European countries, a first degree in psychology or a closely related discipline has become the prerequisite for training as a psychoanalyst or psychotherapist. In the UK, however, where psychoanalysis has tended to remain marginal to mainstream psychology degree programmes, no such requirement exists, and people enter training programmes from a variety of backgrounds. Although some come with prior experience of psychiatric settings, and psychoanalytic training often requires those who do not to spend time in such settings during their training, the tradition of disciplinary openness means that practitioners in the UK have more diverse backgrounds and pathways into psychoanalysis and psychotherapy than is the case in many other contexts.

The legal parameters within which psychoanalysts practise have become more, rather than less, geographically variable in the decades since Freud's original intervention on the question of lay analysis. During his own lifetime, positions hardened, and the disciplinary openness of European developments increasingly contrasted with the effective capture of psychoanalysis by psychiatry in the USA. As a consequence, Freud's plea that those without medical degrees might train as psychoanalysts fell on deaf ears in the USA, where it became and remained the preserve of the medical profession for some fifty years (Wallerstein, 1998).

The legal framing of psychoanalytic practice developed differently elsewhere and has been complicated by the proliferation of other forms of psychotherapy. These have generated a plethora of titles, which are subject to different forms of, and requirements for, licensing and regulation in different places. For example, the relatively new title of "counsellor/counselor" is subject to different licensing arrangements in different states in the USA and provinces in Canada. In the UK, where the regulation of professions is not devolved to the constituent parts of the country, the first decade of the twenty-first century witnessed new twists and turns in the relationship between medicine, psychology, psychoanalysis, and other professions as a result of efforts to bring the so-called psychological therapies into a formal system of regulation. In 2001, the then (Labour) UK government announced its intention to regulate a set of practices including psychology, psychoanalysis, psychotherapy, and counselling. In 2007, the route for this regulation was specified as the Health Professions Council, which is a successor body to what had previously been called the Council for Professions Allied to Medicine. This route was accepted by the body representing psychologists, for whom regulation came into force in 2009, covering a wide range of job titles that include the word "psychologist", such as clinical psychologists, educational psychologists, counselling psychologists, and health psychologists. However, psychoanalysts, psychotherapists, and counsellors vociferously resisted regulation via a body strongly influenced by medicine. In 2011, following the election of a new government in 2010, the plan to regulate these groups via the Health Professions Council (now Health and Care Professions Council) was abandoned. Consequently, at least in terms of regulation, psychology in the UK currently appears to be more closely aligned to medicine than other psychotherapeutic practices, including psychoanalysis, which continue to be legally unregulated.

This recent British story is full of local contingencies. Had the medical profession not been rocked by a series of scandals in the 1990s, had the Health Professions Council not come into being in 2001, or had there not been a change of government in 2010, events might have unfolded differently. But laws and regulations are always geographically framed (even when they are international in scope). Furthermore, whether viewed as a triumph or fiasco, the British experience becomes an example that influences the course of developments elsewhere. What happens in one place influences what happens in others. Just as opponents of the British proposals for the state regulation of psychoanalysts drew on experiences in other countries to make their case (Parker & Revelli, 2008), so the British story is likely to be drawn upon to inform debates and developments elsewhere.

I turn next to geographical variations in psychoanalytic theory. Here, my intention is to illustrate how psychoanalytic thinking bears the impress of its cultural and geographical context. It is commonplace to think about the impact of particular life stories on the work of major psychoanalytic thinkers: examples include the connections between the multiple tragedies of Melanie Klein's life and her emphasis on destructive psychic forces, and the connections between Ronald Laing's highly controlling mother and his concept of the schizophrenic family. It is a small step from this to consider the cultural shaping of psychoanalysis: for example, the influence of anti-Semitism on Freud's work. Cultural influences are themselves intrinsically geographical, as I show with a few brief illustrations.

Before the First World War, psychoanalysis was attracting international interest and an annual International Psychoanalytical Congress was meeting annually. However, as Schwartz (2003) has noted, psychoanalysis lacked a secure institutional framework. Seeking to "strengthen psychoanalysis by seeking acceptance outside the Jewish circles of Vienna" (Schwartz, 2003, p. 109), Freud proposed moving the base of the nascent International Psychoanalytical Association from Vienna to Zurich, where Carl Jung was based. Thus, Freud's attempt to reach beyond his own cultural context was formulated geographically.

Freud's proposal was overtaken by his split with Jung, and the internationalisation and diversification of psychoanalysis proceeded in other ways. In the 1930s, the geography of psychoanalysis was massively affected by the rise of Nazism and the Second World War, which decimated psychoanalysis in Austria and Germany, as well as dispersing refugee psychoanalysts from central Europe to North America, South America, the UK, and elsewhere. Political ideologies and cultural conditions in different places determined not only whether psychoanalysis could be practised at all, but also how it developed as a body of theory (Roazen, 2001).

Language has also influenced the development of psychoanalysis. Translation between languages has been crucial to its travels, but is never a neutral, transparent process. For decades *The Standard Edition* has been the most widely used English-language version of Freud's original, German-language papers. However, some of the choices made by James Strachey, in his capacity as chief editor and primary translator of Freud's works, have long been contentious, generating ongoing debate and discussion. For Birksted-Breen (2010, p. 694), "these discussions and debates which take the translation of Freud into different languages as their focus are an important impetus to the development of psychoanalytic theory". Conversely, the relative paucity of translations of psychoanalytic papers from, for example, Italian, Spanish, or Portuguese into English has impoverished debates conducted solely within the English language.

The local shaping of psychoanalysis has been explored in relation to a number of geographical and cultural contexts. In relation to Scotland, Gavin Miller has argued that classic Scottish contributions to psychoanalytic theory—including the work of Ian Suttie, Ronald Fairbairn, Hugh Crichton-Miller, Ronald Laing, and John Sutherland—bear the impress of a distinctively Scottish philosophical and theological tradition (Miller, 2008). He draws attention to the importance of communion or fellowship within Scottish religious, cultural, and intellectual life, which he traces through the writings of Scottish psychoanalysts, which have, in turn, influenced others within and beyond the psychoanalytic field in Scotland and elsewhere. Developing this theme, Fergusson (2012) points to significant resonances between the work of the Scottish philosopher John Macmurray and the Scottish psychoanalysts Ian Suttie and Ronald Fairbairn in their emphasis on personal relationships. This was applied by Macmurray to relationships between professional experts and their patients, clients, or pupils, and elaborated by Suttie and Fairbairn in their respective contributions to what became the British object relations tradition in psychoanalysis, a distinctly Scottish strand of which has been described as "personal relations theory" (Clarke, 2006; Fergusson, 2013; Kirkwood, 2012).

Perhaps more widely recognised than a distinctive Scottish tradition are different "schools" of psychoanalysis, broadly aligned with national states, including the British school of object relations, the North American school of self psychology, the French Lacanian school, and the Latin American school of analytic field theory. These schools have not remained ensconced within national boundaries, but have themselves travelled, shaping and being shaped by the cultural and political circumstances they encountered and in which they became embedded. Cushman (1996) has explored one highly influential example by tracing the interplay between American psychotherapy and American consumerism. He argues that both the self psychology of Heinz Kohut, who left Austria in 1940 and settled in the USA, and the object relations theory of the British psychoanalyst D. W. Winnicott, foregrounded a configuration of the self as an internal world "peopled" by internal objects, but also characterised by lacks, gaps, and emptiness. This empty self, Cushman (1996) argued, fits perfectly with the logic of consumerism in which ceaseless acquisition promises, but forever fails, to fill these internal voids.

Spatial thinking in and beyond Freud's exposition of psychoanalysis

I turn next to another aspect of Freud's geographies, that is, the value he placed on spatial concepts. In "The question of lay analysis", Freud presented psychoanalytic theory to an imagined interlocutor new to the field. In this context, he drew attention to the importance of a spatial perspective to describe what he called "the pictures we have formed of the structure of the mental apparatus in the course of our analytical studies" (Freud, 1926e, pp. 193–194). He explained that the parts of this "unknown apparatus" need to be understood as having "a fixed spatial relation to one another", and he illustrated "spatial relation" as being "'in front of' and 'behind', 'superficial' and 'deep'" (Freud, 1926e, p. 194). Where his reliance on spatial thinking might have passed unnoticed, he chose to emphasise it:

> we suppose that the ego is the layer of the mental apparatus (of the id) which has been modified by the influence of the external world (of reality). This will show you how in psycho-analysis we take a spatial way of looking at things seriously. For us the ego is really something superficial and the id is something deeper – looked at from the outside, of course. (Freud, 1926e, pp. 195–196)

So, while Freud might have viewed differences between places as local idiosyncrasies that detracted from the rational development of psychoanalysis, he found ideas about space essential to his theory. Sometimes, he drew diagrams to elaborate his topographical understanding of the psyche (Freud, 1923b, 1933a). As the quotation above indicates, as well as drawing on spatial ideas to explain what he proposes as a universal theory, he acknowledged that the position of the knower matters: what is on the surface and what lies deep inside depend upon one's position.

Freud conceptualised the unconscious as simultaneously dynamic and "quite timeless" (Freud, 1901b, p. 274). This timelessness means that the unconscious cannot forget. Consequently, unconscious knowledge persists and returns regardless of time passing, hence the unremitting immediacy of such experiences as traumatic flashbacks, and the reappearance, sometimes in new forms, of apparently long forgotten symptoms. The unconscious does not "obey" normative rules of material space any more than it does time. However, the language of space offers what Lakoff and Johnson (1980) have called orientational metaphors, which, they argue, draw on our bodily experience of negotiating our physical environments. While Freud's interest lay with mental life, he understood this to be biologically grounded and conveyed a strong sense of embodied existence. In this sense, and echoing Lakoff and Johnson's (1980) account of "metaphors we live by", Freud's use of spatial metaphors in "The question of lay analysis" and elsewhere reflected his understanding of the embodied materiality of mental life.

A feature of psychoanalytic theory from Freud onwards is that it offers a framework for thinking about how what is outside our minds—other people (or parts of them), the cultures into which we are born, the material entities that surround us—gets inside, and how what is inside gets outside. Psychoanalysis understands the boundary between inside and outside to be unstable, porous, and endlessly mutable. These ideas—of boundaries, and of the distinction between inside and outside—are intrinsically spatial. Not surprisingly, therefore, subsequent psychoanalytic writers have followed Freud's reliance on a richly spatial language. In some cases, Freud's diagrammatic mapping of the structures of the mind has been taken up, most notably by Fairbairn, who drew on and transformed Freud's topographical model in the development of his "endopsychic structure", elaborating his theoretical ideas by mapping them in two dimensions (Fairbairn, 1952). Another example is provided by Winnicott's concept of potential space, which refers to an area of illusion between inside and outside and between self and other. In addition, Winnicott's notion of the facilitative environment, according to which the needs of a person (archetypically the infant) are understood in relation to a surrounding landscape of provision, the qualities of which support or undermine the person's development and flourishing (Winnicott, 1965, 1971). From Bion, we have the concept of containment, which gives spatial form to the dynamic relationship between container and contained, equivalent in Bion's thinking to the mother's mind and the infant's unconscious experience (Bion, 1963). Indeed, the whole edifice of object relations theory relies heavily on spatial concepts, portraying unconscious life as dynamic figures—or objects—in a landscape (Cushman, 1996). In the Spanish-language tradition of Argentinean psychoanalysis, different but comparable spatial concepts developed. For example, Pichon-Rivière conceptualised the "field of the analytic situation" as a triangular structure in which analyst and analysand interact and communicate unconsciously as well as consciously (Baranger & Baranger, 2008, p. 799; Churcher, 2008).

This reliance on, and development of, spatial concepts continues into contemporary psychoanalytic writing and is evident in different schools. For example, Leader's recent (2008) discussion of depression, mourning and melancholia, which is informed by Lacanian as well as object relations theory, describes the work of mourning in terms of four motifs or elements, each of which is intrinsically spatial. First, he explores "the introduction of a frame to mark out a symbolic, artificial space" (Leader, 2008, p. 168) that enables the loss that haunts us to be represented and, thereby, contained or demarcated. Secondly, he argues that in order to live with the impacts of bereavement we need to lay our dead to rest symbolically, which, in a wide variety of ways, entails performing some kind of spatial separation, such as burial in a demarcated space. On his account "[k]illing the dead is a way of loosening one's bonds to them and situating them in different, symbolic space" (Leader, 2008, p. 124). Thirdly, he points to the need to separate "the images of those things that matter to us from the *place* that they occupy" (Leader, 2008, p.131, original emphasis). In the language of object relations, this requires "the mourner to be able to differentiate, at an unconscious level, between the object and the place of the object" (Leader, 2008, p. 131). In other words, we separate our image of the lost person from the place they occupied in our unconscious life. The final element in Leader's account involves "giving up the image of who we were" (2008, p. 168) for the person we have lost, which, conversely, requires us to separate our image of our place in the life of our lost loved one from our (continuing) sense of who we are.

The language of psychotherapeutic practice is correspondingly rich in spatial concepts, which move easily between practitioners who locate their work within different theoretical frameworks. For example, enormous emphasis is placed on therapeutic boundaries. These include the "clock time" and the physical spaces that frame therapeutic work, limits on the kind of contact between practitioners and clients both within and outside therapeutic sessions, matters of confidentiality through which the communications between practitioners and clients are carefully protected without becoming secrets, and more intangible experiences of psychological safety and impingement, invoked, for example, when practitioners refer to feeling "pushed" or somehow intruded upon by ways in which their clients make conscious or unconscious "use" of them within the therapeutic work. Unconscious dimensions of communication between and beyond practitioners and clients are often conceptualised in terms of projective and introjective processes, which appeal to movement between psyches and, therefore, across boundaries between inside and outside.

Practitioners also invest much meaning in the material spaces in which therapeutic work takes place, placing a very high premium on consistency (i.e., meeting in the same room in the same building with minimum alteration to the furnishings and other contents) and freedom from impingement (i.e., a space protected from the intrusion of others physically, visually, and aurally). The spatial configuration of practitioner and client within the room is equally invested with meaning. Freud adopted the practice of sitting on a chair out of the line of vision of his analysand, who lay on a couch. Chair and couch have been configured differently by others, and many newer approaches have opted for practitioner and client to sit more or less (but not directly) face-to-face in chairs of equal height.

These apparently practical details about physical spaces are invested with significance in ways that connect back to Freud's portrayal of

> the ego as a kind of façade of the id, as a frontage, like an external, cortical layer of it. . . . We know that cortical layers owe their peculiar characteristics to the modifying influence of the external medium on which they abut. . . . The ego lies between reality and the id, which is what is truly mental. (1926e, p. 195)

In psychotherapeutic practice, we engage with our clients' "cortical layers" (translated by Bance (Freud, 2002) as "shells"), as well as what lies underneath those outer layers. The work is often about the complex interconnections between surface and interior, between the ego and the id. To do this work, we provide an "external medium", one into which clients bring the "peculiar characteristics" (translated by Bance as "particular qualities") of the "cortical layers" they inhabit. The external medium of therapy is carefully demarcated from the other environments our clients inhabit and have inhabited, and its consistency is designed, in part, to help the analytic couple to see the nature of the complex adaptations or habits of engaging with the world (inner and outer) that bring the client to therapy. Consistency is not the same as rigidity, and therapists also represent their capacity for thoughtfulness in the care with which therapeutic environments are designed. The environments we make available to clients include our minds, but these are themselves hidden beneath our own outer layers or shells. However, I would suggest that we symbolise our capacity to think, and to serve as container to the client (Bion, 1963), in part through the interior designs and spatial configurations we provide.

Another way of framing this account is to describe psychotherapy as operating in a liminal zone situated at the interface between inner and outer worlds, a space described by Winnicott as "an area of illusion" (Winnicott, 1971, p. 12) and as an "intermediate area of experience, unchallenged in respect of its belonging to inner or external (shared) reality" (p. 14). For Winnicott, this area is the space of play, creativity, and cultural experience. It is what enables meanings to be shared and co-created. One way of understanding psychotherapy is as a body or bodies of theory and practice dedicated to enabling, exploring and enriching this liminal space. In this sense, psychotherapy is intrinsically geographical in its concerns.

Conclusion

Nearly a century ago, Freud offered us an interdisciplinary vision for psychoanalysis. The degree to which this has been remembered varies. In the UK, a degree of disciplinary openness has survived, and, in Scotland, Sutherland helped to institutionalise aspects of the multidisciplinarity Freud had envisaged (Scharff, 2007). The interdisciplinary interface between geography and psychoanalysis has not received a great deal of attention explicitly. However, as I have shown, more implicitly, psychoanalytic thinking and practice, both in and beyond the consulting room, are infused with geographical ideas. Indeed, psychoanalysis and its application might be described as intrinsically spatial practices. As other chapters in this volume testify, making spaces in which psychoanalytic thinking can be put to work has required much effort, but where it has been possible, it has yielded rich rewards. I would suggest that this activity of "making spaces" might be fundamental to psychoanalytic work in all its forms. Perhaps greater awareness of this, together with explicit engagement with geographical thinking, will help to foster the future shape of Freud's and Sutherland's interdisciplinary visions for psychoanalysis.

References

Baranger, W., & Baranger, M. (2008). The analytic situation as a dynamic field. *International Journal of Psychoanalysis, 89*: 795–826.

Bion, W. R. (1963). *Elements of Psychoanalysis*. London: William Heinemann.

Birksted-Breen, D. (2010). Editorial. Is translation possible? *International Journal of Psychoanalysis, 91*: 687–694.

Burman, E. (2008). *Deconstructing Developmental Psychology* (2nd edn). Hove: Routledge.

Churcher, J. (2008). Some notes on the English translation of "The analytic situation as a dynamic field" by Willy and Madeleine Baranger. *International Journal of Psychoanalysis, 89*: 785–793.

Clarke, G. (2006). *Personal Relations Theory: Fairbairn, Macmurray and Suttie*. London: Routledge.

Cushman, P. (1996). *Constructing the Self, Constructing America*. Cambridge, MA: Perseus.

Fairbairn, W. R. D (1952). *Psychoanalytic Studies of the Personality*. London: Routledge and Kegan Paul.

Fergusson, D. (2012). Persons in relation: the interaction of philosophy, theology and psychotherapy in 20th century Scotland. *Practical Theology, 5*: 287–306.

Flyvbjerg, B. (2001). *Making Social Science Matter*. Cambridge: Cambridge University Press.

Freud, S. (1901b). *The Psychopathology of Everyday Life. S.E., 6*: vii–296. London: Hogarth.

Freud, S. (1923b). *The Ego and the Id. S.E., 19*: 1–66. London: Hogarth.

Freud, S. (1926e). The question of lay analysis. *S.E., 20*: 183–250. London: Hogarth.

Freud, S. (1927a). Postscript to "The question of lay analysis". *S.E., 20*: 251–258. London: Hogarth.

Freud, S. (1933a). *New Introductory Lectures on Psychoanalysis. S.E., 22*: 1–182. London: Hogarth.

Freud, S. (2002). *Wild Analysis*, A. Phillips (Ed.), A. Bance (Trans.). London: Penguin.

Glacken, C. (1967). *Traces on the Rhodian Shore: Nature and Culture in Western Thought from Ancient Times to the End of the Eighteenth Century.* Berkeley, CA: University of California Press.

Haraway, D. (1988). Situated knowledges: the science question in feminism and the privilege of partial perspective. *Feminist Studies, 14*: 575–599.

Harvey, D. (1989). *The Condition of Postmodernity.* Oxford: Blackwell.

Johnston, R. J., & Williams, M. (Eds.) (2003). *A Century of British Geography.* Oxford: Oxford University Press.

Kingsbury, P., & Pile, S. (Eds.) (2014). *Psychoanalytic Geographies.* Aldershot: Ashgate.

Kirkwood, C. (2012). *The Persons-in-Relation Perspective.* Rotterdam: Sense.

Lakoff, G., & Johnson, M. (1980). *Metaphors We Live By.* Chicago, IL: Chicago University Press.

Leader, D. (2008). *The New Black.* London: Penguin.

Livingstone, D. (1992). *The Geographical Tradition.* Oxford: Blackwell.

Massey, D. (2005). *For Space.* London: Sage.

Miller, G. (2008). Scottish psychoanalysis: a rational religion. *Journal of the History of the Behavioural Sciences, 44*: 38–58.

Parker, I., & Revelli, S. (Eds.) (2008). *Psychoanalytic Practice and State Regulation.* London: Karnac.

Roazen, P. (2001). *The Historiography of Psychoanalysis.* New Brunswick, NJ: Transaction.

Scharff, J. (Ed.) (2007). *The Psychodynamic Image: John D. Sutherland on Self and Society.* London: Routledge.

Schwartz, J. (2003). *Cassandra's Daughters. A History of Psychoanalysis.* London: Karnac.

Smith, N. (1987). "Academic war over the field of geography": the elimination of geography at Harvard, 1947–1951. *Annals of the Association of American Geographers, 77*: 155–172.

Wallerstein, R. S. (1998). *Lay Analysis: Life Inside the Controversy*. Hillsdale, NJ: Analytic Press.
Winnicott, D. W. (1965). *The Maturational Processes and the Facilitating Environment*. London: Hogarth Press.
Winnicott, D. W. (1971). *Playing and Reality*. London: Tavistock.

PART II

MAKING SPACE TO LOVE

CHAPTER FOUR

The "Fort Da" game and other stories from infant observation

Nicola Chadd

Introduction

Infant observation has played an important part in psychoanalytic training for more than half a century. A form of observation rooted in psychoanalysis, it is an endeavour that introduces practitioners to a very particular way of being subjectively with, while, at the same time, objectively observing, the other. It gives insight into the nature and meaning of relationships, with all the joys and terrors of love and hate, intimacy, separation and loss, and it gives us a privileged view of the crucial early stages of development of the personality. As such, its value goes far beyond the practice of psychoanalysis, and the influence of infant observation, in its original form and its many adaptations, extends into many different spheres. Clearly, it is directly relevant to those concerned with child development, among them parents, teachers, health visitors, general practitioners, psychiatrists, social workers, nurses, psychologists, and psychotherapists, but this unique method of observation has the capacity to enrich our understanding of adults as well as children, groups and organisations as well as individuals. Trowell (2002) describes the value of observational skills derived from infant observations in the training of practitioners in a range of different fields, including community work with older adults, people with mental health problems, and those with disabilities, as well as in training projects with medical students and hospital doctors, police and child protection teams. She further discusses the use of this approach in decision-making for a wide variety of professionals who work with people.

The clinical application of infant observation deserves special mention. The technique in its classical (non-interventional) form can highlight areas of difficulties for mothers and their babies, while adaptations of the observational method have been developed to provide more active interventions for such problems (Rustin, 2009). Where infant development is compromised by difficulties in the mother-baby relationship, brief interventions can help promote more healthy and rewarding interactions. These approaches are of value for a wide range of early developmental difficulties and have, for example, informed work with young children with autism and those with an early history of abuse or neglect. Central to this approach is the understanding of the child's personality development, not in isolation, but within the context of his or her early relationships, the quality of those early relationships and interactions being central for the development of the personality. Finally, alongside these direct clinical applications, we are increasingly recognising the value of infant observation as a research tool, with the findings derived from such research contributing immeasurably to our understanding of the most intimate details of early development (Urwin & Sternberg, 2012).

Theoretical and historical background

Infant observation is, on the face of it, a method both simple and straightforward. The student visits an infant from birth onwards for a fixed hour each week, following the baby's development over time and within the context of the ordinary comings and goings of the family home. However, it raises many challenges: practical, emotional, theoretical. Exactly what the infant brings to his or her early interactions with carers, as well as the ways in which environmental factors shape the personality, are issues that still exercise analysts today as they did in the early days of infant observation. In Freud's early writings, the infant was a creature beset by animal instincts and concerned primarily with seeking pleasure and avoiding displeasure. From the 1920s onwards, however, there was a gradual shift in emphasis away from biologically driven instinctual processes and a correspondingly greater focus on early emotional life and the quality of relationships from birth onwards. Thus, Klein saw babies as less alienated and animal at birth, with an innate capacity for relatedness and a particular sensitivity to their human environment, especially the maternal emotional attitude they encounter (Likierman, 2001). As such, Klein was the first to provide a fully interpersonal model of early psychic life.

Klein was centrally concerned with what was going on in the minds of pre-verbal infants, and her theories attributed complex unconscious processes even to very tiny babies. These ideas about earliest infancy were controversial and, although their usefulness is now widely recognised, they do highlight a particular difficulty, which is this. Infant observation can certainly tell us a great deal about early development, but what can we learn about what is going on in the infant mind simply from observing young babies and children? We can assume that young babies have experiences, both physical and emotional, but they will not yet have the apparatus to think about them, in the ordinary meaning of the word. So, what exactly is happening in the baby's mind, intrapsychically? One way of learning about primitive mental processes is through the accounts of older children and adults, and, in part, psychoanalytic theory depends on the accounts of psychoanalytic patients to piece together the earliest stages of personality development. However, there are problems with attributing mental processes to infants on the basis of adult-derived theory. Winnicott (1957), himself an astute observer of infant and child development, wrote of the tension between theory inferred from adult patients' accounts of early childhood and that derived from direct observation of infants. He was clear that observation of babies and young children could contribute to our understanding of the relational aspects of early emotional development and also provide valuable insights into early intrapsychic development. In addition, it is a central tenet of infant observation that the close observation of babies and young children can indeed contribute to our understanding of both the relational and intrapsychic aspects of early life.

Infant observation as a method takes particular care not to make assumptions or look prematurely to theory to explain what is being observed. Instead, as illustrated in the second half of this chapter, the insights derived from it begin with observers' open-minded attention to the total situation of the baby's experience and their own emotional responses to what they are observing. When Bick (1964) first developed the technique of infant observation in the late 1940s, it was in the context of discussion—and sometimes heated debates—concerning the various psychoanalytic theories about the nature of mental processes and personality development in pre-verbal infants. Before she developed her method, observational material tended to be used as evidence in support of proponents' particular theoretical viewpoints. Rustin (2009) reminds us that newer theories, derived from empirical laboratory-based child development and attachment research and neuroscience, can similarly be used to make premature sense of observations. Bick's method is a very different proposition. It requires the observer to let go of preconceived ideas and to remain fully in the moment, attending with "free-floating attention" to the unfolding drama of the infant's development within the family.

The task, then, is to observe the baby within his or her family for a fixed hour each week, maintaining a reliable, non-intrusive, friendly, and attentive presence (Rustin, 1989). Where the observations are part of a psychoanalytic training, they will continue for a whole year, or sometimes two, supported by regular seminars with fellow students. Bick was concerned about how to gather "objective" observations. This requires more than maintaining an open mind unhindered by theoretical assumptions and pre-existing notions about infant development and childcare, challenging though this is. This aim of objectivity, in the sense of retaining an openness to what is uniquely unfolding within each particular family, must at the same time accommodate the observer's own emotional responses, because to observe in the way required of infant observation—that is, to pay full, emotionally-attuned attention to the other—inevitably has a relational aspect, arousing feelings in both observer and observed. At times, the observer will, in all sorts of ways, feel pulled away from a stable observing position, perhaps wishing to join in the infant's pleasure or provide comfort for his or her distress, perhaps feeling the pressure of a sibling or other family member to adopt a particular role, or perhaps stirred up consciously or unconsciously by personal early experience. Objectivity cannot be maintained at all times, but an understanding of the pressures that compromise this neutral observational stance, and, in particular, the unconscious pressures, is one of the most informative aspects of the observation.

A small baby has no words, no language. Yet, from birth, the infant is "programmed" to relate to others (it is "object-related"), and babies are able to communicate in the most compelling ways and with a complexity that we are still coming to understand. For the infant, without words or an apparatus for thinking (Bion, 1962a), early experience becomes part of the self at an unconscious (un-thought) level. Thus, the relationship between the infant and others, first the mother (or whoever fulfils that role) and then a gradually widening circle of people, such as father, siblings, wider family, and friends, involves unconscious communication, and these unconscious processes have a central role in shaping the personality. Unconscious processes remain just as important throughout the lifespan, and continue to play a part in all human relating and relatedness. In infant observation, we are concerned with the interplay between the baby's internal world and the unconscious processes at work in the mother, the wider family and the observer. From the start, the observer is confronted with a situation of intense emotional impact, the impact made by the arrival of the newborn baby. Primitive, unconscious emotional states are aroused, not just in the baby and in the family, but also in the observer. Thus, the unconscious of the observer, resonating with the unconscious dynamics within the family, will help to inform him or her of what might be going on for infant and family at deeper, more unspoken levels. In this way, infant observation provides a means of understanding the emotional development of the child in a way that goes beyond observable behaviour and conscious thought.

Case illustrations

The family's characteristic ways of relating and, within these, the nature and quality of the infant's relationships are central to emotional development. What we are witnessing in infant observation is no less than the creation of the personality through the interaction between the infant's own constitution and temperament and the particular strengths and weaknesses of the relational environment, with all the complexity of the unconscious dynamics involved. Some of the developmental challenges for infants and their families in this crucial first year of life are illustrated in the following series of vignettes, taken from observations and seminar discussions conducted by students in psychoanalytic training. Seminar groups are central to Bick's (1964) method and uphold the importance of avoiding the premature application of theory to infant observation, supporting observers simply to watch and feel. The emotional responses and unconscious resonance of the seminar group are used to provide further clues to the likely unconscious processes at work within each family. Gradually, within the group, a picture emerges of the characteristic dynamics of family interaction into which each infant is born. Finally, theory is brought in to develop a psychoanalytic understanding of the processes observed. The perspectives of the British object relations tradition provide a particularly helpful way of looking at the developmental processes discussed in this chapter, and the writings of Klein, Fairbairn, Winnicott, Bick, and Bion are particularly relevant (Shuttleworth, 1989).

Unconscious processes in the infant are characterised by particular kinds of fears and phantasies. Klein gave the term paranoid–schizoid position to an early state of acute anxiety for the survival of the self, in which primitive persecutory fears and frighteningly exaggerated versions of good and bad are central (Klein, 1946). The new mother will be a prey to similar anxieties. In the months leading up to the birth, she might have had all sorts of fears and phantasies, not always conscious. If the baby is born with problems, these primitive phantasies might take firmer hold: phantasies of responsibility and blame, for example, or of punishment and retribution (Sinason, 2010). With the birth of a healthy baby, these more exaggerated fears are mostly forgotten or dispelled. Even so, the early days and weeks following a baby's birth remain an anxious time, and it is not unusual for primitive anxieties concerning life and death to come to the fore. For example, Birksted-Breen (2000) writes that the new mother, having given life to her baby, might now fear that she could take that life away, or that it could be taken from her. Early interactions between babies and their families often illustrate unconscious themes of life and death, good and bad, threat and persecution.

These themes are clearly illustrated in the early observations of an infant whose family had previously experienced life-threatening illness in an older sibling. This earlier trauma, unconsciously reinforcing the primitive fears common with any new baby, contributed to ongoing fears for the health and survival of this new baby. Worries about her health, as well as that of her siblings, were a prominent feature of early observations. Doctors represented not trusted, helpful figures, but, instead, became persecutors, critical and withholding, leaving the mother with only her own uncertain judgement upon which to rely. Primitive fears were stirred up in the observer as well, so that she, too, felt caught up in this threatening world, uncertain and unsafe, where it was hard to know if the baby's little sniffles were insignificant or heralded a fatal illness, and where her tiny coughs grew in the observer's mind to life-threatening proportions. Sometimes, she would think how well the baby looked, only to be told of sleepless nights, doctors' appointments, and hospital visits. It became difficult for her to trust her perceptions, and in this she felt she was sharing in the mother's predicament—how could she keep her baby safe and well in a hostile environment? These life and death fears characterised the developing relationship between this mother and her baby. They also appeared more generally to be a part of the dynamics of relationships within the family. Here is an extract from that infant observation, as it was written up for the discussion seminar.

> Stephen (the father) and Emily (baby Alice's four-year-old sister) were playing a computer game together. The game seemed to involve rescuing as many sleeping babies as possible without losing all your lives to some obstructive and predatory monster. Emily took a particular interest in her dad's fortunes, getting very agitated when Stephen lost a life. Stephen started jokingly to blame Emily each time he lost a life. He turned to me and said that this was the good thing about it; you could blame your kids when you got it wrong. He rescued four sleeping babies (interestingly, there are four children in this family) before he lost his last life, and then it was Emily's turn. The following week, they were playing the same game.

For baby Alice's mother and father, the world was a dangerous place, where life often seemed to be hanging in the balance. This computer game, which was a favourite with all the family, contained all those themes described earlier: themes of life and death, good and bad, threat and persecution. In this game, we might say that their unconscious anxiety about keeping babies alive in the face of such dangers was being played out, play being one of the means by which anxieties are worked through and made manageable.

Psychoanalysts from Freud onwards have been interested in the role of anxiety in the development of the personality, and the extent to which babies learn to manage anxiety has a major influence in shaping it. To begin with, it is the mother's task to manage these primitive anxieties. Assuming that she has had a secure enough childhood herself, enabling her in her turn to be able to provide good enough mothering, she will be able to manage her own anxiety so that it does not impinge upon her baby. At the same time, she will be able to contain her infant's primitive fears, tolerating, understanding, and thinking about them in way that helps them gradually to subside. Bion (1962b) calls this "containment". It involves the mother's sensitivity to the infant's emotional experience, her transformation within herself of the infant's anxieties projected into her, and her returning the projections in modified form, naming them and making them more manageable. To give an example, the reader will not find it hard to picture a small baby, red-faced and screaming with the urgency of his hunger. A mother calmly talking to her baby about his hunger and distress as she prepares to feed him is containing his anxieties. She knows that he will not die in the short time it takes for her to provide him with breast or bottle, and he, internalising her less worried state, gradually becomes able to tolerate the short space of time between his hunger and its satisfaction. An excerpt from an observation of an eight-week-old baby gives another example of a mother's calm containment. Given in his own words, it also illustrates the observer's attention to his own feelings.

> Jack was lying in his bouncy chair. I thought he looked very small and vulnerable. James was showing me the monkey suit his mum had made him. He was jumping around the room, making loud monkey noises. At first, Jack watched him with interest, but then he started to make more grumbly, crying sounds. James got more and more boisterous, and kept (accidentally on purpose?) bumping into Jack's chair. I became rather worried that he would hurt him. Jack started to cry more loudly. His mum lifted him out of the chair and sat with him laid against her chest. She rocked him gently and talked softly to him about his noisy brother. Jack soon stopped crying and lay gazing up at his mum, seeming to listen intently to her soothing words. She sat stroking Jack's head and his eyes began to close. He dozed a bit, opening his eyes when James jogged him or made a loud noise, but remaining calm and contented and half asleep.

This excerpt shows the observer's sensitivity to the baby's vulnerability and his growing concern for his safety. However, whereas the observer feels rising anxiety, the mother, familiar with, and attuned to, her baby's grumbly cries, knows just when to intervene, allowing Jack to feel some discomfort and then calmly removing him from the path of his brother's boisterous play, at the same time giving both words and emotional meaning to the situation. It is through the many everyday occurrences of this kind that the baby learns how to manage anxiety and to develop, from the mother's calm containing response, an inner sense of security.

In the very early weeks of life, the new relationship between mother and baby has a particular quality characterised by Winnicott's concept of "primary maternal preoccupation". It is a state in which the mother is taken over by a preoccupation with her infant, enabling her more fully to understand his psychological states and emotional needs. As Winnicott writes (1992), "*ordinarily* the woman enters into a phase, a phase from which she *ordinarily* recovers in the weeks and months after the baby's birth, in which to a large extent she is the baby and the baby is her" (p. 6, original emphasis).

An example of this early and necessary merging is that of a mother who, feeding her four-month-old baby and gazing into his eyes, suddenly exclaims that his eyes have changed colour, they are no longer the same colour as hers. It is as if, in that moment, it has suddenly dawned on her that they are two separate individuals. This dawning separateness marks a new phase in the relationship between mother and baby and in the development of the baby's personality. While this separation is just as essential to development as the earlier merging, it also represents a loss, and there are some mothers who find it very hard to allow their babies to separate and find their own emergent selves. For others, it is the intensity of that early merging that is harder to bear, and here the greater fear is of intimacy rather than separation (although the twin fears of intimacy and separation are often linked). An extract from another infant observation illustrates this difficulty. The situation is of a mother who, although in many respects is loving and attentive, seems unable to bear the intensity of her baby's gaze.

> Sarah was giving Josh his bottle. She sat him on her lap facing away from her, as she often seemed to do, so he was not able to see her face. Instead,

> he gazed at the moving patterns of the television screen. She said he was always looking at the television. Her older son had done this, too, as a baby. Josh, she said, would look at it and smile. Now, gazing at the screen as he sucked on his bottle, he looked small and lost.

Again we see the observer's emotional response to the baby's experience. Here, she sees the baby as "small and lost", although the mother does not seem to regard him as distressed. The impact on the observer can be powerful, and any inferences about what the baby is feeling must be made carefully and cautiously, and with the recognition that the observer's own personality and experiences will have a bearing on their perceptions. Nevertheless, Josh's likely experience in this vignette is something that has been seen in many infant observations, and Bick's (1968) ideas on "second skin" formation provide a useful way of thinking about this particular mother–infant situation. Assuming the observer has accurately tuned into something of the baby's emotional response, and Josh does indeed feel small and lost, then we can understand his need to find another means of holding himself together—in this case, the television screen. Bick's understanding is that too many experiences of this kind can lead to a pseudo-independence and self-reliance that develops of necessity in the absence of adequate maternal containment. This concept provides a way of thinking about Josh's use of the television screen as an attempt to hold himself together in the absence of his mother's containing gaze, and in the face of primitive unconscious fears of a catastrophic falling apart.

Containment requires a mother's capacity to tolerate her baby's anxiety and her own, experiencing fully the feelings stirred up in her without becoming overwhelmed by them, so that she can retain the ability to think about them. It also requires tolerating uncertainty rather than rushing towards premature knowledge and action. These processes are not, of course, restricted to the mother–baby relationship. Many students start their infant observation concerned that their presence within the family will be an imposition, only to find over time how much their quiet, thoughtful presence is valued. More than this, the power for change afforded by properly taking in and thinking about experience cannot be underestimated. To give an example, a student brought a troubling situation to his seminar group. The mother in his observation, initially very keen to be involved in the process, had begun to disengage. She would go out without word or explanation soon after he arrived, a neighbour acting as babysitter in her absence. This state of affairs continued for several weeks and the student became quite worried that the mother would drop out. His considerable anxiety, compounded by the fact that successful completion of the observation was a requirement of his psychotherapy training, was starting to get in the way of his ability to attend to mother and baby. He was even thinking of confronting the mother. Only when he presented the situation to the seminar group was he able to think more about what was going on, to attend to the baby's distress rather than his and to tolerate not knowing, just as the baby did not know, why the mother kept going out. A few weeks later, the mother reappeared and became warmly engaged with the student once more. Quite what led to the change is difficult to say. It was never discussed—the mother never mentioned it and the student managed not to either—but we might wonder about the effect of the student's being enabled by the seminar group (itself functioning as "container") to put aside his own concerns and properly to hold mother and baby in mind again.

The position of observer removes the active role that adults expect to have in the presence of an infant, and Rustin (1989) describes how this creates a space in which the infant's sensations have a more intense impact. It is important that the student does not "act out" with comments, questions, or actions in response to the feelings stirred up in him or her. In the example of the observation with the absent mother, it was the student's capacity to manage his anxiety and to think about the situation that contributed to the change that occurred, not any discussion he might have been tempted to have while temporarily unable to think. Sometimes, however, the urge to act (or speak) can become too much. Another student described to her seminar group how the baby she was observing wore scratch mittens all the time. The mother seemed very afraid of allowing her baby to put her fingers in her mouth, and any attempts to do so were met with stern rebukes. The student was very attuned to this baby and found this extremely difficult to observe, to the point that eventually she could contain herself no longer and lost for a moment her neutral observing stance. In extracts taken from several weeks' observations she describes her growing frustration.

> Katy, aged ten weeks, was lying on her changing mat. She was still wearing scratch mittens. She repeatedly put her hands to her mouth and I was

> longing for her to be rid of the mittens. The following week, her hands were free for once, and I watched her try to put her fingers and thumb in her mouth. Her mum moved her hand away. Katy tried a few more times to suck her fingers and thumb, but each time her mum would stop her. This was frustrating to watch. I wanted her to get her hands to her mouth. I wanted to put *my* fingers in *my* mouth! Two weeks later, I saw with some surprise—and pleasure—that once more Katy wasn't wearing scratch mittens. She looked at me and chewed on her fingers, which seemed to please her. It certainly pleased me, and I smiled at her and said, "Do they taste nice?" She smiled back and carried on chewing. I said, "Are you checking those teeth?" and she smiled some more. Her mum told me she was teething. She gave Katy her own fingers to hold and Katy put them in her mouth. Her mum laughed.

This vignette illustrates the observer's use of her own emotional responses to understand what might be going on for mother and baby. Within the seminar group, where theory is brought in to gain further understanding of the processes observed, Kleinian ideas concerning primitive aggression and its avoidance were discussed (Klein, 1946) in connection with a growing awareness of the avoidance of aggression in this family. But it was in the heat of the moment—the observer's frustration over the scratch mittens—that a more immediate understanding was gained of the emotional state of mother and baby. Following the student's inadvertent comment, Katy continued to be allowed to suck her fingers. Perhaps the student's words, despite being a move away from the neutral observational stance, were in some way containing, allowing a mother who could not allow finger-sucking to think it was permissible after all.

The ordinary frustrations of infancy are vital for development and promote the healthy growth of the personality, provided they are within manageable limits and there is sufficient containment of the upset caused by these early tribulations. To begin with, very little frustration can be tolerated. Things are experienced in extremes, as either all good or all bad (Klein's paranoid–schizoid position), and a baby can go from calm contentment to red-faced rage in a matter of moments. Gradually, however, the infant becomes more able to link different aspects of experience together and so to tolerate a range of emotions and cope with frustration to an increasing degree. Hunger pangs, for example, lose some of their life-threatening urgency, so that a brief wait for breast or bottle becomes more manageable. Initially,

the mother who does not meet the baby's needs immediately is felt to be persecutory; later, the baby can retain a sense of her goodness even when she is, briefly, absent or inattentive. In other words, the baby is learning to tolerate reality, beginning with the reality that his or her mother is not all good or all bad, but a mixture of the two.

The growing capacity to tolerate reality is part of what Klein (1948) termed the depressive position, a new state of mind that also marks the beginnings of concern for the other, rather than anxiety only for the survival of the self. We see this shift beginning when the infant is just a few months old, and it is associated with major advances in development. Now the mother can be seen as a whole person in her own right. With this comes the awareness of separation and dependence, so that, whereas a tiny baby can more easily be passed from one carer to another without apparent distress, a six-month-old is more likely to cry in hurt and protest if his or her mother leaves. In this next extract from an infant observation, the observer is painfully in touch with a six-month-old's distress on seeing her mother leave.

> Amelia gave a shout of protest and tried to snuggle into her dad for comfort, but he held her away from him. Amelia cried and cried as she heard the front door close, and as her dad held her up to the window to wave. I thought she looked sad and hurt and puzzled at her mum's departure. Her dad distracted her with various toys and she turned her attention to them and smiled and played some more. Every now and then during the rest of the observation she would look towards the window, and the expression on her face seemed to be one of deep sadness and longing. Then she would turn back to what she was doing and the sad expression would go again. This was painful to watch. Once, she looked away from the window towards me and I looked back at her, wishing to contain some of her sorrow for her. I thought about how her mum and dad have always talked about how she loves looking out of the window and I wondered for how long her interest had been associated with such sadness and loss.

As with frustration, separations that are of manageable duration are necessary for development. When the mother is present and the baby content, he does not have to know of his need of her. Her absence, together with the infant's developing awareness of her separateness and of his dependence on her, contributes to the capacity to hold her in mind when she is gone, and so to miss her. The mental image of her, and the associated emotions, can be regarded as rudimentary thoughts. There remains the problem of how to deal with these painful thoughts. We have already seen the importance of the mother's capacity to contain her baby's powerful emotions, to think about them for him, and so to make them more manageable, but the baby must himself develop the capacity to think, and Bion (1962a) describes thinking as developing out of frustration, absence, and the need to deal with thoughts. In the excerpt above, the student might have been witnessing the beginnings of thinking; a holding in mind of the absent mother, as the baby looked towards the window with sadness and longing.

Towards the end of their first year, and in connection with the growing sense of physical and mental separateness from their mother, babies start to be able to use play to recreate and master their mother's absence. Here is a baby, eleven months old, doing just that.

> Amy pottered about happily. She would find objects, pick them up, throw them across the floor, then crawl over to retrieve them. She seemed to take pleasure in her ability purposefully to throw and retrieve and in the crawling required of the game she had set up. She was also very interested in the sitting room door, which had a little gadget that prevented its shutting fully, so that little fingers wouldn't get trapped. Amy would crawl up to the door and swing it back and forth. She then developed another little game, crawling out into the hall and peeping back in at us through the doorway. She was quite happy playing on her own, but also very aware of the people around her, looking up at her mum, gran, brother, sister, and me now and again. She seemed more solid and secure this week.

We see here that separateness is recognised and absence tolerated up to a point, thinking and play are developing, and Amy, approaching her first birthday, has made major strides on her lifelong journey of development and growth. Freud (1920g) famously described his eighteen-month-old grandson playing a similar game.

> This good little boy, however, had an occasional disturbing habit of taking any small objects he could get hold of and throwing them away from him into a corner, under the bed, and so on, so that hunting for his toys and picking them up was often quite a business. As he did this he gave vent to a loud, long-drawn-out "o-o-o-o," accompanied by an

> expression of interest and satisfaction. His mother and the writer of the present account were agreed in thinking that this was not a mere interjection but represented the German word "fort" [gone]. I eventually realised that it was a game and that the only use he made of any of his toys was to play "gone" with them. One day I made an observation which confirmed my view. The child had a wooden reel with a piece of string tied around it. It never occurred to him to pull it along the floor behind him, for instance, and play at its being a carriage. What he did was to hold the reel by the string and very skilfully throw it over the edge of his curtained cot, so that it disappeared into it, at the same time uttering his expressive "o-o-o-o." He then pulled the reel again by the string and hailed its reappearance with a joyful "da" [there]. This, then, was the complete game – disappearance and return. (Freud, 1920g, pp. 14–15)

Freud, watching his grandson with the reel of string, was observing not just the child's behaviour, but also his emotional state and his conscious and unconscious efforts to understand and master separation and loss, his mother's departure and return. Amy's play, in the observation described earlier, was concerned with these same important themes of absence and return. The doors that are opened and closed, the toys thrown and retrieved, are aspects of the environment over which the infant can exert actual physical control. At the same time, they are learning to master the emotional impact of separations they cannot control, their play enabling them to bear separation and come to know that it is followed by return. This mastery could be regarded as the culmination of a number of developmental tasks negotiated in the first year of life. These tasks are not mastered once and for all, for these ongoing challenges are part of being human, but, by the time the child is a year old, early primitive terrors will have been replaced by ordinary, more realistic hopes and fears. There will be the beginnings of a capacity for concern; there will be a growing ability to tolerate frustration and, alongside this, a developing capacity for thought; finally, the experience of separateness and separation will be becoming more manageable. All this takes place within the context of ordinary, good enough care and containment and through the developing relationships between the infant and his or her family, beginning with that special early relationship with the mother, or whoever is in that role in relation to the baby.

Summary

Infant observation is a method of studying early development; a privileged viewpoint from which to observe the development of the personality through the interactions between the infant, his or her carers, and the world into which he or she is born. From its early roots in psychoanalytic psychotherapy training, the applications of this unique method of study continue to grow. Its two key elements, the close study of personality development and the training in observational skills, give it an importance that extends far beyond the psychoanalytic endeavour, to professionals in many different fields. Infant observation and techniques derived from it now make valuable contributions in the fields of clinical treatment, developmental research, and more generally in the many areas which require close attention to the subtle and complex dynamics of human relatedness.

To undertake an infant observation is to embark upon a powerful emotional experience. The emphasis is on an open-minded and emotionally attuned approach to that which is being studied, and observers soon find themselves encountering complex unconscious processes, not only within the infant and its family, but also within themselves. Indeed, the observer's emotional responses provide crucial clues as to the probably unconscious aspects of the family drama that unfolds during the course of the observation. The observer tries to stay with uncertainty, rather than rushing prematurely to theory to make sense of experience, but gradually links between observation and theory are made, each informing the other. Thus, the vignettes presented in this chapter, used to illustrate some of the developmental tasks of the first year of life, are discussed in terms of both the observers' emotional responses and psychoanalytic theory.

Klein saw the earliest weeks and months of life as characterised by unconscious fears and phantasies, particularly concerning the survival of the self. Gradually, with sufficiently attuned and loving parenting, these primitive fears diminish and more realistic concerns develop. The infant develops a growing capacity to tolerate frustration and, with this, a capacity for play and for the beginnings of thought and language. Infant observation gives us the opportunity to witness the accomplishment of these extraordinary achievements, made within the context of ordinary, good enough care and containment and through the developing relationships between the infant and his or her family.

References

Bick, E. (1964). Notes on infant observation in psychoanalytic training. *International Journal of Psycho-Analysis, 45*: 558–566.

Bick, E. (1968). The experience of the skin in early object-relations. *International Journal of Psycho-Analysis, 49*: 484–486.

Bion, W. R. (1962a). The psycho-analytic study of thinking. *International Journal of Psycho-Analysis, 43*: 306–310.

Bion, W. R. (1962b). *Learning from Experience*. London: Heinemann.

Birksted-Breen, D. (2000). The experience of having a baby: a developmental view. In: J. Raphael-Leff (Ed.), *"Spilt Milk": Perinatal Loss and Breakdown* (pp. 17–27). London: Institute of Psycho-Analysis.

Freud, S. (1920g). *Beyond the Pleasure Principle. S.E., 18*: 1–64. London: Hogarth.

Klein, M. (1946). Notes on some schizoid mechanisms. *International Journal of Psycho-Analysis*, 27: 99–110.

Klein, M. (1948). A contribution to the theory of anxiety and guilt. *International Journal of Psycho-Analysis, 29*: 114–123.

Likierman, M. (2001). *Melanie Klein: Her Work in Context*. London: Continuum.

Rustin, M. (1989). Encountering primitive anxieties. In: L. Miller, M. Rustin, M. Rustin, & J. Shuttleworth (Eds.), *Closely Observed Infants* (pp. 7–21). London: Duckworth.

Rustin, M. (2009). Esther Bick's legacy of infant observation at the Tavistock – some reflections 60 years on. *Infant Observation, 12*(1): 29–41.

Shuttleworth, J. (1989). Psychoanalytic theory and infant development. In: L. Miller, M. Rustin, M. Rustin, & J. Shuttleworth (Eds.), *Closely Observed Infants* (pp. 7–21). London: Duckworth.

Sinason, V. (2010). *Mental Handicap and the Human Condition: An Analytic Approach to Intellectual Disability* (2nd updated edn). London: Free Association Books.

Trowell, J. (2002). The wider applications of infant observation. In: B. Kahr, (Ed.), *The Legacy of Winnicott: Essays on Infant and Child Mental Health* (pp. 79–99). London: Karnac.

Urwin, C., & Sternberg, J. (Eds.) (2012). *Infant Observation and Research: Emotional Processes in Everyday Lives*. Hove: Routledge.

Winnicott, D. W. (1957). On the contribution of direct child observation to psycho-analysis. In: *The Maturational Processes and the Facilitating Environment: Studies in the Theory of Emotional Development* (pp. 109–114). London: Hogarth Press and the Institute of Psycho-Analysis.

Winnicott, D. W. (1992). The ordinary devoted mother. In: C. Winnicott, R. Shepherd, & M. Davis (Eds.), *Babies and Their Mothers* (pp. 3–14). London: Free Association Books.

CHAPTER FIVE

Learning from experience: developing observation skills and reflective thinking in social work practice with children and families

Debbie Hindle and Alexandra Scott

The Munro Report

A review of child protection in England was commissioned in June 2010 as part of a national drive to improve the quality of child protection services. Led by Professor Eileen Munro, a series of reports ensued that advocated a new approach (Munro, 2011a,b). Previous reforms, which shaped social work practice for several decades, had shifted from relationship-based practice to a more procedural and regulatory approach.

> The managerialist approach has been called a "rationalist-technical approach", where the emphasis has been on the conscious, cognitive elements of the task of working with children and families, on collecting information, and making plans. (Munro, 2011a, p. 36)

In Munro's opinion, this emphasis on gathering data and providing detailed assessments, placed too much emphasis on "the explicit, logical aspects of reasoning and ... contributed to a skewed management framework that undervalues intuitive reasoning and emotions and thus fails to give appropriate support to those aspects" (Munro, 2011a, p. 36). Munro recommended a move away from an emphasis on bureaucratic aspects of social work practice to an emphasis on the importance of forming relationships with children and families. As she says, "Focusing on the centrality of relationship skills draws attention to the roles of intuitive understanding and emotional responses" (Monro, 2011a, p. 37).

If we consider the central task of social work as "forming relationships with children and families to understand and help them", and "engaging the child and family and working with them to promote change" (Munro, 2011b, pp. 8, 88) then practice and training should focus on equipping practitioners to undertake this crucial task. Yet, this aspect of the work is often the most difficult to grasp effectively, given the multiple pressures and competing demands inherent in social work practice with children and families. On the one hand, the duty of child and family social work is to safeguard children, to work with families and carers to overcome problems, and to reduce risk. On the other hand, social work takes place within a framework of law and regulation, codes of practice and accountability. Although social workers aim to work in partnership with the people they are helping, by encouraging them to express their views and to participate in decisions that affect them, they are also required to make difficult decisions in order to protect children. Assessing risk, gaining a realistic perspective on whether change is possible, and bearing the uncertainty that arises when making predictions about a child's future safety, are complex and anxiety-provoking tasks. Workers can feel beset by pressures, whether from within their own or from other agencies: pressures from society and all the issues that might bring their work into public scrutiny, pressures from families, along with often unrealistic expectations of what can be done to alleviate long-standing multi-generational problems, and the pressures which come from within the workers themselves, expressed in their hopes of being able to repair and rescue (Salzberger-Wittenberg, Henry, & Osborne, 1983).

Teaching and learning

If we are to understand other human beings, we have to start from a state of not knowing, an interest in finding out by observing, listening and being receptive to the communications conveyed by others to us,

> both verbally and non-verbally. (Salzberger-Wittenberg, Henry & Osborne, 1983, p. 58)

We draw on our experience of delivering a number of short courses for the Scottish Institute of Human Relations (SIHR) to show that there is a psychoanalytically informed tradition available, which we believe has great potential to help social workers to form the kind of new relationships with children and families that the Munro report envisaged.

SIHR has specialised in delivering training in adult psychotherapy, child and adolescent psychotherapy, family therapy, and counselling. It also offers a number of shorter courses for continuing professional development to many different professionals working in a range of settings. In preparation for writing this chapter, we read through the aims and objectives of a number of these short courses, together with the feedback gathered from course participants. The courses' common, overall approach included developing observational skills, providing relevant reading, linking theory to practice, and encouraging active participation and opportunities to reflect on current practice. Although there was usually some didactic teaching, the shared underpinning for all of these courses was experiential learning, because it encompasses an emotional component such as is encountered in the context of making and maintaining relationships.

Many elements of these courses are based on the Tavistock model of infant observation and work discussion seminars (Briggs, 2002; Miller, Rustin, Rustin, & Shuttleworth, 1989; Reid, 1997; Rustin & Bradley, 2008). This model of teaching and learning is integrally linked with Bion's (1962) concept of "learning from experience". Unlike more mechanistic forms of learning—through acquiring or "having" some "piece of" knowledge (Bion, 1984[1962], p. 65)—learning from experience seeks accuracy based on observations, an awareness of factors that might lead to a tendency to distort or edit what is observed, the engagement of one's emotions in the process, and the development of a capacity to reflect on thoughts and feelings. It is through detailed recordings of observations and work-based encounters discussed in seminar groups that something that might at first seem incongruous or hard to understand begins to make sense. Workers and seminar leaders alike often struggle with having to wait for meaning to emerge, and long for "answers" to difficult questions, or wish to provide or receive more concrete advice about what to do. This tension between fitfully seeking solutions and learning, in which "not knowing" can be tolerated, is intrinsic in these seminars.

Nevertheless, uncertainty and openness to different perspectives does induce anxiety, in contrast to more didactic teaching approaches that aim to reduce uncertainty and, consequently, anxiety. Such approaches expect adults to be rational and reasonable and to be able to solve problems on that basis. They do not take into account the internal motivations and underlying emotional meaning of behaviour. For many of the children and families known to social work, these are the very difficulties they are grappling with—difficulties in processing emotions and managing social relations. We have taken the view that learning that encompasses uncertainty and not knowing, and encourages thinking about and understanding unconscious processes, can be used to make sense of the complex problems faced by social workers. In approaching this chapter, therefore, we have questioned whether providing short courses could facilitate reflective practice and, if so, what key concepts and learning outcomes were particularly relevant.

Our focus in this chapter is on the delivery of some short courses, based on this model of learning, which are listed in Table 5.1. The courses have been designed to address the needs of child and family social workers and other professionals working with children and

Table 5.1. Courses for practitioners working with children and families.

	Course title	Course length
A	Direct Work with Children	10 weeks
B	The Use of Observation in Child Care/ Social Work Assessments	10 weeks
C	Observing Infants – Observation and Assessment Skills: Working with Parents and Very Young Children	4 days
D	Supervising Practitioners using Observation in Childcare Assessments, for Seniors, Supervisors, and Child Protection Advisers	3 days
E	Developing Observation Skills in Relation to Supervised Contact between Young Children and their Families	20 weeks
F	Understanding and Working with Children who are Fostered or Adopted	10 weeks
G	The Impact of Adult Mental Health on Parenting Capacity	3 days

families. We use our experience from these courses to illustrate how psychoanalytic observation can inform social work practice, and we consider the nature of the learning experience offered and the challenges encountered in teaching. We present three examples of participants' experiences that were brought to the course case discussion groups. These examples demonstrate how this kind of learning experience for social workers can address the needs identified in the Munro Review.

Developing observational skills

Whereas many course participants had received training in, and regularly used, observation in social work practice, the concept of psychoanalytic observation was new and different. This model of observation sits particularly well with the principles of reflective practice recommended in the Munro Review reports. Seminar participants are asked to observe for an hour and record in detail afterwards what was seen and felt, paying attention to verbal and non-verbal communication. The observational stance requires the student to be aware of his or her own response as a valuable source of information to be reflected upon. This attention to the countertransference is what distinguishes psychoanalytic observation from other forms of watching or recording human behaviour. The student must refrain from interaction with the subject, as the observer's role is not about doing. Action interferes with the opportunity to reflect.

An experienced social worker attending a course on infant mental health, Observing Infants (Table 5.1, Course C) presented an observation of a young child in a nursery setting.

Liam, aged eighteen months

> Liam was brought into the room and placed on a mat on the floor by his mother, who engaged the nursery worker in conversation. Liam looked round at the toys, his face expressionless. His mother told the worker she was going to get a coffee and left the room. Liam's expression did not change. The nursery worker sat down nearby and picked up a musical ball and spoke to Liam, saying, "Look. What is this?" His face brightened and he looked at the ball the worker rolled towards him. He reached for

> the ball and touched it and there was a nice exchange when she talked to him about the toy and he looked intently at her. Another nursery worker who was sitting nearby said something to the first worker and she replied, turning towards her.
>
> Liam continued to look at the worker for a few seconds. Then his gaze drifted off and he sat quietly looking ahead . . .

The observer reported feeling a bit flat and had difficulty recalling detail about aspects of the observation of Liam, although he had good recall about another child who had been in the nursery that day. The discussion in the seminar group moved away from Liam's experience and became critical of the nursery workers, whom they felt should have been doing more to engage Liam and to help his mother to be more attentive.

The group was asked to think about the painful experience of the child, whose expectation seemed to be that he would be left alone and forgotten, with little hope of contact with adults. When this was noted, group members were surprised that Liam did not protest, make a sound, or even move towards the toys. What emerged from the discussion was an idea that Liam seemed to close himself down from seeking contact, as a way of managing his experience of unresponsiveness. In this state of mind, he could be easily forgotten by his mother, the nursery staff, and the observer, who could not remember the detail of his observation of Liam, but found that his attention was drawn to another, lively and engaging, child. Liam's expectation of the responsiveness of adults was worrying, and seemed to indicate that this way of being was habitual and might reflect his developing internal representation of adults. However, Liam was also seen to be responsive when the nursery nurse actively engaged with him, which appeared to be a hopeful sign and indicated that he still had a desire and willingness to engage. The concern was that if he continued to be left, it was likely that he could withdraw further and become difficult to reach. The observation and the group's discussion had implications for work with Liam's mother and the nursery staff. A more active engagement with this boy, "re-claiming" (Alvarez, 1985) him from this withdrawn state into more lively contact, was a matter of some urgency.

The observation was discussed in relation to the theoretical reading of the course and the research findings that infants need active reciprocal emotional interaction for healthy mental development; that is, they need another person to be sensitively and affectively in tune with them. Emotional attunement (Stern 1977) and feeling understood is vital for the development of affect regulation, social relatedness, and empathy. Neurobiologists have found that emotion is the central organising process in the infant's brain, which develops in response to the emotional environment. Given this context, further discussion in the group centred on the fact that, although workers were often aware of the emotional environment in a home, they did not attribute sufficient significance to this, and neither did they draw on their own emotional responses. Rather, there was a tendency to note more concrete aspects, such as the condition of the home, or the parents' behaviour, and they generally did not feel confident about using their countertransference.

Understanding the child's perspective

The following case vignette was brought for discussion to Understanding and Working with Children who are Fostered or Adopted (Table 5.1, Course F) by an experienced social worker who had known this boy and his family for a number of years.

Adam, aged ten years

Adam, at ten years old, was presenting challenging behaviour in his foster home and there were fears that his placement could break down. He was running away, sometimes to the homes of members of his family, sometimes to sleep rough, sometimes to the home of a well-known local alcoholic. It seemed a matter of urgency to understand why he was running away.

The social worker gave a brief account of Adam's early history. He had been in and out of care since before he was one year old, because of neglect and domestic violence. His mother had chronic alcohol problems, his father had mental health problems, and the home was chaotic and volatile. However, a decision for Adam to remain in foster care was not made until Adam was eight years old.

In the discussion, we developed a picture of what it might have felt like to be Adam as a small child, witnessing violent scenes between his parents, sights and sounds that would have seemed incomprehensible, overwhelming, and frightening. Being repeatedly moved—in and out of care and to different homes—would have compounded his sense of the world as being unpredictable. We began to think of Adam as being driven to seek out the very experiences he had been removed from, but now under his control. The social worker described feeling helpless and frightened about what might happen to Adam.

The discussion in the seminar quickly moved from thinking about how to manage the situation to trying to understand the meaning of Adam's behaviour. Was he running away, or "running to"? On the one hand, we thought about Adam's earliest attachments, his loyalty to his parents, and his concern for them. On the other hand, we thought about how he seemed to be responding to the care he was receiving in his foster home, his development at school, and his enjoyment in being part of this family. The foster parents were aware that Adam often tried to push them to react and to embroil them all in arguments, reminiscent of his own family. It was harder to identify the points when he ran off, leaving everyone feeling that it was inexplicable. It was clear that the social worker and foster parents were in touch with Adam's fear and helplessness—at these points projected into them—but they felt at a loss as to how to help him. Gradually, the group began to consider the *internal conflict* that beset Adam. Unpredictability, waiting, one of his foster parents not being available, seemed to be enough to trigger his flight to something more familiar. Taking a firmer behavioural approach—for example, grounding him for running off—seemed to make things worse. In this case, a more thoughtful approach was needed to understand what felt like a "Catch 22" situation for Adam—the continuous push–pull of competing attachments—now enacted through his running away.

As the discussion continued, we also thought about the re-enacting of Adam's experience of going back and forth, in and out of care. Could what felt inexplicable also be an unconscious communication about his experience, which to him was also inexplicable? We thought about the way in which his running away led to people searching for and finding him—almost a reversal of what one would expect from a young child who needs to keep his attachment figures in sight. Being "re-claimed" again and again seemed to have a reassuring aspect to it. It mattered that someone worried about where he was and what he was doing. The complexity of the situation for Adam, his foster parents, and the social worker were evident and elicited concern and empathy in the group, but anger and blame were not far away. Questions were raised about why decisions had not been made earlier to seek permanency for Adam. Why had his parents not been able to get their act together? There was anger expressed towards the Children's Panel, who seemed so swayed by the parents' promises and longings, as well as anger towards social work management. It seemed harder to express anger towards Adam directly, although his behaviour often led to angry responses and punishment. Might his running away be an expression of anger or a way of avoiding potential angry conflicts? Would it be possible to use these insights to inform a less reactive and a more containing approach to Adam?

Reflecting on the emotional aspect of the work

The following case was brought to a work discussion seminar by a social worker attending The Use of Observation in Child Care/Social Work Assessments (Table 5.1, Course B). She was feeling at a loss about what to do and very uneasy that something was wrong, while feeling helpless and unable to see or understand what was going on. She described a young mother doing all that was asked of her, who clearly loved her children, but whose children were showing an unusual degree of disturbance.

Ben aged four, and Karen aged three

Ben and his sister Karen lived with their young mother, a single parent. The children were beautifully dressed and the house clean, but the aggressive behaviour displayed by both children was very concerning. The worker brought observations of the children at home and in the nursery they attended daily. She also brought examples of her work with the mother, to try to make sense of what was going on.

Over the course of the presentation, a picture began to emerge of the characteristic dynamics of the family interactions and aspects of the children's inner worlds. Paying attention to what was seen and felt (her countertransference), enabled the worker to experience and explore the emotional events happening between the children and their mother at an unconscious level. This helped to bring some understanding to the complicated dynamics of the situation, and highlighted the level of the children's disturbance.

Ben and Karen had to attend nursery at different times because of their aggression towards each other. They were both observed in the nursery where they had been attending for well over a year. Ben was difficult to settle, nipping and biting the member of staff who tried to comfort him when his mother left with his sister. He ran around on his own from one thing to another, carrying things, throwing things about, putting things in his mouth. He had a one-to-one worker who kept saying "pretend" as he tried to eat inedible things. He did not engage with any other children or activities, and seemed isolated and alone.

Karen could play by herself and would play out being a mother with two baby dolls. In her play, there was never enough for both of them, and something always went wrong. However, she, too, was isolated and did not interact with other children. Observing both children increased the worker's sense of unease as she experienced the isolation and lack of emotional connection these children had with others.

When seen at home, their mother did not seem able to keep the children in mind. She would start a game with all three of them, the children would drift off around the room, and their mother would continue playing in an absorbed way by herself. The social worker described occasions where the mother did not contain the children's anxiety, but actually heightened it by, for instance, reminding Ben what he had lost, or pointing out his deficits.

The children's mother was regularly reported to be cut off, difficult to reach, and emotionally unavailable, and it seemed she was unable to attend to her children's needs, even when being supervised in a play situation. This unavailability could be seen in this mother's relationship with both children, but was seen particularly in relation to Karen. In one play session with Karen and her mother, Karen fell and hurriedly got up on three occasions, none of which was noticed by her mother. There had been several occasions at home when the children sustained injuries while their mother was present but which, inexplicably, she had not noticed.

The material was at times very painful for the group. Opening oneself to the emotional experience of the child leads to various processes of identification, and sometimes the feelings of anxiety and distress in response to the children's desperation and isolation were hard to bear. These children did not seem to have an internal world populated by helpful figures, but instead one that seemed barren and frightening; the sense of helplessness and despair was reflected in the group.

In the discussion, the seminar group grappled with the discrepancies described: a mother who was physically present, but emotionally unavailable, and children who were apparently well cared for, but presented as disturbed and disorientated. The group began to consider whether the mother could meet the children's needs, but soon it became clear that the discussion centred on thinking about the mother's needs. The identification with the young woman seemed to make those involved feel guilty and want to distance themselves from responsibility. Identification with parents can lead to feeling cruel and/or sorry for them, and can, in turn, make the worker feel like the abusing parent. Stevenson (1998) describes the difficulty skilled professionals might have in seeing what is in front of their eyes, and how they fail to make some very difficult decisions because of this.

The discussion about the children's disturbance, and whether their mother could meet their needs, led to the group distancing themselves from considering what they might be able to do in this case. The group process mirrored that of the organisational network, and how difficult it seemed to prioritise and hold on to the needs of the children.

Powerful unconscious processes seemed to be at work in this case, perhaps because the reality of the situation was too painful to see. We hypothesised that this led to professionals in the social work network, as in the seminar group, wanting to avoid coming to difficult conclusions. It was felt that this unavailability, in not being able to keep the children in mind, might have been experienced also by the professional network. In the seminar, the power of the social worker's countertransference, now experienced by the group, enabled us to apprehend the level of disturbance in these children and to keep their needs in mind.

Discussion

Analytic skills can be enhanced by teaching and reading. Intuitive skills are essentially derived from experience. Experience on its own,

> however, is not enough. It needs to be allied to reflection – time and attention given to mulling over the experience and learning from it. (Munro, 2011a, p. 48)

In all the courses offered, we have been impressed by the complexity of the social work task, the dedication of the social workers who attended, but also by the competing demands on their time and attention. Also apparent was the way in which these competing demands often led to "losing sight of the child". If the workers took a too "evidence-based" approach to child protection issues, they often found it hard to articulate what seemed most important—the nature of the relationship between the parent and the child (as in the cases of Liam, Ben, and Karen). If they focused on behavioural issues (as in Adam's case), there was a danger in misunderstanding the significance of his inner world. Group presentations and discussions provided a forum where some of these issues could be "mulled over" and thought about, providing an opportunity to integrate theoretical knowledge with experiential learning.

Looking again at the three case discussions presented above, we are struck by the fact that two of these involved a parent who was emotionally unavailable. One had implications for further work (Liam) and the other prompted a discussion about whether child protection procedures should be pursued (Ben and Karen). Glaser and Pryor (1997) identified emotional unavailability as one of the categories of parent–child interaction that, if persistent and pervasive, was characteristic of emotional abuse. Research has indicated that the emotional unavailability, unresponsiveness, or insensitivity of a parent can be particularly damaging to a child, especially in infancy, and can affect neurological, intellectual, and emotional development, and the capacity to form relationships (Glaser, 2000). Yet, these interactions are often the most difficult to describe and tabulate, leaving social workers and other professionals frequently feeling at a loss as to how to make sense of the problems the child is presenting (as with Ben and Karen). Unfortunately, like Liam, without close attention many of these children go "unnoticed" because they do not complain or draw attention to themselves, but have become withdrawn, apathetic, or uncommunicative (Music, 2009).

The course group discussions highlight the importance of the observation of interactions, of offering an opportunity to reflect on the feelings elicited in the workers, and of providing a framework for thinking about what were largely unconscious processes, affects, and actions on the part of the parent. Added to this was the need to consider the way in which children might adapt to an emotionally abusive situation, making it hard to see the true nature of the presenting problem (Boulton & Hindle, 2000).

In feedback on the courses, participants particularly commented on the powerful experience of the observations, the emotional impact of the learning, and, in some cases, such as that of Liam, the painful awareness of what it is like for an infant to be left alone and not attended to. One student on a ten-week Use of Observation in Child Care/Social Work Assessments course (Table 5.1, Course B) noted, "Never again will I just accept that a quiet undemanding infant is happy and contented. It is normal for a child to protest and seek attention. I will now pay attention to the nature of the child's experience." Another student on the Direct Work with Children course (Table 5.1, Course A) said,

> "I am very conscious of the validity of simply "sitting with" someone even when it feels like doing nothing—the enormous usefulness of how we find ourselves feeling at these times, why that happens, where it is coming from and what it leads to—our understanding of someone who seems to be telling us nothing—not engaging."

This type of understanding and learning also raised some anxiety and feelings of guilt. Awareness of not fully understanding or being able to articulate what workers had felt or observed, experiences of powerlessness or hopelessness engendered by complex or chronic situations, generated painful feelings about lost opportunities. This led participants to question their practice and their intervention. In seminars, thought was also given to the way in which institutional processes could conspire to "not see" the damage done to young children.

The structure of the courses reflected their aim of linking theory with practice. The discussion groups helped students to think about how their observations and experiences could be used in assessments and reports, extending their observations from practical and concrete descriptions to more qualitative observations of the interactions between parents and their children. But focusing on the emotional interaction and experience of the child or children was not an easy task. We have come to think about the tendency to minimise difficulties, or to subtly "turn a blind eye" to more disturbing interactions, as an unconscious response to the pain of facing what was happening, and as a defence against recognising the degree of damage done to some children. Defences against this awareness, such as forgetting or denying, were encountered in many discussions. Generally, the seminar groups helped to contain anxieties and enabled workers to reflect on and process their experience.

This way of learning presents challenges for seminar participants and leaders alike.

> Learning arises in a situation in which we do not yet know or are as yet unable to achieve what we aim to do. It thus invariably involves uncertainty, some degree of frustration and disappointment. This experience is a painful one and if it cannot be tolerated then it may be evaded . . . or else dealt with omnipotently and angrily. (Salzberger-Wittenberg, Henry, & Osborne, 1983, p. 53)

The capacity to bear uncertainty and not knowing is essential, and providing containment in the group is, therefore, a key part of the learning process. The seminar leaders also have to manage the pressures from group members who look to them for "answers", and, thus, to relieve anxiety by providing theoretical understanding. Theoretical knowledge can itself be used as a defence against the anxiety of not knowing.

Conclusion

Research findings and developments in neuroscience provide valuable evidence for what psychoanalysts and psychotherapists have been saying for a very long time: that healthy infant development is a crucial foundation for long-term mental health. Much has been learned in the past decade about the way in which the human brain develops in response to early experience. Findings from neurobiology and psychoanalysis have been converging and producing a new understanding of emotional life. Developments in neurobiology and biochemistry have found that emotion has been seen to be the central organising process within the brain (Pally, 2000; Siegel, 1999). Damasio (1999) has argued that cognition depends on emotion, and that the rational part of the brain cannot work without the basic regulatory and emotional parts of the brain.

During the past decade, SIHR's courses, as listed above, were delivered many times over, reaching a large number of social workers in a variety of settings. At times, the course organisers felt as if they were "swimming against the tide" of the "managerialist approach" identified by Munro (2011a), and the aims of the courses seemed at odds with the prevailing climate in social work departments. Yet, these learning opportunities were well, and often enthusiastically, received by workers struggling to engage with children and families and really wanting to make a difference to their lives. Like the findings in neuroscience, the Munro Review has provided further evidence and support for psychoanalytic practice, emphasising the need to observe, to be receptive to verbal and non-verbal communication, to be aware of conscious and unconscious processes, and the essential importance of creating space for reflective practice.

References

Alvarez, A. (1985). The problem of neutrality: some reflections on psychoanalytic attitude in the treatment of borderline and psychotic children. *Journal of Child Psychotherapy, 11*: 87–104.

Bion, W. R. (1962). *Learning from Experience.* London: Karnac, 1984.

Boulton, S., & Hindle, D. (2000). Emotional abuse: the work of a multidisciplinary consultation group in a child psychiatric service. *Clinical Child Psychology and Psychiatry, 5*: 439–452.

Briggs, A. (Ed.) (2002). *Surviving Space: Papers on Infant Observation.* London: Karnac.

Damasio, A. (1999). *The Feeling of What Happens.* London: Heinemann.

Glaser, D. (2000). Emotional abuse and neglect and the brain: a review. *Journal of Child Psychology and Psychiatry, 41*: 97–116.

Glaser, D., & Pryor, V. (1997). Is the term child protection applicable to emotional abuse? *Child Abuse Review, 6*: 315–329.

Miller, L., Rustin, M., Rustin, M., & Shuttleworth, J. (Eds.) (1989). *Closely Observed Infants.* London: Duckworth.

Munro, E. (2011a). *The Munro Review of Child Protection – Interim Report: The Child's Journey* (DFE-00010–2011). London: Department of Education.

Munro, E. (2011b). *The Munro Review of Child Protection. Final report – A Child-centred System* (Cm 8062). London: Department of Education.

Music, G. (2009). Neglecting neglect: some thoughts about children who have lacked good input, and are "undrawn" and "unenjoyed". *Journal of Child Psychotherapy, 35*: 142–156.

Pally, R. (2000). *The Mind–Brain Relationship*. London: Karnac.

Reid, S. (Ed.) (1997). *Developments in Infant Observation*. London: Routledge.

Rustin, M., & Bradley, J. (2008). *Work Discussion: Learning from Reflective Practice in Work with Children and Families*. London: Karnac.

Salzberger-Wittenberg, I., Henry, G., & Osborne, E. (1983). *The Emotional Experience of Learning and Teaching*. London: Routledge.

Siegel, D. (1999). *The Developing Mind: Towards a Neurobiology of Interpersonal Experience*. New York: Guildford Press.

Stern, D. (1977). *The First Relationship: Infant and Mother*. Cambridge MA: Harvard University Press.

Stevenson, O. (1998). *Neglected Children: Issues and Dilemmas*. Oxford: Blackwell Sciences.

CHAPTER SIX

Scotland the Brave: freedom to roam between individual, family, systemic, and social perspectives in psychoanalytic work with children and young people

Joan Herrmann

This chapter is an account of the development of my ideas about the role of child psychotherapists working within organisations such as the NHS; in fact, within any organisation that provides mental health services and support to individuals and their families. Over the years my ideas about the value and usefulness of a psychoanalytic training have significantly changed. I began, as I think many of my colleagues began, with a faith in the power of insight into one's self, which therapy can offer to individuals in distress, and ended in a firm conviction in what Jeremy Holmes describes, with reference to Sutherland's work, as "outsight". This refers to the belief that "man is a person sustained by his social relatedness" (Sutherland, 1966, in Holmes, 1993a, p. 16), and that for psychoanalytic insight to be useful it must attend to the larger context within which the individual is placed: the family, the community (including the wider community of the helping professions), and the complexities of social reality.

John Sutherland belongs to a tradition of psychoanalytic and psychiatric thought with deep roots in Scottish intellectual and religious life, extending back at least to Adam Smith and probably before (Miller, 2004, 2008). This tradition stresses the fundamental roots of the self as developing within, and constituted by, relationships; the individual is born into a community of others, and the aim of therapy is to promote interpersonal relations, to restore the individual to the community. These ideas were not central when I trained as a child psychotherapist, a training that depended heavily on the ideas of Melanie Klein and Anna Freud. Both these formidable and brilliant women grew their originality within the constraints of classical Freudian theory, with its stress on the individual's need to mature in order to regulate primitive emotional states: "Where id was, there ego shall be" (Freud, 1933a, p. 80). Interpretation of the inner world was the prime objective; the actual past and present experience of the individual was seen as formative but, in one sense, irrelevant. Bowlby, for example, was concerned at the lack of attention to the real deprivations in the life of the boy who was his training case while in supervision with Klein (Holmes, 1993b). Psychoanalysts at that time were not at all receptive to his ideas about attachment needs, and he encountered intense resistance to his focus on the real life experience of the individual.

The tension between a focus on individual pathology and defences, and a larger, more inclusive focus on interpersonal relations and systems (family therapy, organisational dynamics, etc.), has in recent years, stimulated the development of a strong "post-Freudian" current of thought throughout the psychoanalytic community. In the field of child psychotherapy, there is a growing literature about the complex relationship between the inner and outer worlds and, especially relevant to this chapter, about the importance of attending to the dynamics around a child, in the family, the residential unit, and the professional network (Emmanuel, 2002; Henry, 1974; Sprince, 2002, 2009; Williams, 1997). Nevertheless, I find it interesting that, even at the beginning of my training, I found an exclusive focus on the individual both confusing and unsatisfying. I was drawn to the writings of Fairbairn and fascinated by the maverick tradition of people such as Laing. As an "incomer" to Scotland, having moved from the USA, the peculiarly Scottish perspective, with its stress on the central importance of community, has been a great discovery for me.

I have worked in Scotland for all of my professional life as a child psychotherapist, first as a trainee in a residential school for emotionally disturbed children, and, later, as a member of a CAMHS team (Child and Adolescent Mental Health Service in the NHS), situated in one of the most deprived communities in the country. For most of this time, I was the only child psychotherapist available in the work setting. At first, I tried hard to cling to my professional identity, as someone who offered individual work to children and young people who undoubtedly needed it. I often felt very alone, in despair at what I experienced as the inability of my colleagues to value my way of thinking and my work. At times I felt attacked, sidelined, or oddly elevated to the position of a super-specialist unable to comprehend the ordinary burden of, and demands on, a desperately over-subscribed service.

My colleagues also held a deeply felt hope that the child psychotherapist could provide solutions to extraordinary difficulties. The referrals that came my way frequently involved children and young people whose past history and, most significantly, current circumstances contained no hint of anything remotely good enough to sustain developmental growth. Common to all these referrals was the fact, often unacknowledged, that the causes for the referral lay not only with the child, but also within the family. Sometimes, the child had been taken into care, or placed in a residential setting, and this allowed me to observe that one can remove the child from the family without removing the family from the child. It was my growing realisation that the system dynamics around a child often replicate those of the original family, which first led me to explore ways of extending my training, and to use my psychoanalytic thinking in ways which are often described as "applied psychotherapy".

Shuttleworth (1999) describes the dilemmas for child psychotherapists confronted with the demands of working in multi-disciplinary settings, in close alliance with colleagues whose training is based on very different models of the mind, and who have different ways of formulating and treating mental and emotional disturbance. He argues that in recent years, the workplace has changed in ways that make it impossible for child psychotherapists always to work psychoanalytically. Sometimes, for example, the child psychotherapist must also serve as case manager, which requires a great deal of transparency and shared information about a child. Much of Shuttleworth's disquiet stems from arguments by psychoanalysts about the overriding need to resist pressures to breach confidentiality and the boundaries of the sessions (Bollas & Sundelson, 1995). The suggestion he makes is that we develop a "dual citizenship", which allows us to separate purely psychoanalytic work from more "applied" ways of working, and to develop a "second language" which our non-psychoanalytic colleagues can understand and use.

I want to argue that all of our work is applied, and that one very important way in which we apply our thinking is in the ability to link one way of working with another. Erikson (1950) describes a sense of identity as "the ability to experience one's self as something that has continuity and sameness and to act accordingly" (p. 37) and this must refer to our professional as well as our personal identity.

My first workplace, as a trainee in a residential school, was something of a trial by fire. The therapy room was situated in the midst of the school grounds; teachers and children passed it on every trip into and out of the main building. This situation and the problems consequent upon it led me to question my identity as a child psychotherapist whose work was confidential, specialised, and isolated from the general tasks of the school. The children knocked on the door when they knew another child was in therapy; they banged on the windows and the child in therapy would often answer these territorial breaches by shouting or leaving the room to chase the transgressors. The staff would often deliver a child to me with what I considered most unhelpful comments: "Tell Joan what you have been up to today". There was a general counsel of despair among the staff, which often led them to behave in ways that undermined the therapy: for example, by forgetting to bring children to their sessions, or the sudden cancellation of therapy sessions because of school activities. The referrals for psychotherapy tended, at times, to reflect the needs of the school rather than a full consideration of the needs of the child. One child would be singled out as the "troubled one" and there would emerge the rather magical thought that psychotherapy would sort him or her out. This would then permit the school to function as if the population of highly deprived and emotionally disturbed children was, with the exception of one very troubled bad egg, capable of an ordinary school day. There was always the pressure to join in a culture of despair, a blaming culture, and to protect one's professional activity by tucking it away in the safe corner we describe as "individual work".

I can now understand the confusions, ambivalence, and conflicts I was encountering as a form of transference. The staff in residential units have in general not been analysed, trained, or given access to the sort of supervision that is so integral to a psychoanalytic training. The more sensitive and well-intentioned the worker, the more vulnerable they are to the unconscious projections of the children, who are often desperately trapped within a very damaged inner world, populated with monstrous figures. Their identification with these spectral and persecuting inner figures is absolute and "transferred" in many complex ways to the external world.

In the psychoanalytic literature, these figures are often referred to as "objects", in order to differentiate between the actual real person who failed them and the very primitive internalised representation of these figures. The "bad object" describes the child's distorted attempts to personify an experience in their inner world. The witch of fairy tales is a prime example of a "bad object". In actuality, this very subjective representation can be because the child's mother was depressed, or a drug addict, or, for some other reason, unavailable emotionally. In these situations, the real mother might want to provide good care, but her inability to do so provokes the experience of a "bad" mother for the child. It is this very "bad" relationship that determines that the child will respond to new and more trustworthy figures in terms of their earlier expectations, and these expectations are very powerful. For the reasons described in more detail below, they can lead to the most well-intentioned individuals behaving in accordance with the child's expectations, and to the most caring individuals behaving in ways which seem very remote from their good intentions.

In reality, the painful fact is that the children are often still living within a family that is unable to meet their needs. One reason for this is an understandable wish to keep the family together. This can, at times, mean that admission to a placement in a residential setting, designed to keep the family intact, often follows upon a series of failed options. Very often, too often, there is a "worm" of hopelessness and despair (Blake, 1794) concealed in the referral: a family on the verge of collapse, a deep uncertainty about the safety of the home environment, a series of failed placements, and a child whose capacity for relationships is deeply damaged. Even when children have been placed in care, with good foster parents or in specialised units, or when the family has been receptive to change, we often find that children test this new reality to breaking point; the systems around the child collapse into a strange re-enactment of a past where good, well-intentioned people find themselves feeling (and, at times, acting) like monsters.

Most children in residential care have experienced huge and traumatic environmental failures, which are intergenerational, and the child, who is very resistant to change, perpetuates these. In their inner world, they maintain a great deal of loyalty to the parents who have failed them, because their attachment needs have developed around these figures and they are, in a profound way, unable to respond to the better alternatives on offer. Fairbairn recognised that the worse one's internal objects are, the less one is able to differentiate from them, and his theories are extremely useful in understanding this paradox (Celani, 2010; Fairbairn, 1952; Ogden, 2010). He found, for example, that sexually abused children often defend their parents in order to preserve the poignant belief that if they are better children, they will gain access to better parents. Without this belief, there is a total loss of hope, a world with no goodness in it. As Fairbairn describes it,

> In a world ruled by the Devil the individual may escape the badness of being a sinner; but he is bad because the world around him is bad. Further, he can have no sense of security and no hope of redemption. The only prospect is one of death and destruction. (Fairbairn, 1952, p. 67)

As Fairbairn (1952) also noted, this is precisely Satan's dilemma in *Paradise Lost*, when he finds himself in hell, without hope and proclaims,

> So farewell hope, and with hope farewell fear
> Farewell remorse: all good to me is lost
> Evil, be thou my good.
> (Milton, 1667, Book iv, ll.108–110, in Fairbairn, 1952, p. 27)

When there is a total loss of hope in the restoration of a good internal relationship, when reparation feels impossible, the individual can become dedicated to being "bad", a state of mind which we describe as "psychopathic".

Such a catastrophic loss of hope is, fortunately, not common, but it is important to do more than recognise the unmet needs of a child, and to offer respite and a restored or substitute family or home. It is also vital to acknowledge that the repairs necessary in the internal world are far more challenging. The inner world is a closed system, very resistant to change. Fairbairn (1958) recognised that the real challenge for the therapist is to "effect a breach in this closed system and to provide conditions under which, in the setting of a therapeutic relationship, the patient may be induced to accept the open system of outer reality" (p. 92).

We now realise that for children whose lives are dominated by this sort of closed system, the most effective interventions involve attending not only to the child in therapy, but also to the world around the child. My work in the residential school began to change when I realised how, instead of being able to offer the child an alternative and better reality, we had become press-ganged into various and complex confirmations of the child's internal version of reality. This involved recognition of not only our attitudes and behaviour towards the children, but, most importantly, our relations with each other.

Child psychotherapists now have a deeper understanding of how children who have suffered early trauma convey their experience to others (Sprince, 2002; Williams, 1997). This can be understood as a pathological form of projective communication. What is projected into others is not only a fragmented and chaotic bundle of indigestible experience, but also a whole way of operating, of dealing with it. The aim is not to be understood, but to evacuate the self, often to achieve some degree of control over the other, who is given very little freedom to respond to, or process, the projection. The unfortunate outcome of this process is the replication of the child's inner world in the world around him. The carer feels monstrous, the well-intentioned professional feels helpless and bewildered, the residential school feels like a prison, and the staff is hopelessly divided not only as to how to deal with a child, but also how to think about the child.

I was fortunate to find a supervisor trained in group dynamics, from whom I learnt that the transference relationship between the school and the therapist was fundamental in the understanding of the children who lived there. This understanding was not solely or mainly to protect the child's therapy; rather, it was put to good use, providing the staff with time to consider how information about the child was contained in the dynamics of the referral, in the attitudes we had towards each other, and, most fundamentally, in the nature of the splitting between the care and education teams. I learnt that being a child psychotherapist in a residential setting meant understanding the unconscious of the workplace, and that this was wholly compatible with my identity as the school's psychotherapist.

This way of working and thinking continued to develop when I moved to work in a CAMHS team, although again the initial expectations about my role were that I would, in the main, be offering individual therapy. This was an entirely different setting; referrals came from across the community and there was not, as there is in a residential unit, an easily accessible and enclosed system with which to work. A great deal of my work was with parents and carers, but slowly I also developed ways of working with my colleagues, offering case discussion time to reflect on the emotional demands, which are so pervasive and so draining, that permeate all work with deprived and troubled children. I discovered new ways of drawing together the professionals and carers whose work was often fragmented into specific tasks, and who often found these tasks to be in conflict with each other. The unconscious is always there, and we can always put our understanding of it to good use.

Close attention to the network dynamics around a child can often help the workers involved gain some clarity about the young person's dilemmas and the intergenerational issues involved. The example below, the details of which are a disguised and composite description about a typical series of events in a CAMHS team, demonstrates how useful psychoanalytic thinking is, even when the setting for it is extremely dispersed in both time and space.

Harry is a fifteen-year-old who was referred by the social worker then involved, ostensibly because of worries about his state of mind. In infancy, he had experienced prolonged, frequent, but life-saving, surgical interventions. Harry was living in a residential unit because both of his parents had effectively abandoned him. The consultation was to be a joint one, between my adolescent team, the citywide LAC (Looked After and Fostered Children) team, the residential unit, and the social worker. The effort to bring four workers from these different teams together has, at times, seemed Olympian in its ambition. As case manager, this effort fell largely on my shoulders.

After an initial consultation, the social worker cancelled several carefully planned sessions at the last minute, possibly with the hope that we would proceed without her. There is always the wish in these referrals that complex problems can be resolved by the offer of individual therapy. After a period of silence, I wrote to the social worker suggesting that, since she had cancelled the last two sessions and had not been in contact, perhaps she no longer felt the need for a consultation. She wrote back with an expression of surprise, as she thought it was very important to meet. I then attempted to locate a time when we could meet, and was greatly shocked when I rang the area team to learn that the social worker had been on placement and was due to move at the time she wrote to me. The case remained unallocated.

This long procedure had by now dragged on over many months, until, and inevitably, a social worker rang me to say the case had now been allocated to her and could we arrange a consultation. As it proved impossible for the LAC team representative to attend, I arranged to see the social worker and Harry's key worker without her. On the day, the key worker arrived but the social worker was unable to attend, due to pressing concerns about another case. Despite, or because of, my incandescent irritation, which I was having a great deal of difficulty containing, the residential worker and I decided to meet; she was very keen to do so. As the session developed, my angry response became more understandable as a form of countertransference. I was experiencing a feeling of frustration about inadequate care, which belonged not only to Harry, but which was also a widespread experience for all those who were trying to provide him with a new and better reality.

It will not come as a surprise to learn that one item, which the residential worker was quick to share, was the disappointment Harry experienced as the social worker continually failed to appear, often cancelling her appointments with him at the last minute. In my CAMHS team, we were familiar with the rage and disappointment generated by an overstressed and under-resourced social work department. It would be easy to generalise the experience and to incorporate it into a widely shared attitude towards an agency that seems doomed to replicate the bad experiences that overwhelm it.

I asked the residential worker to tell me about Harry. At first, her descriptions were carefully organised around the dire circumstances of Harry's life. His parents were in hate with one another and used Harry to communicate this. Although his father did maintain contact with his son, this was entirely on his terms; the demands and conditions he imposed about their contact time contained the most unrealistic expectations of his behaviour. When he was allowed home, his father would sometimes drive him to his mother's home, where he could then experience the full impact of a severely depressed mother, who told her son that the only reason she did not kill herself was because her pets needed her and that she would not, on any terms, have any more to do with Harry. Although his father had allowed his son to live with him for a while, this approach broke down once the tensions and hatred Harry felt towards the new wife and, especially, their children emerged. His father maintained he could not offer a home to his son because his current wife was frightened for her children.

It became apparent that one reason his father maintained any contact with Harry at all was to use him to keep alive the active and vengeful relationship with his former wife. Harry's special needs, because of his early problems as a baby, probably exacerbated what sounded to me like a long-term sadomasochistic relationship between the parents. His mother might have felt left with the product of a very damaging and destructive coupling and, once her husband had left, was unable to cope with a child who was filled with terrible and hateful feelings, in which his status as a child with special needs was effectively ignored.

I then asked about Harry: what was he like? The revelation that he was a person with whom it was incredibly hard to be emerged slowly, and only after I had addressed the issue of how angry we both were with the social worker. He was described as someone who had no loyalty, was incredibly manipulative, and who had no real affections. He could, for example, after ingratiating himself with a peer, have no compunction about dropping one friendship for a more advantageous alliance. As the key worker was keenly sensitive to the impact of these rebuffs on the vulnerable youngsters in the residential unit, she clearly had difficulty in coping with Harry's opportunism. The residential worker thought that one reason Harry had been school refusing, although bright and able in school, was because he was worried about the dominance hierarchy in the residential unit. She was able to empathise with Harry's belief that if he absented himself from the peer group, it would effectively eject him.

A picture developed of a child whom no one liked or wanted, who maintained his right to exist only by a very active vigilance, and whose rage expressed a suspicion that without active coercion his very existence might be extinguished: all these elements were, in retrospect, evident in the difficult process of establishing the consultation. My early disinclination to persevere with it and my provocative letter to the social worker are clear indications that I was as susceptible as my colleagues to a potentially destructive process of infection. I could, however, in large part because of the supports provided by my training, understand that some very toxic process had found fertile ground, and that some very powerful devils had been unleashed.

When eventually we did manage to establish an inter-agency meeting, I was fascinated to learn of Harry's unique relationship with a pupil support teacher in the school, who attended the meeting with some reluctance. She presented herself as someone whom Harry would listen to and obey. This was because, as she described it, she was "not close" to him. Whenever she had to interact with Harry, she deliberately conveyed to him the air of someone quite emotionally unavailable, concerned only to establish rules and to monitor Harry's ability to follow them. She believed this approach to be effective, and her teacherly advice to the rest of us was undoubtedly meant to be helpful. The fact that Harry was not attending school seemed to be ignored.

We might conjecture that what Harry most required was for someone to experience how deeply unlovable he felt. The teacher's approach allowed us to experience at first hand Harry's sense of living in a world in which acceptance was dependent on submission to authority. This had the qualities of a paternal figure who could enforce the terms of access, while remaining impervious to his qualities as a person. The teacher's reactions and responses, very like my own initial irritation, demonstrate the power of the transference and countertransference in situations where the real experience of the individual can seem too awful to contemplate. I have very little doubt that this teacher was caught up in an enactment of Harry's internal world. She seemed to be acting very much in identification with his father, a person who refused to admit his son's needs, but was determined that if he was to have any access to a family, he must become obedient and suppress his anger.

However, it is also important to recognise how much Harry felt unlovable and behaved in the most unlovable ways. He acted in ways that made it very difficult to offer the tolerance and containment he needed. This is the paradox that lies at the heart of so many traumatised children and young people; their internal world is projected into

assumptions about the nature of the group and that undermines its conscious task: for example, that the group has an enemy who must be identified and managed, either by blame or evasion. In Harry's case, there was a clear invitation to form an alliance with the key worker and to level blame at the social worker. Similarly, the pupil support teacher's harsh attitude, which could easily invite censure, demonstrates how Harry's internal world had become fragmented and projected into the people in contact with him. The task of a reflective group would be to identify these elements, in order to further our understanding of how identified we had all become with these internal objects and the dynamics between them, which dominated his internal world.

The insights from such discussions, however, once gained, are hard to hold on to, and are, without great vigilance, fated to return to obscurity, to return to the realm of the unthinkable. It is so easy to "forget" the deep unhappiness of family life and its repercussions. One reason is fear about the potential for demonisation of the family. We can see this in our own profession, where the very important contributions of Bettelheim (1967) and Laing (1969) resulted in distortions about the complexities of family life and have led to the effective loss of some of their most original insights (Kanner, 1941; Wing, 1978). There is also a pervasive fear of blame that infects the professional system, and a sense of organisational helplessness in the face of rage, especially if it takes the form of parental complaint.

There is no doubt that, at times, it does require courage to address environmental failures and this is no less true whether we are attempting to help families reflect on their contributions to a child's distress or casting a reflective eye on the ways in which professional networks can repeat these failures. This is one reason why psychoanalytic theory can be so helpful in uncovering the unconscious determinants for patterns of behaviour occurring within and across generations; it is not simply a question of "bad mothers", as Bettelheim (1967) suggested, or "bad families" as Laing (1969) believed. Rather, it is about the possibility of discovering the defences against unacknowledged and often unconscious pain and the anxieties it gives rise to, which have been uncontained and thus fester, like unattended wounds, dominating family life.

Our work teaches us to listen to the unconscious. It is a language all psychoanalytically trained workers learn, and it is not possible to unlearn a language, to decide to be deaf to communications that arrive at unexpected times, or in situations that do not meet the requirements for transference interpretations. I have learnt, rather, to think of our training as akin to that of musicians who have developed a capacity to listen in a particular way, and to use our ability to "hear" the sounds of the unconscious in the most apparently random of circumstances in a creative way. This is because of the power of the mind to convey information with an uncanny immediacy, through a process we describe as "projective identification". Receptivity to this kind of communication is the hallmark of a psychoanalytic worker, and provides us with a wealth of information unavailable through ordinary channels, as the following example demonstrates.

I was approached by the team leader of a group of teachers, tasked with supporting a group of learning-disabled children who were being moved from their separate specialist learning groups into ordinary classroom situations. He was very concerned about his team because they were having difficulty dealing with the emotional stress of helping the children adapt to the classroom. The source of their distress was not clear to him. He wanted my help to support the teachers with their problems. I asked what these problems were; what was their task? He attempted to explain the theory of "inclusion" to me, how the idea was that learning-disabled children are no different from ordinary intellectually able children, except in terms of the time needed to learn. He described this as a sort of ruler, which instead of being based on twelve inches, was—and he stretched his arms to encompass the walls of the consulting room in order to demonstrate this to me—much, much, much longer. Learning-disabled children were no different from ordinary children, except in terms of the time required to incorporate and use the teaching available.

I sat listening to him, but had the odd experience of not understanding most of what he was trying to tell me. I felt very defensive about my inability to understand what, on the surface, seemed a clear-cut description of the task. I had the strong sense that I must not let him see my confusion or he would think me very stupid and not up to the kind of reflective help he required from me. In some very extraordinary and unconscious way, and within a very short period of time, he had conveyed to me the dilemma that he, the children, and their support teachers experienced. There was a sudden change of message to the children, from teachers who had supported them in special units to these same teachers telling them they were now just like everyone else. I thought there must have been very intense demands on the support teachers, as they were really not permitted to acknowledge how frustrating the classroom experience must feel to children who felt different, unable to benefit from the dictates of the well-intentioned inclusion policy. The team leader was, in turn, charged with supporting the teachers, and he was insightful enough to realise that there were unconscious pressures at work, but, like me, he could not understand them. Instead, there was a shared need to deny felt experience; that the children were at sea in this new ordinary world. They were now to be just like everyone else. The experience I had in the consultation was deeply linked to the children's belief that the frustration of not being up to what was required of them would expose them as "stupid". To challenge this proposition would be tantamount to admitting there was no hope of integration into the ordinary world. This sense of "stupidity", of not understanding what was required, described the experience of the teachers, their team leader, who had the courage to think more deeply about the dilemma and seek help, and me. The roots of all of our confusion was based on the children's belief that they could not admit their deep sense of inadequacy and difference.

In this way, and through this common but not usually recognised mode of communication, I gained some understanding of the dilemma the teachers faced; in order to accomplish their task, they felt obliged to ignore the fears and anxieties of children placed in a highly frustrating and potentially humiliating situation. To admit this was to invite exposure of their sense of inadequacy. Thus, one might conjecture that my experience of stupidity was the result of something akin to an intergenerational failure, in this case involving the children, their special support teachers, the team leader, and, finally, me. The winds of this complex transference would blow unimpeded until it reached a transforming object. Bion (1962) termed this process "alpha function", and it is the capacity to offer this sort of reflective containment that is the hallmark of a psychoanalytic worker, in any form and in any setting.

A few months before his death in January 1971, Winnicott gave a talk to the Association of Workers for Maladjusted Children, the David Wills Memorial Lecture. He began that paper, entitled "Residential care as therapy", with these words:

> A great deal of growing is growing downwards. If I live long enough I hope I may dwindle and become small enough to get through the little hole called dying. I do not need to go far to find an inflated psychotherapist. There's me. In the decade called the thirties I was learning to be a psychoanalyst, and I could feel that, with a little more training, a little more skill, and little more luck I could move mountains by making the right interpretations at the right moment. (Winnicott, 1970, p. 220)

This is a courageous statement for a person to make towards the end of his life. Winnicott, in what I think of as a gesture of loyalty to his internal professional parents (Freud and Klein), was highly critical of the work of Fairbairn and the Scottish tradition. There is irony here, because, in fact, Winnicott's own theories challenged the psychoanalytic orthodoxy in ways he could not freely acknowledge. What is "the facilitating environment" if not the family and the community that provides its mores and beliefs? More than most psychoanalysts of his day, Winnicott devoted much time to popular talks about the role and responsibilities of the community and of society towards its children, and he was very active in supporting the aims of therapeutic communities.

His views are entirely commensurate with those of Sutherland, who, as Jeremy Holmes describes,

> saw that psychoanalysis had most to offer the psychotherapy community when it develops an interactive relationship with other institutions. The attempt to dominate the helping professions is based on an omnipotent phantasy and leads to sequestration and a closed society. Like a good parent, a psychotherapy institution needs to offer attunement, modulation, regulation and communication as well as instruction and example, not domination or avoidance. (Holmes, 1993a, p. 21)

We all need courage to think like this, to take on the task of understanding unbearable realities we would rather not know about, to be receptive to the power of the transference to communicate the unthinkable to us. We also, as professionals, need courage to broaden our skills, to explore ways of supporting and sharing skills with colleagues who are struggling at the coalface with these realities, often with very limited resources. It might, at times, be hard for us to recognise how much bravery is involved, when individuals, parents, carers, or professionals with very specialist skills, but who have little knowledge of the unconscious, become receptive to ideas that can seem at first very alien to them. They are receptive because psychoanalysis is, foremost, a fund of practical knowledge, and should and must be more easy to access than it is.

I have called this chapter "Scotland the Brave" because so many of these ideas, about the central role of relationships, about families, about community, about empathy and sympathy are deeply embedded in Scotland's intellectual history, its traditions, and its poetry:

> Oh wad some Pow'r the giftie gie us
> To see oursel's as others see us!
> It wad frae monie a blunder free us
> An' foolish notion
>
> (Robert Burns "To a Louse, On Seeing One on a Lady's Bonnet at Church")

References

Bettelheim, B. (1967). *The Empty Fortress: Infantile Autism and the Birth of the Self.* New York: The Free Press, Simon and Schuster.

Bion, W. R. (1961). *Experiences in Groups and Other Papers.* London: Tavistock.

Bion, W. R. (1962). A theory of thinking. *International Journal of Psycho-Analysis, 43*: 306–10.

Blake, W. (1794). The Sick Rose. In: *Songs of Innocence and Experience* (p. 39). Oxford: Oxford University Press, 1970.

Bollas, C., & Sundelson, D. (1995). *The New Informants: Betrayal of Confidence in Psychoanalysis and Psychotherapy.* London: Karnac.

Burns, R. (1786). To a Louse, On Seeing One on a Lady's Bonnet at Church. In: *Poems and Songs, Volume VI: The Harvard Classics.* New York: P. F. Collier & Son.

Celani, P. (2010). *Fairbairn's Object Relations Theory in the Clinical Setting.* New York: Columbia University Press.

Emmanuel, L. (2002). Deprivation x3. *Journal of Child Psychotherapy, 28*: 163–179.

Erikson, E. (1950). *Childhood and Society.* London: Penguin.

Fairbairn, W. R. D. (1952). *Psychoanalytic Studies of the Personality.* London: Routledge and Kegan Paul.

Fairbairn, W. R. D. (1958). On the nature and aims of psychoanalytic treatment. In: D. Scharff & E. Birtles Fairbairn (Eds.) *From Instinct to Self, Vol. 1* (pp. 74–92). Northvale, NJ: Jason Aronson, 1994.

Freud, S. (1933a). *New Introductory Lectures on Psychoanalysis. S.E., 22.* London: Hogarth.

Henry, G. (1974). Doubly deprived. *Journal Child Psychotherapy, 3*(4): 15–28

Holmes, J. (1993a). Bowlby, Fairbairn, Sutherland: the Scottish connection in psychotherapy. Unpublished Inaugural Lecture of the Sutherland Trust, March 1993, Edinburgh.

Holmes, J. (1993b). *John Bowlby and Attachment Theory.* London: Routledge.

Kanner, L. (1941). *In Defense of Mother: How to Bring Up Children in Spite of More Zealous Psychologists.* New York: Dodds, Mead.

Laing, R. D. (1969). *The Politics of the Family.* London: Tavistock.

Miller, G. (2004). *R. D. Laing.* Edinburgh: Edinburgh Review.

Miller, G. (2008). Scottish psychoanalysis: a rational religion. *Journal of the History of the Behavioural Sciences, 44*: 38–58.

Milton, J. (1667). *Paradise Lost,* C. Ricks (Ed.). London: Penguin Classics, 1968.

Ogden, T. (2010). Why read Fairbairn? *International Journal of Psychoanalysis, 91*: 101–118.

Shuttleworth, A. (1999). Finding new clinical pathways in the changing world of district child psychotherapy. *Journal of Child Psychotherapy, 25*: 29–49.

Sprince, J. (2002). Developing containment *Journal of Child Psychotherapy, 28*: 147–161.

Sprince, J. (2009). The devil and the deep blue sea: dyadic narcissism and the problem of individuation. *Journal of Child Psychotherapy, 35*(1): 13–31.

Sutherland, J. D. (1966). The psychotherapeutic clinic and community psychiatry. *Bulletin of the Menninger Clinic, 30*: 338–350.

Williams, G. (1997). *Internal Landscapes and Foreign Bodies.* London: Routledge.

Wing, J. K. (1978). *Reasoning About Madness.* Oxford: Oxford University Press.

Winnicott, D. W. (1970). Residential care as therapy. In: C. Winnicott, R. Shepherd, & M. Davis (Eds.), *Deprivation and Delinquency* (pp. 220–228). London: Tavistock, 1984.

CHAPTER SEVEN

The perinatally depressed couple and the work of mourning: a developmental imperative

Molly Ludlam

Introduction

In this chapter, I focus on the impact of perinatal depression on relationships in families and especially on couple relationships. Such is the cumulative effect of the timing of this experience in a couple's life, I want also to suggest that their relationship *itself* might sometimes be considered to be "depressed".

My interest in this subject emanates from meeting a number of couples who were expecting a child or who recently had become parents. They had come for couple psychotherapy because depression was preventing one or both partners from enjoying together life as a couple, and life as parents.

We know that a couple's relationship is most vulnerable and most likely to break down during pregnancy and their children's infancy (Cowan & Cowan, 1992; Shapiro & Gottman, 2005; Twenge, Campbell, & Foster, 2003). This is the time when the couple has to manage a number of demanding developmental tasks in order to grow as individuals *and* as a couple. It is generally understood that anxiety and depression are commonly experienced by new parents. The increasing recognition of maternal "postnatal depression" led, in the latter part of the twentieth century, to the development of special treatment programmes for new mothers. Nevertheless, it has recently been estimated that *pre*-natal depression now affects one in ten women in the UK, and that mental health problems constitute the largest identifiable cause of death in the perinatal period (CEMD, 2001). Enquiries such as *Why Mothers Die* (CEMD, 2001) question whether depression experienced by women during the perinatal period differs significantly in its characterisation from depressive illness at other stages in life. Thus, we might now wonder whether the term "postnatal depression" has not only served to obscure the whole nature of mental health problems in the broader *perinatal* period, but also whether it has fostered an undue focus on women. Furthermore, might any such focus on hormonally triggered illness have been reinforced by societal anxieties about the catastrophic consequences of breakdown in new mothers? Increasing reports of paternal depression (Cox, 2005) now add to a wider picture and might enable us to define a couple context for this phenomenon.

While the occurrence of depression in new parents is familiar, I suggest that if we consider that *couples* can be "perinatally depressed", we might find another way of understanding the complexity of the developmental tasks required of new parents. This is important because the relationships that couples and their infant children make and remake during this crucial period are fundamental to emotional learning. So, we should never underestimate the long-term transgenerational consequences of what parents and children learn at this time and its effects on how future couple relationships are made.

What makes this developmental change, whereby a couple becomes a threesome, of such phenomenal significance? The transition occurs at a time that is full of expectation and uncertainty. This is when the experience of transitions made in earlier life, and notably the management of oedipal conflicts, become especially meaningful. How these earlier developmental hurdles were managed and survived will affect new parents' abilities to take on their new roles. This transition, therefore, like all others in human experience, presents a crisis. Like all crises, it is both a challenge and an opportunity for personal growth. Seen from this perspective, depression might serve as an unconscious means of putting off, or of resisting, feared uncertainty and change.

Jane and Richard

The following description of a couple may assist in considering the effect on a couple relationship when both new parents become depressed. (For the purposes of this account, names and details have been disguised.)

Jane requested some meetings for herself and Richard to talk about their difficulties. Richard explained that he had agreed to come along for Jane's sake, having no need himself. Jane said that communication between them had broken down. Indeed, Richard left her to tell their story: they were in their early forties and had made a late marriage, three years before. Their two-year-old son, Simon, was born prematurely at thirty weeks, and during his first months was frequently hospitalised. Jane decided to give up her career ambitions to look after him. On his discharge home, Jane was referred for counselling for "postnatal depression".

All of this would have been stressful enough, but, soon after their wedding, Richard, who had recurrent inflammatory arthritis, had become ill again. His symptoms flared up acutely during Jane's pregnancy and meant that he was often too ill to work. Jane now felt as if she had acquired *two* sons who were irritable, fragile, and impossible to satisfy. In the short space of time between Richard and Jane's heady romance and coming for couple therapy—barely three years—the outlook for this family appeared challenging. In my countertransference, it felt bleak and quite hopeless.

From their presentation at the initial consultation, it seemed to me that *both* Jane and Richard were depressed, and that in many senses this was a natural, understandable, and even healthy reaction to difficult experiences. But depression had set in at such a level and so chronically that it seemed impossible to shift. Richard saw no need to seek help because he felt that the problem was manageable if no attention was paid to it. This was because, having decided against any treatment interventions, whether medical or psychotherapeutic, he believed that essentially nothing could be done. For him, it was simply too dangerous to hope. Always a reserved man, he had once found Jane's outgoing spontaneity attractive. Now her need to express her feelings and to put into words her impression of the feelings he wished to hide was unwelcome and intrusive. He shrank visibly in his chair as she tried to cajole him to speak to me, and she smarted visibly, hurt at his dismissal and withdrawal from her. In my experience, this reflected a characteristic male–female dynamic, in which the woman is more expressive, and the man is less emotionally articulate.

If Jane and Richard were going to make any use of couple therapy, it would require some engagement, but engagement in itself implies some hope. Richard was too angry with Jane for deserting him for Simon, and Jane was too angry with Richard for becoming seriously ill, and therefore unavailable to her. They recalled their wedding of three years ago with nostalgia, since when both felt betrayed by the other's failure to live up to the ideal they each sought. So, each blamed the other for standing in the way of some resolution. The pain of their exchanges was excruciating to witness. The loss of their youthful, hopeful selves was poignant; they clung determinedly to anger as a defence against acknowledging the change that Simon had introduced, and against the fear of separation and abandonment. I felt fearful for them both, and also for Simon. Their couple psychotherapy with me was short-lived; it was not able to survive the ambivalence with which it had been begun.

Discussion

The complexity of this couple's story illustrates how new parenthood brings together many potentially overwhelming demands in a couple's life. Our brief series of meetings raised more questions than answers, but I hope that by asking the questions we might be better able to explore the deadening impact that depression has on a couple relationship, and how it acts to stifle growth in relationships at a crucial developmental stage.

We might begin by speculating about why this couple had come to marriage so late. Perhaps Richard, with his chronic illness, feared that no woman would truly be able to love him "in sickness and in health". As much as Jane wanted children, I wonder if she also feared losing the autonomy she had struggled hard to achieve by investing in a career. If their late marriage was a marriage made "before it's too late", we might consider that a marriage that is made in the hope of rescue can become a trap.

A colleague, Joaquin Canizares (personal communication), has hypothesised that problems which are current for a couple at the moment of conception become bound up with the pregnancy. So, problems such as the loss of Jane's identity and Richard's preoccupying concern about becoming an invalid might have become encapsulated in the pregnancy with their ambivalence about being a couple. Did the pregnancy, therefore, threaten Richard in his status as Jane's principal object of care? If Richard felt ambivalent about the impending addition of a rival to him for his wife–mother's love, we might wonder how he felt when Simon was born prematurely and began life in such a vulnerable way. If he felt resentment, did he also feel guilt? He might also have identified with Simon as the sick son of the family. Can such conflicting feelings be safely expressed? Birksted-Breen (1986) notes that if the baby does not conform to the parents' expectations, the "ideal baby" is therefore lost and must be mourned. Indeed, Simon was not at all a "bouncing baby". He must have arrived being far more fragile and needy than either Jane or Richard had anticipated.

Parenting the infant is not the only parenting needed when a baby is born. Partners' capacities to parent one another during their child's infancy play an important part in enabling them to separate from their own parents. Birksted-Breen (1986) observes that the immediate postnatal period is a time when a woman re-evaluates her relationship with her own mother. Perhaps the worsening of Richard's arthritis during her pregnancy caused Jane to fear that he would not, after all, be able to "mother" her so that she could separate from her own mother. Joaquin Canizares (personal communication) has also hypothesised that if a man is subject to depressive feelings, his partner might also become depressed, so that unconsciously she can enable him to feel relatively better about himself, and valued as the carer. We might wonder, however, whether Jane's preoccupation with Simon and her subsequent collapse into depression aroused such fear in Richard that it exacerbated his arthritic symptoms, leading him to shut down all engagement and focus on self-preservation and looking after himself.

If depression is seen as a way of managing anger by internalising it, we can see that this couple easily made their angry feelings inaccessible to change. Indeed, if being angry is a way of managing external threats, anger can become identified with the force that keeps one alive and, thus, it is impossible to let go. Whatever the triggers were, we can see that having begun, the dynamic of exchanged depressive feelings took hold and built up in a way that was hard both for them and for me as their therapist to address. As a result, they were quite stuck.

The impact of maternal depression

As observed above, emotional turbulence, both pre- and postnatal, has been mostly associated with women. Hormonally triggered "baby blues" do affect about 80% of women for a few days after a birth and usually subside spontaneously. Some 10–15% mothers continue to experience depression, presenting as exhaustion, with feelings of guilt and inadequacy. Sometimes this leads to panic attacks, despair and even to fears of harm to the baby or themselves. If untreated, this condition may persist for months or even years. Puerperal psychosis, a relatively rare illness, affects between one and two women in every 1,000, and in this group the suicide rate is estimated at two per every 1000 (CEMD, 2001). Its severity is such that care of both mother and baby is generally undertaken in hospital.

Close observations of parent–child relationships tell us about the ways in which, even in infancy, children can "self-regulate" in response to a lack of attention or holding by their adult carer (Tronick, 1989). One description of the potentially traumatic life-long impact on a child whose mother was severely depressed comes from the psychoanalyst, Harry Guntrip. His relationship with his mother suffered when she withdrew from him following the birth and death of his younger brother (Guntrip, 1975). Modell (1999) defines the range of reactions in children to an emotionally withdrawn, chronically depressed mother as a "dead mother complex". Happily, human beings are also capable of sublimation and of self-repair. Guntrip's own dead mother complex made him hyper-sensitively aware of schizoid withdrawal in others, which he turned to good account as a psychoanalytic thinker and practitioner.

A recent study (Murray et al., 2011) which followed up 100 first-time mothers over sixteen years, found that children of postnatally depressed mothers bear an increased risk of suffering from depression themselves. Insecure attachment to mothers during infancy, marital conflict and further maternal depression, extending beyond the perinatal period, were also correlated with offsprings' experience of lifetime depression.

Because of its potentially devastating impact, not only on the woman and her baby, but on her partner too, it is important that depression is recognised and addressed early on. Indeed, the study lead by Murray lends urgency to calls for routine screening and parenting support for perinatally depressed mothers. Sadly, many women feel they must hide their symptoms, out of shame and guilt for not coping as a parent. Their partners, therefore, might be the recipients of most of their complaints, often in the form of projected anger and resentment. Partners later often report a sense of responsibility, coupled with powerlessness to help to put things right. These feelings might also be perceived as having been introjected, their projection by the woman being a communication of her sense of feeling overwhelmed in her new role as mother. Murray's research, together with other studies cited below, highlights the importance of looking at the impact on the whole family, and the need to take a systemic approach to include the family and/or parental couple in any treatment.

Fathers are important, too

It might help us to hold on to a couple and family perspective when we recognise that men may also experience depression before and/or after their child's birth. A longitudinal study *When Partners Become Parents*, begun in California in 1975 by Philip and Carolyn Cowan, is still running (Cowan & Cowan, 1992). From all the data collected, the authors have traced recognisable and predictable patterns. For example, they say,

> Individuals and couples who are doing well in pregnancy will probably continue to do well after the baby arrives: those in difficulty in the early phases of the transition tend to be struggling later on, with each other and with their children. (Cowan & Cowan, 1992, p. 204)

Moreover, the less that the father is involved in the baby's care, the more likely it is that there will be dissatisfaction in the couple relationship. Unsurprisingly, those fathers who are more involved in parenting have lower parenting stress and report fewer symptoms of depression, and mothers whose partners are more involved in their child's care express higher satisfaction in their couple relationship.

The first UK study (Ballard, Davis, Cullen, Mohan, & Dean, 1994) of fathers' experience examined postnatally a small sample of 200 couples. Whereas more women than men showed psychiatric symptoms both at six weeks and six months after the birth, fathers were more likely to experience depression if their partners also suffered. This link was particularly noticeable at six months. Another study (Cox, 2005) noted that while maternal depression has been extensively researched, fathers "have been kept in the wings . . . at most . . . seen as welcome playmates, but with only marginal effects on infants' development" (Cox, 2005, p. 982). Surveying records of over 8,000 fathers two months after the birth, it was found that over 300 appeared to be suffering with depressive symptoms such as mood swings, feelings of hopelessness, and anxiety. Following up the children of all these men at three-and-a-half years, it was noted that, irrespective of other factors, including depression in their mothers, those children, and especially boys, whose fathers had suffered postnatal depression were at an increased risk of behavioural problems between the ages of three and five. The study concluded that fathers' influence has probably been previously underestimated and suggested that postnatal depression in fathers has a "specific and persisting impact" (Cox, 2005, p. 982) on children's early behavioural and emotional development. Indeed, Crockenberg & Leerkes (2003) found that those women who, as children, experienced parental rejection, or whose mothers had depressive symptoms, bear an increased risk of developing perinatal depression. Happily, however, this risk is reduced if the woman's relationship with her father was positive and "accepting".

So, is paternal depression following a baby's birth a recent phenomenon, or have we been slow to recognise it and to appreciate its significance? It might have risked being dismissed as a "me too" reaction to a partner's depression. Seglow and Canham (1999) drew attention to ways in which men in our society identify with their pregnant partners, citing an increased incidence of nausea and vomiting in expectant fathers, as a somatic parallel to the male "couvade" exhibited by expectant fathers in some cultures in the developing world. Might depression in fathers be understood in the same way?

The impact of early relationships on adult couples

The character of early attachment patterns between parents and children has been shown to be very significant in later adult relationships. Hazan and Shaver (1987) showed that adult partners function as attachment figures for one another in patterns that reflect the attachment styles that predominated for them as infants. Bradburn (1997) further demonstrated that partners who are both rated as securely attached as individuals manage relationship difficulties moderately well. Heterosexual couples comprising men who are securely attached and women partners who are insecurely attached, in fact, fare just as well. However, if the gender/attachment status is reversed, that is, with the women being securely attached and their male partners insecurely attached, these couples show the highest potential for relationship breakdown. Discussing the striking findings of Bradburn's study, Cowan and Cowan (2001) wonder whether one explanation might lie in the possibility that when conflicts arose, securely attached women could feel relatively free in expressing angry feelings. Insecurely attached men, however, might have sought partners who were "qualitatively different from their mothers – that is more nurturing, responsive and accepting" (Cowan & Cowan, 2001, p. 72) as one might expect of a securely attached woman. When their partner did not behave as expected, the men became angry. The women might also have been drawn to insecurely attached men, in the hope that they could make them feel loved and cared for. Cowan and Cowan speculate that this nurturing might be perceived as a "central task of the relationship" (Cowan & Cowan, p. 72), and that if this task proved too difficult, the management of the relationship in the long term was threatened. As I shall explore later, these dynamics might play a special role in new relationships, which might occur predominantly in young adults who have children. However, they will also be features of couple relationships at later points in life, whenever it seems crucial for the couple to recognise and address the unmet "central task" of the relationship.

What can couple therapy contribute?

Despite an international interest in researching the impact of perinatal depression on couple and family relationships, it appears that services are much more readily offered to individual mothers and fathers than to address the crisis with the couple involved. This is the more unfortunate because we know that during the course of a couple's relationship, there is an increased risk in partners of those who are mentally ill of also developing a mental illness (Hagnell & Kreitman, 1974).

Where should the focus of intervention be? On the mother, father, parental couple, or on the couple? One study has demonstrated that by enhancing a father's appreciation of motherhood, distress and depression is significantly reduced in first-time mothers who have low self-esteem (Matthey, Kavanagh, Howie, Barnett, & Charles, 2004). Other research supports taking a couple-focused approach. For example, in the treatment of depression, couple therapy has been shown to be more acceptable and at least as efficacious as antidepressant drugs (Leff et al., 2000). Recently, interest has been shown in the potential efficacy of couple counselling as a primary health care resource, along with support for fathers' involvement throughout the pregnancy and their baby's infancy. In a study in Greenwich, London, to explore the efficacy of three different kinds of interventions to support new parents, parenting workshops, postnatal support groups, and relationship counselling, the Tavistock Centre for Couple Relationships collaborated with MIND (Clulow & Donaghy, 2010). Although all three interventions were found to be effective in improving the depression experienced by the women who participated, only the relationship counselling raised the levels of satisfaction in the couples' relationships. Moreover, it was the only intervention that consistently involved their male partners, who were otherwise relatively hard to reach. Promoting the role of fathers, and with it an awareness of the centrality of the couple relationship, seems to make sense, given the way in which our society views parenting nowadays. Pressures on both parents to work outside the home add to uncertainties about gender roles. Many new families find themselves geographically and emotionally separated from extended family networks. This awareness, however, would appear not to be reflected in the creation of accessible couple-focused services.

Transition to parenthood and developmental tasks

If we view crises as opportunities for personal growth, what are the developmental tasks for new parents *and* for the couple? They are so complex that perhaps we should not be surprised that new parenthood is the time of greatest vulnerability for the survival of couple relationships; it is remarkable that so many couple relationships survive and even grow in response. Four key tasks are identified here.

Reviewing relationships with parents

Those who can plan for parenthood, ideally before the pregnancy, may also be able to reflect on the new role of becoming a parent and the likely impact on their relationships with their own mother and father (Birksted-Breen, 1986). Reflection in anticipation of parenthood allows both a reconnection with parents and the kind of separation that might allow a different dependency to evolve, so that there can be recognition and a further affirmation of the new parent as adult. Not all of this may happen, however, if planning for the baby or the pregnancy itself is cut short, or becomes fraught with anxiety, such as when the pregnancy is unplanned, and particularly if it is unwanted. We might wonder what happens in the sometimes relatively accelerated process of adoption, or after a previous history of infertility, stillbirth, or premature birth. If, like Richard and Jane, the expectant parents are preoccupied by illness, or other major life changes, such as the death of a parent, or moving country, or house, or job, then there might not be enough time to re-evaluate relationships with parents, so as to free the person to step into mother or father's shoes. In addition, since rivalry with one's own parent might be feared and avoided, feelings of lack of confidence or inadequacy as a parent, so often a feature of perinatal depression, will be exacerbated. Thus, postnatally, depression might offer time out for the re-evaluation and adjustment which was needed before the baby arrived; alternatively, it offers time to resist attending to these altogether.

Anticipating psychologically becoming a parent and that one's partner will also

If a crucial individual developmental task on becoming a parent is to find a meaningful role as mother or father, then a complementary couple task will be for the expectant and/or new parental couple to allow and even assist one another to assume their new mother and father roles. A couple who can do this might be described as having a "creative couple state of mind", as elaborated by Morgan and Stokoe (Morgan, 2002, 2005). Such a state of mind necessitates being able to tolerate being part of a threesome, and part of a relationship in which one is sometimes one of a pair and, at others, excluded by the other two. One of the main imperatives, therefore, that parenthood demands is to clear the hurdles thrown up by oedipal conflict.

Working to resolve oedipal conflict

Many women nowadays actively decide to parent alone. In a recent psychoanalytic re-evaluation of the importance of fathers, Marks (2002) discusses the difficulties which women might have in "letting fathers in" to their relationship with their baby. She suggests that the degree to which a woman includes her sexual partner in the relationship she has with her baby *and* whether the man will feel able to get involved as a father will depend on whether or not each has a sexual mother and father couple in their minds. Furthermore, if each partner has an internalised sexual coupling, this will help to foster in their child's mind a notion of a father and mother couple, and "a certain creative kind of mind and that capacity as an adult and parent to welcome a sexual and potent father" (Marks, 2002, p. 93).

In the case of Jane and Richard, oedipal conflicts were unresolved. Illness seemed to have recreated childhood experiences of rejection as disappointing/disappointed children. In successive depressive phases, they withdrew sexually from one another. Each found loss of their honeymoon excitement painfully rejecting, but they resisted my attempts to explore it. I felt like a teenager's intrusive parent. It seemed to me that for this, as for many other couples, lovers could not lie in the same bed as a dependent patient and a new mother. I wondered, therefore, if they both lacked a belief in themselves as adult lovers.

This problem of being simultaneously both a partner and a parent may also be "resolved" in other ways, such as by serially excluding fathers from the maternally dominated family. A colleague described a sad and marginalised father in such a family who adopted an apparently masochistic, helpless position, and even labelled himself as a "spare part" (F. Calvocoressi, personal communication).

Mourning

When change occurs, we must mourn what has been lost. On becoming parents, the couple must let go what might be a delicious twosome fusion to allow a completely dependent third to join them. Freud (1917e) perceives mourning as enabling the recovery of self and a capacity for loving after the loss of a beloved, and he identifies the failure to mourn as a source of melancholia. Although mourning might be considered a fact of life, it is often avoided or resisted, especially where it involves letting go a relationship complicated by unresolved conflict.

Loss and grief can strike couples with young children in various ways: for example, when a pregnancy ends in stillbirth, or a child is born with disabilities. Grieving couples who can share their feelings are immensely enriched by their mutual support. Those who experience grief as a more solitary preoccupation, however, as Jane and Richard probably did, do so because revelation of loss and disappointment risks exposure to criticism and rejection. A failure to grieve together is a common feature of the troubled relationships that couples bring for therapy. Crucially, what is evident in meeting couples like Jane and Richard is the breakdown in each partner's capacity to be available, whether physically or emotionally, to the other. This breakdown might mirror, in a potentially re-traumatising way, the preoccupied state of mind with which the depressed mother excludes her infant.

The depressed couple relationship

Depression constitutes a cry for help. Nevertheless, help that is offered might not be accepted. The depressed person often rejects the help she/he seeks as not to be trusted; it is too little and too late. The partner whose love is so spurned is vulnerable to suffering a deep, narcissistic wound. Could perinatal depression really degenerate into a depressed couple relationship? In couple psychotherapy, I have encountered couples, in both new and longstanding relationships, where both partners have become depressed, and I hypothesise that the depression is, for one or both of them, a defence against embracing a developmental imperative. It may present at a number of different times in the life-cycle of the couple, and not only when the couple become, or fail to become, parents, but also, for example, when the nest empties, or at mid-life, or at the point of retirement, or when a life-threatening experience has occurred. Indeed, a depressed relationship may present when there might appear to be no incidence of depression in either partner; rather, there has been a "silent" or unconscious recognition that the "central task" of the relationship has not been addressed.

With Bannister and Pincus's concept of a shared fear and shared belief in mind, it could be said that the depressed couple relationship lacks belief in its capacities for self-repair and self-renewal; it becomes stuck (Bannister & Pincus, 1965). Notably, such couples lack faith in their relationship's potential for creativity; when I meet them in therapy, my countertransference is instead pervaded with a sense of emptiness and futility. In these instances, I wonder whether the couple relationship has had to manage an envious attack on hope and creativity, an attack which is embedded in a shared belief that their relationship was not meant to succeed. Morgan and Ruszczynski (1998) identified a capacity vital to successful couple relating as the ability to become a "creative couple". This Morgan defined as "a primarily psychic development . . . in which it is possible to allow different thoughts and feelings to come together in one's mind, and for something to develop out of them" (Morgan, 2005, p. 22). Extrapolating from this idea, one might perceive that the creativity that the depressed couple will require to allow development, to explore difficulties and repair hurts, to mourn loss and to harness change, cannot be tolerated. When it is unused, creativity atrophies. The depressed couple, then, is the antithesis of the creative couple.

Reflecting again on Richard and Jane, and recalling Jane's sociability, which once attracted and now repelled Richard, we might imagine that Richard had been drawn to and promoted Jane's liveliness and creativity, these being qualities which he denied in himself. But this had led in turn to the creation of a rival in the form of their son, Simon. Feeling abandoned by Jane, Richard now enviously attacked the creativity and vitality he could not own. It is possible, too, that I, as the female therapist, was also identified with a maternal creative process which could not be allowed to thrive. In such a scenario, it is easy to imagine that in Richard's management of hurt at rejection and abandonment, resentment became a powerful defence against hope.

Conclusion

Can we be hopeful? Perhaps we can, provided that a couple can find a containing relationship, which, if not found within the family, may be offered by couple therapy, until such time as they can adapt to the profound changes and losses incurred in becoming parents. Research I have drawn upon (Clulow & Donaghy, 2010; Matthey, Kavanagh, Howie, Barnett, & Charles, 2004) shows that if a woman becomes depressed in the perinatal period, she and her children are more likely to recover if her partner is in an emotionally resourceful state to support her through their period of vulnerability. If he is not, the prognosis for the couple's relationship is poor, and the future relationships of parents and children alike will suffer.

I have argued that perinatal depression is a crisis that belongs in a particular way to the parental couple, as well as to the new family. Where possible, the intervention of couple therapy should be offered, because it aims to involve both partners creatively. The emotional well-being of the couple and their children depend upon fostering *all* their creative resources.

References

Ballard, C. G., Davis, R., Cullen, P. C., Mohan, R. N., & Dean, C. (1994). Prevalence of postnatal psychiatric morbidity in mothers and fathers. *British Journal of Psychiatry, 164*: 782–788.

Bannister, K., & Pincus, L. (1965). *Shared Phantasy in Marital Problems: Therapy in a Four-person Relationship*. Hitchin: Codicote Press [reprinted London: Institute of Marital Studies, 1971].

Birksted-Breen, D. (1986). The experience of having a baby: a developmental view. *Free Associations, 4*: 22–35.

Bradburn, I. S. (1997). Attachment and coping strategies in married couples with pre-school children. Unpublished doctoral dissertation, University of California, Berkeley.

CEMD (Confidential Enquiries into Maternal Deaths) (2001). *Why Mothers Die 1997–1999*. London: Royal College of Obstetricians and Gynaecologists.

Clulow, C., & Donaghy, M. (2010). Developing the couple perspective in parenting support: evaluation of a service initiative for vulnerable families. *Journal of Family Therapy, 32*: 142–168.

Cowan, C. P., & Cowan, P. A. (1992). *When Partners Become Parents: The Big Life Change for Couples*. New York: Basic Books [reprinted Mahwah, NJ: Lawrence Erlbaum, 2000].

Cowan, P. A., & Cowan, C. P. (2001). A couple perspective on the transmission of attachment patterns. In: C. Clulow (Ed.), *Adult Attachment and Couple Psychotherapy* (pp. 62–82). London: Brunner-Routledge.

Cox, J. (2005). Postnatal depression in fathers. *The Lancet, 366*(9490), 17 September.

Crockenberg, S., & Leerkes, E. M. (2003). Developmental history, partner relationships, and infant reactivity as predictors of postpartum depression and maternal sensitivity. *Journal of Family Psychology, 17*: 1–14.

Freud, S. (1917e). Mourning and melancholia. *S.E., 14*: 239–258. London: Hogarth.

Guntrip, H. (1975). My experience of analysis with Fairbairn and Winnicott. *International Review of Psycho-Analysis, 2*: 145–156.

Hagnell, O., & Kreitman, N. (1974). Mental illness in married pairs in a total population. *British Journal of Psychiatry, 125*: 293–302.

Hazan, C., & Shaver, P. (1987). Romantic love conceptualised as an attachment process. *Journal of Personality and Social Psychology, 52/3*: 511–524.

Leff, J., Vearnals, S., Brewin, C. R., Wolff, G., Alexander, B., Asen, E., Dayson, D., Jones, E., Chisholm, D., & Everitt, B. (2000). The London depression intervention trial. *British Journal of Psychiatry, 177*: 95–100.

Marks, M. (2002). Letting fathers in. In: J. Trowell & A. Etchegoyen (Eds.), *The Importance of Fathers* (pp. 93–106). London: Brunner-Routledge.

Matthey, S., Kavanagh, D. J., Howie, P., Barnett, B., & Charles, M. (2004). Prevention of postnatal distress or depression: an evaluation of an intervention at preparation for parenthood classes. *Journal of Affective Disorders, 79*(1–3): 113–126.

Modell, A. (1999). The dead mother syndrome and the reconstruction of trauma. In: G. Kohon (Ed.), *The Dead Mother* (pp. 76–86). London: Routledge.

Morgan, M. (2002). The therapist's couple state of mind. In: F. Grier (Ed.), *Brief Encounters with Couples* (pp. 17–32). London: Karnac.

Morgan, M. (2005). On being able to be a couple: the importance of a "creative couple" in psychic life. In: F. Grier (Ed.), *Oedipus and the Couple* (pp. 9–30). London: Karnac.

Morgan, M., & Ruszczynski, S. (1998). The creative couple. Unpublished paper presented to the Tavistock Marital Studies Institute 50th Anniversary Conference.

Murray, L., Arteche, A., Fearon, P., Halligan, S., Goodyer, I., & Cooper, P. (2011). Maternal postnatal depression and the development of depres-

sion in offspring up to 16 years of age. *Journal of the American Academy Child and Adolescent Psychiatry, 50*(5): 460–470.

Seglow, R., & Canham, H. (1999). Inter-uterine life and the experience of birth. In: D. Hindle & M. Vaciago Smith (Eds.), *Personality Development, a Psychoanalytic Approach,* (pp. 13–47). London: Routledge.

Shapiro, A. F., & Gottman, J. M. (2005). Effects on marriage of a psycho-education intervention with couples undergoing the transition to parenthood, evaluation at 1-year post intervention. *Journal of Family Communication, 5*(1):1–24.

Tronick, E. (1989). Emotions and emotional communication in infants. *American Psychologist, 44*: 112–119.

Twenge, J. M., Campbell, K. W., & Foster, C. A. (2003). Parenthood and marital satisfaction: a meta-analytic review. *Journal of Marriage and Family, 65*: 574–583.

PART III

MAKING SPACE TO WORK

CHAPTER EIGHT

Temenos or ivory tower? Academic pedagogy through a psychodynamic lens

Lindy Barbour

Introduction

"It may be that universal history is the history of the different intonations given [to] a handful of metaphors" (Borges, 1964, p. 227). This chapter will explore some of these metaphors and intonations as they are deployed consciously or unconsciously in both psychodynamic thinking and in the field of academic pedagogy, in theories of learning and teaching.

At one time, I used to have lunch with a group of philosophers in a Scottish university. After the stress of facing the masses of the Philosophy Ordinary class, they would often respond to the topics of the day by remarking, "Now, this is how philosophy can help!" This always raised a laugh, which doubtless discharged some of their tension, but the habitual joke was a defence. Behind the laughter hid the real belief that their academic discipline could affect and clarify the thinking of others, and a fear that it might not.

This chapter emerges from my participation in a Postgraduate Certificate in Academic Practice, the aim of which is to encourage the self-reflective practice of university teaching, together with an experience of simultaneously teaching on postgraduate courses on counselling and counselling skills. In encountering the discourse and themes of academic pedagogy, I found many points of intersection with the theory and habits of mind of psychotherapy, and found myself inwardly echoing the philosophers, "Now, this is where psychodynamic thinking can help." I was aware of taking a similar stance, that of being engaged by, but not making any statement of, this intellectual conviction. This might be understood in terms of an observing third position (Britton, 1998), perhaps with a sense of the importance of the ideas of my discipline, but was also defensive and wary of overstatement. In academic life, as in psychotherapeutic circles, one treads cautiously when stepping out of the silo of disciplinary culture and identity. This defensiveness, it seems to me, represents a potential loss. Lehrer (2012) emphasises that creativity emerges out of the encounter with difference, in horizontally interacting groups, or the "mash-up", to use a current term. In psychodynamic theory, we hold that the self emerges from identification with the other, into difference and agency in a dialectic of playful exploration. The therapeutic encounter, in its dissolving of fixed and repetitious relations of transference, re-enacts this, to enable, if all goes well, greater flexibility and toleration of difference. In this chapter, I set out, using my experience on this academic course, to endorse the belief of psychoanalyst Jock Sutherland, one of the founders of the Scottish Institute of Human Relations, of the importance of engaging creatively with wider fields of professional practice, culture, and intellectual exploration. In so doing, I also invite reflections on the possibilities for creative connection between the idea of the *temenos*, or sacred space, a space for thinking, and the phallic ivory tower more conventionally associated with the academy.

In the views of Sutherland and Fairbairn, "Psychoanalysis ceased to be merely a method of treatment and became a method of scientific investigation profitably employed within the whole group of psychological and sociological sciences" (Scharff, 1994, p. xxi). As Holmes points out in his 1993 inaugural lecture to the Sutherland Trust (Holmes, 1996), Sutherland's thinking is democratic. He quotes Sutherland as follows:

> The attitude sometimes conveyed by psychoanalysts that this kind of work [social work in this instance] is a poor substitute for what more thorough-going analysis might achieve is more a professional fantasy than an established fact. (Sutherland, 1971, p. 75)

In Sutherland's model of a helpful connection between psychoanalysis and other professions, psychoanalysis underpins and advises rather than supersedes the expertise of other professions.

I propose to look at four strands of research in the sphere of academic pedagogy, examining them in both their own terms and through the lens of psychodynamic thought, and to do this in a spirit of dialogue, looking for resonances without privileging either sphere. The first pedagogical strand considers the importance placed on holding open a space for teaching. The second considers the recent emphasis on the importance of developing a "way of thinking, perhaps and practising". The third strand is about "threshold concepts" and "troublesome knowledge" and what helps to make a breakthrough to a new realm of understanding. Finally, the fourth looks at an exploration of the "knowledge object": how knowledge is internalised through memorising and revision. My aim throughout is to offer an experience of these themes rather than a didactic exposition.

Holding open a space for teaching

Theatre director Peter Brook writes, "I can take any space and call it a bare stage. A man walks across this empty space whilst someone else is watching him, and this is all that is needed for an act of theatre to be engaged" (Brook, 1990, p. 1). This concept of what he calls "The Immediate Theatre" conjures something of the essence of pedagogy and psychotherapy, observing that great theatre, like teaching, or therapy, takes place in the present moment and in the context of relationship. "The word representation no longer separates actor and audience; it envelops them: what is present for one is present for the other" (Brook, 1990, p.156). Brook discusses a dichotomy between, on the one hand, filling up the empty space with the content of the director's mind, the traditional interpretation with "safe" production values, and, on the other hand, the notion, for which he argues passionately, of eliciting and enlisting the thoughts and feelings of the "other", the audience, in the present moment. The philosopher of education, John Dewey, describes this either/or dilemma in his *Experience and Education* when he remarks, "The history of educational theory is marked by opposition between the idea that education is development from within, and that it is formation from without" (Dewey, 1938, p. 17).

In another seminal text on education, *Hard Times*, Charles Dickens shows Gradgrind, the teacher whose God is Facts, teaching his pupils and his own children in an "entirely rational and scientific manner" by stuffing them with facts.

> Thomas Gradgrind presented [himself] to the little pitchers before him, who were to be filled so full of facts. Indeed . . . he seemed a kind of cannon loaded to the muzzle with facts, and prepared to blow them clean out of the regions of childhood at one discharge. He seemed . . . charged with a grim mechanical substitute for the tender young imaginations that were to be stormed away. (Dickens, 1854, p. 48)

In all fields of knowledge, detailed content is important. It is not the facts that are the problem, but the "stuffing". In *Hard Times*, Dickens makes a passionate case for the place of the imagination in education.

> Louisa had been heard to begin a conversation with her brother one day, by saying "Tom, I wonder" – upon which Mr Gradgrind stepped forth and said, "Louisa! Never wonder!"
>
> Herein lay the spring of the mechanical art and mystery of educating the reason without stooping to the cultivation of the sentiments and affections. "Never wonder." (Dickens, 1854, p. 89)

Gradgrind blights the development of his own children. The heroine of *Hard Times* is an orphan adopted from the circus and dismissed by Gradgrind as incurably stupid. Sissy Jupe, "Girl Number Twenty", is the possessor of emotional and moral intelligence and an active imagination, nourished in childhood by a diversity of experience and that sense of adventure of which the circus has always been a compelling symbol.

Gradgrind brings two psychoanalytic thinkers to mind: Winnicott, with his description of the neglectful or impinging mother, either encroaching on the transitional space for creative play, or abandoning that space, thus endangering the capacity to be alone in the presence of the other (Winnicott, 1965, 1971), and Bion, whose theory of container–contained considers the origin of thinking (Bion, 1967). Bion's theory is, above all, about the generation of meaning and the detoxification of the new and disturbing idea, making it digestible.

Thinking with Bion in an educational context, the words "penetrating" and "receptive" come to mind, with their separation of active and passive. Bion's theory emphasises the active nature of both container and contained. Stuffing does not aid metabolism. Container–contained is not a metaphor of an empty vessel containing settled contents. It is, rather, like the active, generative contact of genitalia engaged in intercourse. I am indebted here to Jonathan Delafield-Butt (2012) for the idea, drawn from developmental biology, that our thinking about the processes of conception, intercourse and parturition tends to have a false split between active sperm and phallus and passive receptive ovum, vagina, and uterus, whereas all these processes, when closely observed, can be understood as co-operative. We think of a phallic occupation of space, when, for generative purposes, the "space" is actively collaborating in eliciting and containing content. To put it in the educational context, the student is not a vessel for the ideas of the teacher. The teacher's role is to be drawn upon, like an active feeding breast, but also at times to function as a container for hopes, dreams, and fears, not just to project, but to be projected upon and into.

One teacher, who has attended to the importance of the teacher's holding an open space is Parker Palmer. In his book, *The Courage to Teach: Exploring the Inner Landscape of a Teacher's Life* (1998), he stresses the importance of the teacher's integrity and use of self, and the importance of subjective engagement as well as objective knowledge. He echoes Dewey when he asks, "How can we reconcile the demands of space and stuff?" (Palmer, 1998, p. 124) and he goes on,

> As the debate swings between the teacher-centered model, with its concern for rigor, and the student-centered model, with its concern for active learning, some of us are torn between the poles. . . . We are caught in yet another either/or. (Palmer, 1998, p. 118)

His suggestion for a synthesis recognises the teacher's anxiety. "Waiting out the silences" is hard, says Palmer, and any teacher might worry about whether they have provided enough.

> Like most professionals, I was taught to occupy space, not open it. After all, we are the ones who know, so we have an obligation to tell others all about it. . . . If I am not filling all the available space with my knowledge, I am not earning my keep. (Palmer, 1998, p. 135)

The teacher's dilemma and anxieties about not providing enough resemble those of the nursing mother.

Palmer suggests that in teaching from the polarities of either a teacher focused transmission model, one that might be described as authoritarian, or the student focused model, one that might be described as permissive, "community easily slips into narcissism, where either the teacher reigns supreme or students can do no wrong" (Palmer, 1998, p. 119). He suggests, powerfully, that the antidote to "slipping into narcissism" is to put at the "center of the pedagogical circle" neither teacher nor student, but what he calls "the third thing, a great thing", the importance of which is recognised by students and teachers alike: commitment to the subject itself (Palmer, 1998, p. 119). Acknowledgement of the importance of "the third thing", the subject, holds open the space for thinking. This resonates strongly with Britton's idea of the triangular space for thinking, which "provides us with a capacity for seeing ourselves in interaction with others and for entertaining another point of view" (Britton, 1993, p. 85).

Palmer works with his students through questioning focused on an example, in his own phrase, "teaching from the microcosm", where the chosen example contains the "inner logic of the discipline". This opens up the space to the possibility of interrogating and deconstructing apparently fixed concepts. Students learn to question the norms of categorisation and concept formation within the subject, and, thus, to approach a point where they can discern for themselves new patterns and uses for data. Waiting is important here. Palmer, in resonant words that echo Winnicott, puts it this way: "I needed to wait for the moment when my students could experience it as their own, as a way of naming a discovery that they had made for themselves but were not yet able to put into words" (Palmer, 1998, p. 138).

Ways of thinking and practising

Academic teachers are now encouraged to reflect on their "ways of thinking and practising" (WTP). In broad terms, the WTP approach constitutes a critique of unreflective disciplinarity and over-emphasis on learning outcomes, and

> . . . describes the richness, depth and breadth of what students might learn through engagement with a given subject area in a specific context . . . understandings, forms of discourse, values or ways of acting which are regarded as central to graduate level mastery of a discipline or subject area. (McCune & Hounsell, 2005, p. 257)

Reimann explores the boundaries of disciplinarity and the tensions between teaching within a discipline-specific WTP, and the more generic approach that tends to be favoured by departments of academic practice and pedagogy. She asks if the very idea of a WTP helps academics to become more reflective practitioners, and if it can, thereby, change how they teach (Reimann, 2009). One of Reimann's most significant findings is that thinking about and discussing the WTP in any subject or disciplinary context of itself evokes more of a focus on students' understanding as opposed to the teacher's transmission of content. It does not seem surprising that the habit of reflection on process, having to make the taken-for-granted explicit, encourages this change in practice, increasing awareness of the needs and progress of the learner.

For a therapist, attention to process is ingrained. For the teacher of counselling and psychotherapy, reflecting on our WTP constitutes the greater part of our subject content. Making the taken-for-granted, and unconscious, more explicit and conscious is not something of which therapists require to be convinced, and neither is the valuing of context that is underlined by the WTP approach. Often, the problems that we find in life stem from an interpretation of self as an object with fixed characteristics in relationships with others who are equally unchanging. An important part of the learning process within therapy is precisely the realisation that behaviour varies with context, and that there is no fixed order of meaning. This could be frightening compared with a belief in the fixed order, however stultifying it might have been. Reimann establishes that academics can find interdisciplinarity challenging. Disciplinarity in a university can constitute a fixed order of meaning within the transmission of culture, and can act as a family acts upon its members. Disciplinary silos prevent creative horizontal interaction with other academic families. They are both fortress and prison, alleviating, but, at the same time, creating anxiety and stifling creativity. Phillips quotes Garber:

> If at the beginning of any discipline's self-definition, it undertakes to distinguish itself from another "false" version of itself, that difference is always going to come back and haunt it. Differentiation is one strategy that disciplines employ to protect themselves against incursion and self-doubt (Garber, 2001, in Phillips, 2006, p. 149).

In "On teaching psychoanalysis" (Ogden, 2009) Thomas Ogden outlines his WTP of psychoanalytic teaching. He sounds like Parker Palmer when he begins "Psychoanalytic teaching at its best opens up a space for thinking and dreaming in situations where the understandable impulse [because of anxiety] is to close that space" (Ogden, 2009, p. 50). He continues, "To fill that space *as a teacher* is to preach, to proselytise, to perpetuate dogma; not to fill it, is to create conditions in which one may become open to previously inconceivable possibilities" (Ogden, 2009, p. 50, my emphasis). Ogden goes on to describe his experience of teaching and learning psychoanalysis within long-running open groups where it is the practice to read papers aloud, listening to the writer's use of language, and thus absorbing their thinking, through consideration of the group's countertransference. This creates a community for thinking and collective dreaming. The seminar is described by Ogden as a Winnicottian "going concern", and the group unconscious as a form of the analytic third (Ogden, 2009, p. 57).

To illustrate this further, Ogden describes his participation in a Balint group of seven GPs in NHS practice, giving us in an apparently simple anecdote the essence of his WTP. He reports how Dr L described a case in which he had been summoned to the house of a woman patient whose mother has just died. He had immediately called an ambulance to collect the body. Ogden notes that Dr J asked, "Why did you do that?" Dr L, surprised by the question, replied, "Because she was dead." Dr J had then asked, "Why not have a cup of tea with the daughter?" (Ogden, 2009, p. 67). Ogden says that the feeling of being with the daughter, and the frightening presence of her mother's body lying in the next room, became real for the group. "We . . . fell silent and simply lived for a period of time with the imagined felt presence of the mother's body" (Ogden, 2009, p. 67). Ogden elicits from this ordinary question about an ordinary act that "to have a cup of tea with the daughter" is to allow the event to remain timeless for a while, and for the daughter to do some unconscious psychological work in the presence of the doctor. He goes on to say that this experience in the group has continued to affect him deeply:

> I find that the idea of "Why not?" has . . . become central to the way I think and speak with patients. So often, I find myself asking the patient, "Why not feel frightened or sad or jealous? Why not keep to yourself the dream you find so embarrassing?" (Ogden, 2009, p. 69)

Ogden finds that his WTP consists in holding open the space for dreaming and for undreamt of possibilities. Within its boundaries, the space is, in that highly loaded term, "permissive". Ogden's "Why not?" is a simple, yet profound, amplification of the pedagogical question posed by Palmer.

Threshold concepts and troublesome knowledge

The term "threshold concepts", which is discussed by Meyer and Land (2005, pp. 373–375) using the terms "transformative", "irreversible", "integrative", "troublesome", "bounded", "discursive", and "reconstitutive", has become influential in the literature on curriculum development. Examples of threshold concepts might include precedent in Law, opportunity cost in Economics, entropy in Physics, or irony in Literature. A threshold concept for psychotherapists might be the idea of the communicative countertransference. By grasping the threshold concept, the learner passes into a new understanding of the subject. They learn a new language, the discourse of the subject, but also there is an ontological transformation, "a shift in the learner's subjectivity, a repositioning of the self" (Meyer & Land, 2005, p. 374). Meyer and Land report that the recognition for first year students of Cultural Studies of the implications of the concept of hegemony can lead to a sudden (and perhaps difficult) illumination of the ways in which their own personal choices and behaviours might have been culturally constrained (2005 p. 375).

Cousin says that "a focus on threshold concepts enables teachers to make refined decisions about what is fundamental to the subject", as opposed to "stuffing the curriculum with content, transmitting vast amounts of knowledge bulk" (Cousin, 2006, p. 4). Threshold concepts are seen as "jewels in the curriculum": holding something distinctive about the subject and the discipline, and allowing for the development of more complex insights (Land, Cousin, Meyer, & Davies, 2006, p. 198). Meyer and Land argue that learning involves transforming the internal view of the subject matter or of parts of the subject matter (the stuff) of what is being taught. Would these not also be definitions of therapy? Threshold concepts, moreover, require a recursive approach, not a linear model of learning outcomes, but something more like a "working through". They can define critical moments of irreversible conceptual transformation in the educational experience of learners and teachers. Meyer and Land locate this transformation in an area of liminality, and use the metaphor of the portal to illustrate this. They briefly reference Winnicott's *Playing and Reality* (1971), saying that the holding environment might enable the necessary shift in perspective when students encounter "epistemological obstacles". Drawing on the ethnographical studies of rites of passage by van Gennep (1960) and Turner (1969), which draw attention both to their transformational aspects and the ritual humiliation entailed, Meyer and Land (2005) explore what learners might experience as de-skilling. This "troublesome" aspect of learning threshold concepts is analogous to the anxious passage in therapy towards relinquishing old defences and patterns of resistance.

There is a parallel between the threshold concept and the idea of the paradigm shift in science described by Kuhn, who wrote,

> I have in mind statements of an individual's best guesses about the proper way to connect his own research problem with the corpus of accepted scientific knowledge. ... Tests of this sort are a standard component of what I have elsewhere labelled "normal science" ... the scientist must premise current theory as the rules of his game. (Kuhn, 1970, p. 4)

New theory is not forged through straightforward empirical progress. Scientists refer over time to an existing body of theory, what Kuhn describes as "normal science", until such time as it cannot any longer support the theoretical burden and the paradigm must be radically shifted. One might see patients in psychotherapy as enmeshed in the theories of "normal science" within their families and other relationships. Normal science, after all, is no less than everything we have ever known to be true.

Some learners might not be able to withstand this uncertainty. The transformation, as in a rite of passage, could involve "oscillation between states, often with temporary regression to earlier status" (Meyer & Land, 2005, p. 376). The learner might remain stuck with what Meyer and Land describe as "mimicry": a shallow, naïve, and imitative form of the new concept (Meyer & Land, 2005, p. 377). Struggle, however, if it can be tolerated, is beneficial and precedes insight. The realisation that new knowledge and its terminology might be counter-intuitive and not amenable to conformity with "normal science" is a powerful point of learning and growth. As Symington and Symington point out, "It is part of psychoanalytic experience that it only becomes possible to understand an emotional constellation when it begins to cede to a different pattern" (Symington & Symington, 1996, p. 5). Another example is provided by Leader, who remarks,

> Clinicians working with the bereaved . . . have noticed a peculiar phenomenon. A mourning is often accompanied by dreams which, unlike others do not call out for interpretation, they are more like indications of where the mourner is in the process, a kind of mapping of their situation, and among these dreams a special motif frequently emerges: doorways, arches, stages, *and the many other features that serve to frame a space.* (Leader, 2008, p. 100, my emphasis)

Leader points out that the frame draws attention to the space within its boundaries and draws it into another register from the surrounding reality.

Land (2012) quotes the classical writer Quintilian as saying that the role of the teacher is to arrange victories for the student. He firmly opposed, however, the idea that an education should be a passage through a pre-designed series of threshold concepts, a "kind of intellectual golf course" towards a prescribed set of learning outcomes. The threshold concept, if it has meaning and value, must exist in a "troubled" context where uncertainty abounds. Consider the following dream recounted by Freud in "On dreams":

> Thus, I dreamt on one occasion that I was sitting on a bench with one of my former university teachers, and that the bench, which was surrounded by other benches, was moving forward at a rapid pace. This was a combination of a lecture theatre with a *trottoir roulant.* (Freud, 1901a, pp. 650–651)

The *trottoir roulant* was a moving roadway, or travellator, installed at the Paris exhibition of 1900. In his usual witty manner, Freud says, "I will not pursue this train of ideas any further". In education, as in therapy, difficulty, resistance, support, and transformation must go side by side, but not on a fixed path.

Understanding and the knowledge object

Noel Entwistle (1997) and Marton and Säljö (1976) have taken a phenomenographic approach in gathering students' own accounts of their experiences of studying, revising, and reaching understanding. From this, they have developed the idea that there are different approaches and strategies for learning and understanding, for which they have used the terms "deep", "shallow", and "strategic". Säljö (1997) found that students who adopted a "surface" approach to their learning had difficulty reading and explaining the text *in the way in which it was written.* They had difficulty in seeing the intended gestalt, in distinguishing the background from the foreground of the argument, and in perceiving the status of an example. They adopted what Säljö calls an atomistic approach, mining the text for parts that seemed useful to them and associating only to those parts. When asked, "What did the person who wrote it want to say?" a typical response was "Hmm, it's difficult to say, really." For these "surface" learners, knowledge equated with information or facts, they looked for "targets for learning" and their attention was skewed towards these targets and away from the intended message of the writer of the article. This led to a "flatness" of understanding, with little appreciation of background, foreground, salience, or the relation of example to overall argument. The "deep" approach learners, on the other hand, who, in some cases, had tested lower in standard vocabulary and reasoning tests, had no difficulty in appreciating the gestalt and structure of the article as evidence of the author's intentions. They approached the text with the desire to understand, and regarded it as a communication from the author.

We might wonder what has happened to these "surface" learners to bring about what might be seen as a failure of "other mindedness", a turning away from an offered communicative relationship and a, perhaps, narcissistic unwillingness to engage with the terms set down by the other. If, as Säljö suggests, we can view students' approaches and conceptions of knowledge and understanding as social phenomena, evolved in response to exposure to educational and social situations, we might wonder what, in their prior experience, has affected their ability to take in and contain the products of other minds. Connecting once more to Bion, "The statement that something cannot be taken in must not therefore be dismissed as a mere way of speaking" (Bion, 1962, p. 6).

For Säljö (1997), a static and factual conception of knowledge is a part of common sense thinking in modern western culture, and sign-posts the dominance of a factual point of view, the construing of knowledge in absolutist, rather than situational and contextual, terms. He says that, on the other hand, a dynamic conception of knowledge, a commitment to seeing reality from new, previously unfamiliar perspectives is built into the scientific enterprise itself (Säljö, 1997). A similar commitment to the creation of new knowledge is surely also built into the psychotherapeutic way of thinking and practising.

Discussing the "deep" approach to learning, Entwistle and Entwistle (1997) make the point that if its defining feature is the intention to understand, then the intention itself "evokes the processes which allow deep levels of understanding to be reached" (p. 145). They ask a profound question, "What is understanding? In spite of its centrality in descriptions of learning, its meaning has been rather taken for granted" (Entwistle & Entwistle, 1997, p. 145).

Entwistle and Marton (1994) explored understanding by asking students about their learning experiences and, in describing the "understandings that were constituted in the process of intensive study", they began to use the term "knowledge objects" (p. 161). This framing came from interviews with students about their experiences of revision for final examinations, including both their strategies for revision and all the feelings and sensations they experienced in developing understanding (Entwistle & Entwistle, 1997). Revision strategies were diverse, but had in common what might be described as a process of "remembering, repeating and working-through" (Freud, 1914g): distilling and condensing many pages of notes, memorising and checking at each stage. Extracts from the interviews emphasise the importance of linking. For example, understanding "is the interconnection of lots of disparate things . . . you can make sense of it internally" (Entwistle & Entwistle, 1992, p. 9), and irreversibility as in "It's when I could . . . explain it so that I felt satisfied with the explanation" and "when you understand it like that . . . you can't 'de-understand' it" (Entwistle & Entwistle, 1992, pp. 9–10). Entwistle and Marton report that students described understanding as "always involving a feeling of satisfaction . . . this feeling was derived from a recognition of the meaning and significance of the material learned. It also emanated from a perception of coherence and connectedness" (Entwistle & Marton, 1994, 164–165). Students described an awareness of a tightly integrated body of knowledge, which Entwistle and Marton infer is the result of repeated rehearsal, condensation, and reconstruction of the material. They conclude that the students were

> . . . describing a feeling that the material . . . was experienced as an entity with form and structure. Only some aspects of these entities could be visualised but additional associated knowledge was readily "available" when needed. It was this recurring experience which we came to describe as a "knowledge object". (Entwistle & Marton, 1994, p. 166)

Characteristic of the knowledge object is what they call its "quasi-sensory" nature, a three-dimensional shape and structure (Entwistle & Marton, 1994, p. 169), its seeming to have an independent existence *and* the ability to exert a directive associative force. As well as the experience of integration and wholeness, however, it seemed that the visualisation of the knowledge object connected to unfocused, perhaps unconscious, aspects of knowledge, and seemed to be "no more than a trigger to remind students about related information and ideas at the margins of awareness" (Entwistle & Marton, 1994, p. 168). Entwistle and Entwistle quote one student describing their knowledge object as follows:

> it pulls in pictures and facts as it needs them . . . Each time I describe [a particular topic], it's likely to be different. Well, you start with evolution, say, and suddenly you know where you're going next, then you might have a choice to go in this direction or that direction . . . and follow it through the various options it's offering. . . . Then it says, "OK, you can go on to talk about further criticisms in the time you've got left". (Entwistle & Entwistle, 1997 p. 152)

Marton had been previously involved in a study of scientific intuition with Nobel laureates and found that students and scientists seemed to be describing experiences with elements in common (Entwistle & Marton, 1994, p. 165). The scientists' responses indicated that most of them had an experience of a "metaphorical 'seeing' of the phenomenon searched for, an anticipatory perception of its shape or its gross structure, there was an awareness of an entity with a sensory flavour" (Entwistle & Marton, 1994, p. 173). This description illuminates and resonates with psychodynamic thinking about processes of object representation and internalisation and the psychology of memory. Research about the knowledge object gives us a striking description of minds in a creative process, taking in information in order to express it. There is a sense in all of the work on the knowledge object that pressure and form are significant; it might be that the container, so to speak, forms a knowledge object when placed under pressure and within constraints.

The knowledge object as introjected knowledge, condensed and shaped, has acquired alterity, and is perceived as a controlling but benign introject, a kind of genie of the lamp, as it were, in a time of crisis and pressure. We might describe the knowledge object as an object representation, a helpful internal projection. The condensed learning has been internalised as part of the inner world, part of the intellectual furniture, but in the process acquires the significance of an external object. It has something of the quality of what Lacan in various places has called *extimité*, or "extimacy", a term combining exteriority with intimacy, associated with his fascination with the Möbius strip in which the continuity between what appear to be two sides disrupts the possibility of differentiating between an "inside" and an "outside". We may hold the knowledge object inside us, having taken in the thoughts and teachings of others, and, in so doing, we might feel held by another mind. If we express the thoughts held in the knowledge object out into the world, the product continues to hold our internal processes within it. Many writers and artists refer to this process. Entwistle and Marton (1994, p. 174) refer to a letter from Mozart in which he says "The work grows; I keep expanding it in my head . . . it is in its entirety that my imagination *lets me hear it*" (my emphasis). Mozart conceives of his imagination as separate from himself, and in control of the process. The Russian formalists used the word *ostranenie* (estrangement) for this phenomenon. The sculptor, Anish Kapoor, interviewed recently in the *Financial Times*, had this to say: "The psychoanalytic method is somewhat the studio method. The speculative process, the space between analyst and patient where there's a third object, the fantasy object – that's very much like sculpture" (Kapoor & Wullschlager, 2012).

Conclusions

It does not surprise me when Entwistle and Entwistle say,

> The introduction of the term, the "knowledge object" has provoked a variety of reactions; some people accept the concept as describing a recognisable reality but others have challenged the use of the term "object", its generality and its stability. (Entwistle & Entwistle, 1997, p. 153)

Referring to the knowledge object, they continue, "This experience invites further consideration of the role of metaphor and imagery in teaching and learning" (Entwistle & Entwistle, 1997, p. 153). If we isolate the underlying metaphors of these strands of pedagogical research, they resonate close to the pitch of psychodynamic thought.

How can the *temenos*, or sacred space, coexist with the phallic ivory tower, and how may they be brought into creative and generative intercourse? How are ideas digested and processed? How do we sublimate and idealise the product?

Perhaps we should think of the containing function of maternal reverie as ever dilating and thinning over the whole period of human growth and development, until it expands to encompass the analyst or the teacher, or the institution as "alma mater" and the whole of culture functioning as a containing sphere, if we are to have healthy generative cultural institutions and ways of thinking that are, as Bion (1962, 1967) would have it, adequate to the process of containing the anxiety and excitement of thoughts.

Locating cultural experience was a theme taken up by Winnicott (1971), who emphasises its liminality and condenses his theory of cultural experience around the question of play. For Winnicott, the ability to play is dependent on trust, and on not being made to wait too long. Failure of dependability or loss of object means, to the child, a loss of the area for play; the creative area of potential space is intruded upon and "it seems that whatever is in this space is *persecutory material* and the baby has no means of rejecting it" (Winnicott, 1971, p. 102, my emphasis). Here is the psychodynamic confirmation of the importance of keeping open a creative learning space.

Imagination, empathy, and the ability to wait, wonder, and play are at the heart of both education and therapy. Furthermore, when considered broadly in psychoanalytic terms, education, learning itself, and that sense of "making progress" is not just a social good. It is, in Freudian terms, a sublimation, a defence against loss and the awareness of transience and mortality. The university and the shapes of its subjects and disciplines might shift slowly, but they are cultural forms. The disciplinary adherents, like so many medieval knights in their castles, or like the characters in Hermann Hesse's *Glasperlenspiel*, may choose to dwell within the ivory tower, or to escape and engage outside it. They may be resistant to the efforts of academic pedagogy to encourage generic thinking, interdisciplinary co-operation or reflexivity, or they may act, like Parker Palmer (1998), as benevolent protectors of the creative space.

Phillips (2006) tells us that Freud mentions "education" over three hundred times in the *Standard Edition* compared with his one hundred uses of the word medicine. If the ideas presented here confirm that there are others engaged in a cognate endeavour to understand how ideas are internalised, expressed, and transmitted over time, perhaps these resonances will encourage communication across divides. Thomas Kuhn, in his argument with Karl Popper, asks,

> How am I to persuade Sir Karl, who knows everything I know about scientific development, and who has somewhere or another said it . . . How am I to show him what it would be like to wear my spectacles when he has already learned to look at everything I can point to through his own? (Kuhn, 1970, p. 3)

This "showing" is an endeavour to which psychodynamic thought must continue to apply itself. Immordino-Yang and Damasio assert that "We feel, therefore we learn", and they continue, "No matter how complex and esoteric they become, our repertoire of behavioural and cognitive options continues to exist in the service of emotional goals" (Immordino-Yang & Damasio, 2007, p. 7). Aiding and interpreting this recognition is how psychodynamic thinking can help.

References

Bion, W. R. (1962). *Learning From Experience*. London: Heinemann.
Bion, W. R. (1967). *Second Thoughts*. London: Heinemann.

Borges, J. L. (1964). The fearful sphere of Pascal. In: *Labyrinths* (pp. 224–227), D. A. Yates & J. E. Irby (Eds.), A. Kerrigan (Trans.). New York: New Directions.

Britton, R. (1993). The missing link: parental sexuality in the Oedipus complex. In: D. Birksted-Breen (Ed.), *The Gender Conundrum; Contemporary Psychoanalytic Perspectives on Masculinity and Femininity* (pp. 82–94). London: Routledge.

Britton, R. (1998). *Belief and Imagination: Explorations in Psychoanalysis.* London: Routledge.

Brook, P. (1990). *The Empty Space.* London: Penguin.

Cousin, G. (2006). Introduction to threshold concepts. *Planet, 17*: 4–5.

Delafield-Butt, J. (2012). Unpublished presentation given in Counselling and Psychotherapy, School of Health in Social Science, University of Edinburgh.

Dewey, J. (1938). *Experience and Education.* Indianapolis, IN: Kappa Delta Pi.

Dickens, C. (1854). *Hard Times.* London: Penguin, 1994.

Entwistle, A., & Entwistle, N. J. (1992). Experiences of understanding in revising for degree examinations. *Learning and Instruction, 2*: 1–22.

Enwistle, N. J. (1997). Introduction: phenomenography in higher education. *Higher Education Research and Development, 16*: 127–134.

Entwistle N. J., & Entwistle, A. (1997). Revision and the experience of understanding. In: F. Marton, D. J. Hounsell, & N. J. Entwistle (Eds.), *The Experience of Learning* (pp. 145–158). Edinburgh: Scottish Academic Press.

Entwistle, N. J., & Marton, F. (1994). Knowledge objects: understandings constituted through intensive academic study. *British Journal of Educational Psychology, 64*: 161–178.

Freud, S. (1901a). On dreams. *S.E.*, 5: 629–686. London: Hogarth.

Freud, S. (1914g). Remembering, repeating, and working-through. *S.E., 12*: 145–156. London: Hogarth.

Garber, M. (2001). *Academic Instincts.* Princeton, NJ: Princeton University Press.

Holmes, J. (1996). *Attachment, Intimacy, Autonomy: Using Attachment Theory in Adult Psychotherapy.* Northvale, NJ: Jason Aronson.

Immordino-Yang, M., & Damasio, A. (2007). We feel therefore we learn: the relevance of affective and social neuroscience to education. *Mind, Brain and Education, 1*(1): 3–10.

Kapoor, A., & Wullschlager, J. (2012). Lunch with Anish Kapoor. *Financial Times Life and Arts,* 5th May 2012.

Kuhn, T. S. (1970). Logic of discovery or psychology of research? In: I. Lakatos & A. Musgrave (Eds.), *Criticism and the Growth of Knowledge* (pp. 1–23). Cambridge: Cambridge University Press.

Land, R. (2012). Unpublished presentation to Institute of Academic Development seminar, University of Edinburgh, April.

Land, R., Cousin, G., Meyer, J. H. F., & Davies, P. (2006). Conclusion. Implications of threshold concepts for course design and evaluation. In: J. H. F. Meyer & R. Land (Eds.), *Overcoming Barriers to Student Understanding. Threshold Concepts and Troublesome Knowledge* (pp. 195–206). Abingdon: Routledge.

Leader, D. (2008). *The New Black*. London: Penguin.

Lehrer, J. (2012). *Imagine: How Creativity Works*. Edinburgh: Canongate.

Marton, F., & Säljö, R. (1976). On qualitative differences in learning. I. Outcome and process. *British Journal of Educational Psychology*, *46*: 4–11.

McCune, V., & Hounsell, D. (2005). The development of students' ways of thinking and practising in three final-year biology courses. *Higher Education*, *49*: 255–289.

Meyer, J. H. F., & Land, R. (2005). Threshold concepts and troublesome knowledge (2): epistemological considerations and a conceptual framework for teaching and learning. *Higher Education*, *49*: 373–388.

Ogden, T. (2009). *Rediscovering Psychoanalysis: Thinking and Dreaming, Learning and Forgetting*. Hove: Routledge.

Palmer, P. J. (1998). *The Courage to Teach: Exploring the Inner Landscape of a Teacher's Life*. San Francisco, CA: Jossey Bass.

Phillips, A. (2006). *Side Effects*. London: Penguin.

Reimann, N. (2009). Exploring disciplinarity in academic development. Do "ways of thinking and practicing" help faculty to think about learning and teaching? In: C. Kreber (Ed.), *The University and its Disciplines. Teaching and Learning beyond Disciplinary Boundaries* (pp. 84–95). New York: Routledge.

Scharff, J. S. (Ed.) (1994). *The Autonomous Self: The Work of John D. Sutherland*. Northvale, NJ: Jason Aronson.

Säljö, R. (1997). Reading and everyday conceptions of knowledge. In: F. Marton, D. Hounsell, & N. Entwistle (Eds.), *The Experience of Learning* (2nd edn) (pp. 89–105). Edinburgh: Scottish Academic Press.

Sutherland, J. (1971). *Towards Community Mental Health*. London: Tavistock.

Symington, J., & Symington, N. (1996). *The Clinical thinking of Wilfred Bion*. London: Routledge.

Turner, V. (1969). *Ritual Process: Structure and Anti-Structure*. London: Routledge and Kegan Paul.

Van Gennep, A. (1960). *Rites of Passage*. London: Routledge and Kegan Paul.

Winnicott, D. W. (1965). *The Maturational Processes and the Facilitating Environment: Studies in the Theory of Emotional Development*. London: Hogarth Press.

Winnicott, D. W. (1971). *Playing and Reality*. London: Routledge.

CHAPTER NINE

Precious gift or poisoned chalice: what does psychoanalysis offer to social research?

Sue Jervis

Introduction

At the turn of the twenty-first century a new academic discipline known as "psycho-social studies" emerged. This evolving approach explores how people's feelings influence the society in which they live and *vice versa*. Psychoanalysis is especially helpful to psycho-social studies because it uses data-generating free association and addresses the role played by the unconscious. In particular, psychoanalytic theories shed important light on the interpersonal psychodynamics that inevitably underlie research relationships (Clarke, 2008; Clarke & Hoggett, 2009; Hollway, 2008a). Since these unconscious dynamics are potentially very informative, attending to them closely can facilitate deep understandings of research participants' experiences. Hence, what psychoanalysis offers to social research is extremely valuable.

However, as the title of this chapter suggests, researchers could regard psychoanalysis as a mixed blessing. The use of the phrase "poisoned chalice" is not intended to imply that psychoanalysis might be injurious to social research; rather, that while it appears to offer something wholly beneficial, its contribution is also proving to be problematic. A number of ethical issues and interpretative difficulties arise when psychoanalytic theories and techniques are used in research. Many of these problems were highlighted at the inception of psycho-social studies (Clarke, 2000, 2002; Hollway & Jefferson, 2000; Wengraf, 2000, 2001). Among the various dilemmas discussed then were: the risk of evoking distress in research participants, the possibility of arousing anxiety by introducing participants *and* researchers to unconscious thoughts and feelings that they would really rather not explore, the difficulty of determining which psychic products belong to whom, and the ever-present danger of "wild analysis" (i.e., making erroneous interpretations, either through simple ignorance or by mistakenly relying on presumed expertise). To illustrate some of these problems, this chapter focuses primarily on a single research relationship. Before discussing that relationship, however, I want to outline why the ethical issues that psycho-social researchers must consider are so challenging.

As Clarke and Hoggett (2009) argue, since the unconscious influences every aspect of social research: what researchers choose to study, the methods that they use, how they perceive and relate to research participants, and so on, researchers must pay careful attention to ethics at all stages of a research project. In particular, they need to recognise that both researcher and participant cannot help but bring unconscious aspects of themselves into their encounter. These elements are unwittingly communicated through similar processes to those known in psychoanalysis as "transference" and "countertransference". If researchers are to attempt to address and to learn from the analogous communications underlying their research relationships, they must constantly employ a critical reflexivity. This means not only remaining aware of, and being honest about, all that they themselves bring into a research project (e.g., gender, ethnicity, social position, beliefs, prejudices, personal agenda), but also carefully scrutinising each element of that project. It is demanding for researchers to maintain such a suspicious self-consciousness, continually checking on how they might be influencing the research and perpetually questioning their own assumptions, especially assumptions about what they think they are discovering.

In addition, psycho-social researchers need to develop a mental capacity that enables them to maintain their emotional engagement with research participants while simultaneously noticing and reflecting on the experience in a manner akin to that exemplified by effective psychoanalytic therapists. Researchers, however, are not usually trained in psychoanalysis, so their adoption of its theories and techniques carries the danger that psychoanalytic thinking might be used indiscriminately, or even distorted to fit research needs. For example, Frosh and Baraitser (2008) argue that, by equating reflexivity as it is used in research settings with the way that countertransference is employed in clinical situations, there is a risk of researchers privileging their feelings unquestioningly and regarding them as providing definite information about the unconscious content of research participants' minds. Meanwhile, those researchers who *are* trained counsellors or psychotherapists, already familiar with using countertransference responses as a source of information, face a different problem. The danger, for them, is of unwittingly responding to research participants' (unconscious) requests for attention, or for help with unmet needs. As I have discussed previously (Jervis, 2012), in highlighting my own experience of feeling guilty about not providing support for a troubled interviewee, this potential problem can lead to role confusion or role conflict.

It is precisely because such difficulties can arise that psycho-social researchers must maintain clear boundaries and high ethical standards throughout their research. Since these standards have been described in detail in other publications (Clarke, 2002; Hollway & Jefferson, 2000; Jervis, 2011), I do not revisit them here. What I want to stress, however, is that they amount to a taxing "duty of care" (Clarke, 2008, p. 123). Moreover, as Beedell (2009) argues, the sort of emotional work that researchers need to undertake, indeed cannot avoid if they are to achieve an in-depth understanding of research participants' experiences, is in itself extremely demanding. It requires researchers not only to feel, tolerate, and examine sometimes uncomfortable, even painful, emotions, but also to subject the whole process to rigorous, time-consuming intellectual enquiry (Beedell, 2009; Clarke & Hoggett, 2009). Given all of the challenges involved, it is perhaps not surprising that the very idea of taking psychoanalysis outside the consulting room and into social research remains controversial.

However, it must be remembered that the objectives of psychoanalysis and psycho-social research are quite different. Researchers are not concerned with interpreting events and unconscious ideas from the past as a means of analysing entire personalities. Rather, they use psychoanalytically informed reflexivity for more limited aims: to glean some hint of research participants' present-day psyches and to discover what, if anything, might be learnt from their research relationships by closely observing how each member relates to, or becomes positioned by, the other (Brown, 2006; Clarke & Hoggett, 2009; Hollway, 2008b). Just as psychoanalysts scrutinise their countertransference to discover how analysands unconsciously "use" them, thereby potentially learning about their analysands' early lives, so reflexive psycho-social researchers might learn about research participants' experiences by considering how their own feelings, thoughts, and behaviour are influenced, or pressured, by their research relationships (Jervis, 2009). To discuss how this can work in practice, I describe various aspects of my relationship with a research participant who has kindly given permission for information relating to her experiences to enter the public domain, but whom I refer to by the pseudonym "Fiona" in order to protect her anonymity.

Fiona

I met Fiona when I was researching the emotional experiences of relocated "military wives", a group to which I, too, belonged. A full account of that study is described in *Relocation, Gender and Emotion: A Psycho-Social Perspective on the Experiences of Military Wives* (Jervis, 2011). Throughout my research, I endeavoured to empower participants in a variety of ways, including giving them a choice as to the timing and location of their interviews. Fiona chose her current workplace as the venue for our meetings and I wondered what that might mean. Had she told me that she shared adjoining offices with a colleague, which meant that privacy was not assured, I would have considered Fiona's choice even more striking, and discussed with her the possibility of using an alternative venue. Not knowing this, however, I found myself thinking instead about an inference that Fiona had made: that, having previously worked for organisations providing support to military families, she held specialist knowledge that would be particularly useful to me, which left me wondering whether her choice of meeting place was intended to emphasise her professional expertise.

Since I was more interested in Fiona's *own* experience of military relocation than in what she knew professionally, it felt important that I should be very careful to follow my normal practice of explaining the aims of my research at the outset, clarifying the sort of personal information that I was seeking. After hearing my explanation, Fiona remained willing to be interviewed. Nevertheless, she was surprised, during our first interview, to find herself disclosing some very private material and said, "I can't believe that this is all coming out of my mouth." Earlier, Fiona had been shocked when she began to cry as she told me that military relocation had meant sending her children away to boarding school. Unfortunately, just as Fiona started weeping, her colleague briefly entered the office adjoining the room where we were talking. Shortly afterwards, I was concerned when Fiona's colleague re-entered the adjoining office, especially given Fiona's tearfulness and the deeply personal nature of what she had been saying. So I asked Fiona, who seemed oblivious to her colleague's presence, how she felt about continuing and she replied, "Fine, fine." Still concerned, I said, "I'm aware that there's somebody else here", to which Fiona responded, "Yes, yeah, yeah, that's fine," before apparently changing her mind and asking her colleague to leave.

Later, Fiona and I heard voices immediately outside her open office window. I was very conscious that anyone standing there might hear what Fiona was saying, but she seemed untroubled. It occurred to me that perhaps I was more worried about safeguarding Fiona's confidentiality than she was, so I said nothing. After several minutes, Fiona asked what was going on outside, but made no move to investigate or to shut out the intrusion. Closing the window myself, I found it striking that Fiona, a capable woman who had taken on a variety of caring roles throughout her life, seemed unable to protect herself, in her own workplace, from other peoples' intrusions into her privacy.

After the interview, however, I began to wonder whether *I* had been too intrusive. As Brown (2006) argues, important ethical considerations in psychoanalytically informed research include the risk of intruding into, or misusing, research participants. Both of these concerns applied to my interview with Fiona. In addition to my worries about intruding, I now felt slightly uneasy that I had interviewed Fiona about her personal experiences when, originally, she had intimated that she wanted to tell me about her professional knowledge. Although I had explained my research interests carefully, and Fiona had seemed content to talk about her private life in some detail, I became concerned, nevertheless, that I might have been somehow "dishonest" with her. This vague unease increased when I realised that one of Fiona's themes during that first interview was about a lack of honesty, or openness, between military families regarding their difficulties.

Eventually, of course, I was to discover that there were unconscious elements underlying both my behaviour and my disquiet. My concern to ensure that what Fiona said was not overheard by her colleague or by other people meant something else, too, as did Fiona's amazement about her somewhat dramatic outpouring. Moreover, these unconscious meanings proved to be significant, not only for us but for other research participants as well, and also for my research as a whole. I will say more about uncovering those dynamics later. For now, I want to highlight how my ethical responsibilities to Fiona were apparently compromised from the start. Her surprise that she had disclosed so much suggested that, while I had obtained Fiona's consent to participate in my research, perhaps that consent was insufficiently informed. Moreover, my research had evoked distress and risked embarrassing Fiona, particularly in front of her colleague. However, Fiona's willingness to continue speaking through her tears and after her subsequent recovery, and then to participate in a second interview, suggests that she did not feel harmed by the experience. Indeed, since both of Fiona's interviews lasted for longer than any of my other research interviews, I think it is reasonable to conclude that she was content with the direction that they took.

When Fiona and I met for a pre-arranged second, and final, interview, she began to talk immediately, apparently spilling out everything that was in her mind. She spoke in such a way that I felt it would have been rude, cruel even, to interrupt her to ask for permission to turn on the tape recorder. So, I just sat and listened. Some time into the interview, Fiona's phone rang, allowing me an opportunity to remark that I wished I had been recording what she was saying, whereupon she readily agreed that I could turn on the recorder. Among other things, Fiona talked about suffering from panic attacks, describing a recent one when something was placed in her mouth at the dentist's. Fiona had been distressed about being controlled in this way, but now felt rather silly about becoming so upset. She made a connection between her feelings about that experience and her surprise that she became distressed during our previous interview:

> Fiona: It was the same with the dentist's chair, I just burst into tears . . . and you think, "Why?" I just felt so foolish, Sue. I couldn't believe it . . . all of a sudden, everything feels out of your control, you know? When I have these panic attacks it's, "I'm not in control" and that is what is so fearful. . . . I found myself in, in floods of tears and I thought, "What on earth happened there?" And that is what I don't like.
>
> Sue: The being out-of-control?
>
> Fiona: Yeah, because that is not me. . . . [but] I'm not a control freak . . . Well, I don't think I am.

Fiona then described how her religious beliefs enable her to hand over control of her life to God. She continued talking about the importance of her faith for a long time, explaining how much she relies upon it for support. Fiona said that it was "nice to have the freedom to talk to somebody who . . . understands how I feel and is open to listening to me". Although I did indeed empathise with Fiona's feelings about her faith, I felt mildly discomfited by her remark because, for several minutes, I had been wondering why she was telling me about her relationship with God at such length.

Thereafter, Fiona raised various other themes, including how military families do not want to be seen as "weak", or not coping, and the stigma associated with them seeking support. She remarked that people who visited military welfare services often engaged in seemingly trivial "chat", but "all of a sudden everything has spilled out". Eventually, Fiona indicated that she had said everything that she wanted to say. As I thanked her, Fiona surprised me by asking whether we would be having another interview in a few months' time. Then, after I had turned off the tape recorder, she went on to talk for several minutes more, returning to a theme that she had raised earlier about the harsh way in which her husband would be "cut off" by the Armed Services when he retired. Even though Fiona herself had brought the interview to a close, and knew in advance that it would be the last time we met, I was left wondering whether she felt cut off by me.

When I reflected on this interview, several aspects of it caught my attention. First, the way that Fiona had spilled everything out, like the welfare clients that she had mentioned; secondly, how Fiona linked her feelings during her dental treatment with her distress in our previous interview; thirdly, various issues relating to control. Conversely, I was much less interested in Fiona's personal relationship with God, even though it clearly meant a great deal to her as she had talked about it for so long. Before I add some of my thoughts about these aspects, I must emphasise that they did not all occur to me right away; they evolved over a period of some months. It is important for me to stress this point because, as Frosh (2010) argues, retrospective accounts produced by researchers run the risk of making neat, normative sense of messy, irrational experiences. While Fiona had presented her experiences in a lucid, rational way, leaving me feeling that I was in possession of a considerable amount of rich and potentially useful data, the subsequent process of trying to understand what those experiences might mean, in the context of my research, was by no means neat. Rather, I found it bewilderingly difficult to use Fiona's abundant material, a problem that I discuss later in this chapter.

My thoughts turned, first, to how Fiona began with a flood of material, continued talking beyond the (apparent) end of our interview, and asked whether there would be another interview, all of which evoked in me the idea that she was "full to overflowing", and yet she wanted more. Secondly, I wondered about the meaning of the issue of control that appeared to link Fiona's two experiences of being distressed and then feeling foolish about becoming so emotional. Thirdly, what Fiona said about control seemed contradictory; for example, she did not like feeling out of control, or being controlled, as she had been at the dentist's, but she was happy to hand over control to God. I thought, too, about the way in which Fiona and I had each, to some extent, unwittingly controlled the other. In Fiona's workplace, where she is normally in charge, I had taken control over who might hear her. Meanwhile, Fiona had effectively controlled what I could take (or use?) from our second interview with a flow of words that initially prevented me from switching on the tape recorder and then extended beyond my turning it off. Before discussing the relevance of these ideas to my research, I want to try to unravel some of what I believe happened between Fiona and me.

The problem of untangling the intersubjective

As already mentioned, an important premise of psycho-social studies is that research relationships inevitably involve potentially informative "projective communications" (Clarke, 2002, p. 182), which researchers attempt to decipher by reflexively addressing their own emotions. The aim is for researchers to identify empathically with research participants, internalising their experiences in order to learn from them, but without becoming so merged that all objectivity is lost (Clarke, 2008; Hollway, 2008b). In psychoanalytic terms, this process involves exploring the transference–countertransference relationship and any identifications therein. In the research context, meanwhile, the direction in which any transference–countertransference dynamics might operate has been called into question. Frosh and Baraitser (2008) argue that whereas, in psychoanalysis, the patient seeks the analyst's help, in psycho-social research the situation is reversed; it is the researcher who seeks out the research participant, the researcher who has an agenda. Consequently, it is the researcher's emotions and responses that should be regarded as transference, and the research participant's state of mind that should be regarded as countertransference.

While this is an interesting point, I find two other arguments persuasive when considering the potential complexity of the unconscious dynamics underlying research relationships: first, a tenet of relational psychoanalysis, that emotional communications operate not just in one direction, but in the opposite direction, too (Hoggett, 2008), and second, Ogden's view of transference and countertransference, not "as separable entities that arise in response to one another", but as "a single intersubjective totality" (Ogden, 1995, p. 25). Applying these ideas to social research suggests to me that *either* member of a research relationship could unwittingly influence the feelings of the other. Furthermore, it is what they create *together* that is potentially informative.

The difficulty comes in making sense of these intersubjective psychic creations. My experience of interviewing Fiona was that I felt flooded with a vast amount of material, lots of potentially useful data, and yet, when I tried to describe it, there did not seem to be anything solid there. Something essential appeared to be missing. That is, having imagined Fiona as "full to overflowing" but wanting something more, that description now fitted how I felt in relation to what she had told me. I subsequently listened to the recording of our first interview with my academic supervisor and, between us, we listed numerous different themes that had emerged, including issues around what could or could not be said in military communities, the difficulty for service families in being honest about their feelings, and the lack of control that they have over their lives. While I have no doubt that those themes accurately represented aspects of Fiona's experience, I was still struggling to utilise them in a meaningful way in my research.

What finally enabled me to use Fiona's material was an event which happened several months after our interviews, and that, as I have discussed elsewhere (Jervis, 2011, pp. 165–167), involved me becoming distressed while talking about Fiona during a researchers' consultation group. The task of the group, which I shared with three other psycho-social researchers and with the help of a consultant, was to explore whatever problems had arisen in our research. I had not expected to discuss Fiona. Initially, I set out to talk about my concern that, being a much relocated "military wife" myself, there was a significant risk that I might unconsciously misrepresent the experiences of the women I interviewed by projecting my personal feelings about service life into them. Although I had anticipated that some blurring of the psychological boundary between us might occur, I was worried that my position as an "insider researcher" might make it particularly difficult for me to work out later which material belonged (just) to me and which belonged to research participants. I had become especially preoccupied with the problem of how to represent participants' experiences accurately after hearing another researcher highlight the complexity of this issue, and comment on the danger of describing research participants only as they appear to be, as if the way that they present themselves is all that they are.

Having embarked on a discussion of those concerns, I found myself thinking about Fiona and the bewildering difficulty that I was experiencing in using the abundance of research material that she had provided. I could feel tears bubbling up inside me as I recalled Fiona, and when I started to talk about her, I began to cry. The level of distress that followed came as a complete surprise to me and I was embarrassed about my emotional outburst. It felt messily out of control, as if I had vomited on the carpet, and I was aware that my fellow researchers were shocked to see me so extraordinarily upset.

Before exploring the meaning of this incident, I must briefly recapitulate. I have mentioned Fiona's shock about becoming upset during our first interview when she spoke of her regret about sending her children to boarding school. After she recovered, Fiona told me how surprised she was to have become so distressed, especially about something that had happened long ago. Other data that Fiona provided indicated that she perceived herself, and was perceived, as someone who coped well with any difficulties that she encountered, someone who remained in control. So, Fiona's expression of distress was unusual and, together with what she had said about the difficulties that she faced as a mobile military wife, it had taken her by surprise. Similarly, when I discussed my problem of how to represent research participants' experiences accurately, without either projecting into them something that did not belong, or producing only a superficial account, I, too, was surprised, both by unexpectedly talking about Fiona so long after our interviews and by how distressed I became in the consultation group.

Reflecting on that distress some time later, I became aware of two contradictory feelings: a concern that there might have been something contrived about the way that I had begun to cry, and that, nevertheless, my subsequent tearfulness felt completely honest. I did not realise it immediately, but this oppositional quality to the experience, as seemingly pretentious and yet feeling deeply authentic, was similar to what I felt after I presented a paper about my research in which I had quoted participants in an unusually dramatic way. My intention during the presentation had been to convey the feelings that I sensed were behind the women's stories, but afterwards I wondered whether, instead, I had put on some sort of "act" (Jervis, 2011, pp. 130–131). With the help of other researchers, I thought about this anxiety, that I might have unwittingly over-dramatised participants' experiences, and I began to recognise how frequently research participants, including Fiona, had "played down" or *under*-stated their feelings, especially anything that was painful.

To explain: all of the research participants belonged to a military community, as did I, which expected its members to "get on with it" stoically and not to complain. Servicemen's wives commonly collude with such expectations, often discouraging, even privately among themselves, anything that might be construed as "moaning". Typical of the women who participated in my research, Fiona told me, "I've never been a person that has ever felt sorry for myself. I've never been one . . . that complains." Since complaining is not countenanced, and the problems associated with military life are habitually denied, whatever pain those problems evoke tends to remain unexpressed and unheard. This taboo means that any distress felt by servicemen's wives, including, I suggest, that experienced by Fiona when she was obliged to send her children away to boarding school, is treated as though it does not actually exist, as if it is "unreal". No wonder, then, that Fiona was amazed about the dramatic outpouring of her distress when she burst into tears during our first interview.

No wonder, too, that my anxiety about how to describe faithfully research participants' experiences increased after I heard another researcher discuss a participant who was not (only) what he seemed, at face value, to be. Having unconsciously identified, *myself*, with the stoicism demanded of military families, I was unaware, at that time, of how difficult it was for me to accept fully the reality of, much less publically reveal, the depth of distress that my research had uncovered beneath the mask of control ordinarily worn by servicemen's wives, including Fiona and me. My membership of the military community meant that, without realising it, I shared with most of the women whom I interviewed a reluctance to break ranks and speak up about the painful losses associated with repeated relocation. As Sullivan (2002) argues, "an individual's thoughts, feelings and actions reflect not only intrapsychic processes but also the conditions of the groups of which the individual is a member and the relations between those groups" (p. 381). It was not until I unwittingly replicated Fiona's distress and, in a separate incident, dramatically quoted from the narratives of other research participants, really taking in their experiences and then noticing the anxiety that they evoked in me, that I began to understand better participants' underlying feelings and also the institutional dynamics that had contributed to those feelings being silenced. Following the two incidents, it occurred to me that perhaps servicemen's wives' distress could be heard *only* if it was (re)presented dramatically.

Later reflections

My unconscious enactments of aspects of research participants' experiences confirm that a researcher's psychic material can become confusingly intertwined with that belonging to participants, raising the danger of wild research analysis. However, without such intertwining, I do not think that it would have been possible for me to understand how the women who participated in my research *really* felt. I believe that a deep understanding of participants' experiences requires the researcher to first *feel* those experiences, which means losing themselves, to some degree, in the transference–countertransference. It was only through experiencing distress myself that I got in touch with what I now think of as the "hidden honesty" of Fiona's feelings of loss. Reflecting on our interviews later, I found myself wondering whether my sense that Fiona "wanted more", and also my anxiety that I might have "cut her off", was evoked by one, or both, of us unconsciously realising that something deeply felt and real existed beneath the surface of the interview that was not being allowed full expression, or full recognition, because neither of us regarded it as entirely trustworthy.

If this is so, my concern after interviewing Fiona that I might have been somehow dishonest makes more sense. Consciously, I wanted to hear all about her experiences, intending to represent those experiences and Fiona's underlying feelings as fully and as faithfully as possible. At first, however, all that I could do was regurgitate superficial bits of her narrative. My understanding now is that, because I was not just a researcher, but also part of the same military community that perceives wives' distress as "mere stories" (Jervis, 2011, p. 167), I had not digested Fiona's material properly. I felt stuffed with pieces of data that I could not use. The material seemed to be rich, but it *felt* insubstantial because I had not yet reached the depth of feeling behind it. Having argued elsewhere (Jervis, 2009, p. 149) that researchers can identify with research participants both emotionally and somatically, I think that it is probably no coincidence that when I started to write this chapter and revisited my interviews with Fiona and their aftermath, I suffered from a painful bout of indigestion. Instantaneous relief came when it occurred to me that there had, indeed, been something indigestible for me in our encounters.

There is some evidence that Fiona herself had been unable to digest completely her distressing experiences. The way that she flooded me with words and tears (unprocessed emotions?) suggests as much. So, too, does Fiona's shock about having become so upset while talking about sending her children to boarding school many years earlier; she said, "I'm so surprised that it . . . set me off. I can't believe that it did actually." Perhaps, then, one link between that distress and what Fiona experienced at the dentist's was that, on both occasions, she found something unwanted in her mouth; in the dental surgery, a solid instrument that controlled and silenced her, and in our interview, words that ordinarily remained unspoken, which aroused emotions that left Fiona feeling out of control. Her description of experiencing feelings of "emptiness" after sending her children away, and how she subsequently filled the "void" in her life with her faith (Jervis, 2011, p. 183), certainly implies that Fiona's loss aroused such pain at the time that its open expression within the military community was unlikely to have been well tolerated. Hence, Fiona might have had no alternative but to repress that pain. While she later found support in her beliefs, Fiona speculated during our interviews that her reliance on God may have amounted to "opting out". Apparently questioning whether her faith had allowed her to avoid thinking about the difficulties in her life, Fiona remarked, "You can say . . . everything's not rooty-toot, but then, God's in control and He'll make it right, you know, so I can just opt out by handing it to Him all the time."

It is hardly surprising that Fiona's personal relationship with God remained so important to her. Fiona saw God as unchanging, ever-present, always listening, and entirely accepting of both her strength and her weakness. She felt that God even accepted her dissent against what she regarded as His plans for her. In contrast, Fiona's life as a military wife involved constant change, a frequently absent husband, and a social context that demanded both stoicism and unquestioning compliance. Moreover, Fiona felt that the military controlled significant aspects of her life. For example, she was told when to move house and when her husband would be required to work away from home. However, she said that there were times when it did not "suit" the military to be in control of wives and "then they don't want to know".

Other research participants shared Fiona's feeling that while the military intruded markedly into their private lives, it remained largely uninterested in their personal concerns and needs. Given both my anxiety about being intrusive and my indifference to hearing about Fiona's relationship with God, perhaps I unwittingly replicated that dynamic within our research relationship. It is possible, too, that Fiona unconsciously chose a venue for our interviews wherein intrusions might be enacted that would reproduce, and thus demonstrate, the intrusiveness of the military and its disregard for personal feelings, a dynamic with which she was already familiar and, to a degree, had compliantly accepted. Of course, some of my ideas about Fiona's states of mind might amount to mere conjecture. Moreover, alternative interpretations could be made. It has been suggested to me, for instance, that perhaps Fiona tolerated the intrusions into her privacy that occurred during our first interview because, unconsciously, she *wanted* to reveal what she was ordinarily required to conceal. I find this suggestion persuasive. Furthermore, it serves to underline that Fiona's experiences might be understood in various different ways or have several meanings. As Frosh (2010) argues, there are always limits to how much anyone can understand about another person because "all subjects – analysts as well as analysands, clever and reflective researchers as well as recalcitrant participants – relate *partially*" (p. 216).

As discussed earlier, however, the aim of psycho-social research is not to attempt to decipher entire personalities, but, rather, to learn something about the social context under investigation, in part through exploring what happens within research relationships. Interviewing Fiona and other research participants who provided similar material helped me to discover that relocated servicemen's wives frequently sustain multiple personal losses, the distressing impact of which usually passes unnoticed within their communities. I also learnt that servicemen's wives become incorporated into the military institution, unwittingly identifying with their husbands' stoicism about the hardships of military life. While this stoicism can be understood as a collusive defence against the anxieties aroused by the dangerous, sometimes life-threatening, situations that service personnel face (Jervis, 2011, p. 95), one consequence of its replication among servicemen's wives is that they seldom express, and might not even recognise themselves (the depth of), their own distress. In such an environment, painful emotions remain concealed, making it more difficult for them to be worked through.

Since completing this research, my findings have been corroborated by a number of informal discussions, both with other servicemen's wives and with representatives of several charities that support military families. Additional supporting evidence came from the unlikely source of a reality television programme. *The Choir*, screened in 2011 by BBC2, followed a group of servicemen's wives as they learnt to sing together, highlighting how the women coped with the demands of the military lifestyle by hiding their often very painful feelings, even from each other. So, quite literally, their real voices were hardly ever heard. The group's transformation, amid considerable anxiety and tears, into a "Military Wives Choir" was inspirational. However, the means by which those servicemen's wives finally achieved emotional expression, through several televised and extremely moving public performances culminating in extraordinary chart-topping success, could hardly have been more dramatic.

Conclusion

This chapter has argued that psychoanalytic thinking offers valuable insights to researchers who seek to explore beneath the surface of human experience. Among other contributions that it makes to social research, psychoanalysis illustrates that, by paying close attention to, and carefully reflecting on, the feelings and ideas evoked in them, researchers might learn from the unconscious communications that inevitably underlie their research relationships, thereby enhancing their understanding of participants' experiences. This sort of understanding can inform the entire research project, as I found when I reflected on my interviews with Fiona. For example, thinking about our (unconscious) attempts to control each other helped me to recognise various ways in which control functions within military communities. These include the expectation that servicemen's wives will remain stoically "in control", repressing any disturbing emotions, the control that wives exercise among themselves to prevent moaning, and the military's patriarchal control over wives' lives (Jervis, 2011).

However, a necessary concomitant to using psychoanalytic ideas to inform social research is that researchers must consistently meet taxing ethical responsibilities. In addition, the requirement to explore unconscious communications is challenging and can involve unravelling complex problems. One such dilemma, which I encountered in my research relationship with Fiona, is that psychic material belonging to the researcher can become transiently entangled with that belonging to research participants in a complicated transference–countertransference. Psychological boundaries are especially likely to become blurred, increasing the risk of wild research analysis, if the researcher concerned is an "insider", as I was. My aim in describing my personal struggle to make sense of these processes has been to demonstrate that this task is both emotionally and intellectually demanding. Given the demands associated with its use, it would be understandable if some social researchers regard psychoanalysis as offering them more of a burden than a gift.

For me, however, meeting these challenges is an effort worth making, because utilising psychoanalytic thinking, especially to address the underlying complexities of their research relationships, enables researchers to explore factors that would otherwise be missed. It was only through noticing similarities between my unwitting reproduction of Fiona's distress and my somewhat theatrical delivery when quoting from other research participants' interviews that I began to recognise the collusion that exists within military communities. Being a mobile serviceman's wife myself, hence subject to similar social and institutional pressures to those that influenced the women who participated in my research, I was initially blind to the risk that I, too, might collude to deny the depth of distress that several of them had experienced. Using psychoanalytically informed reflexivity enabled me to consider whether my unusual behaviour was saying something about my research relationships or about participants' experiences. That reflection helped me to recognise how research participants had minimised or denied their distress, leading me to explore the ways in which servicemen's wives' voices become so silenced that something quite dramatic must happen before they can be heard.

References

Beedell, P. (2009). Charting the clear waters and the murky depths. In: S. Clarke & P. Hoggett (Eds.), *Researching Beneath the Surface: Psycho-Social Research Methods in Practice* (pp. 101–119). London: Karnac.

Brown, J. (2006). Reflexivity in the research process: psychoanalytic observations. *International Journal Social Research Methodology, 9*(3): 181–197.

Clarke, S. (2000). On white researchers and black respondents. *Journal for the Psychoanalysis of Culture and Society, 5*(1): 145–150.

Clarke, S. (2002). Learning from experience: psycho-social research methods in the social sciences. *Qualitative Research, 2*(2): 173–194

Clarke, S. (2008). Psycho-social research: relating self, identity and otherness. In: S. Clarke, H. Hahn, & P. Hoggett (Eds.), *Object Relations and Social Relations* (pp. 113–135). London: Karnac.

Clarke, S., & Hoggett, P. (2009). Researching beneath the surface: a psycho-social approach to research practice and method. In: S. Clarke & P. Hoggett (Eds.), *Researching Beneath the Surface: Psycho-Social Research Methods in Practice* (pp. 1–26). London: Karnac.

Frosh, S. (2010). *Psychoanalysis Outside the Clinic: Interventions in Psycho-social Studies*. Basingstoke: Palgrave Macmillan.

Frosh, S., & Baraitser, L. (2008). Psychoanalysis and psychosocial studies. *Psychoanalysis, Culture and Society, 13*(4): 345–365.

Hoggett, P. (2008). What's in a hyphen: reconstructing psychosocial studies. *Psychoanalysis, Culture and Society, 1* (4): 379–384.

Hollway, W. (2008a). Doing intellectual disagreement differently? *Psychoanalysis, Culture and Society, 13*(4): 385–396.

Hollway, W. (2008b). The importance of relational thinking in psycho-social research. In: S. Clarke, H. Hahn, & P. Hoggett (Eds.), *Object Relations and Social Relations* (pp. 137–161). London: Karnac.

Hollway, W., & Jefferson, T. (2000). *Doing Qualitative Research Differently; Free Association, Narrative and the Interview Method*. London: Sage.

Jervis, S. (2009). Use of self as a research tool. In: S. Clarke & P. Hoggett (Eds.), *Researching Beneath the Surface: Psycho-Social Research Methods in Practice* (pp. 145–166). London: Karnac.

Jervis, S. (2011). *Relocation, Gender and Emotion: A Psycho-Social Perspective on the Experiences of Military Wives*. London: Karnac.

Jervis, S. (2012). Parallel process in research supervision: turning the psycho-social focus towards supervisory relationships. *Psychoanalysis, Culture and Society, 17*: 296–313.

Ogden, T. H. (1995). *Reverie and Interpretation: Sensing Something Human* (pp. 21–63). London: Karnac, 1999.

Sullivan, C. C. (2002). Finding the thou in the I: Countertransference and parallel process analysis in organizational research and consultation. *Journal of Applied Behavioral Science, 38*(3): 375–392.

Wengraf, T. (2000). Uncovering the general from within the particular: from contingencies to typologies in the understanding of cases. In: P. Chamberlayne, J. Bornat, & T. Wengraf (Eds.), *The Turn to Biographical Methods in Social Science: Comparative Issues and Examples* (pp. 140–164). London: Routledge.

Wengraf, T. (2001). *Qualitative Research Interviewing: Biographic Narrative and Semi-Structured Methods*. London: Sage.

CHAPTER TEN

The inner voice: building the institution in the mind

Eileen Francis

Introduction

This chapter is concerned with how we talk with each other in professional relationships and how we think about dialogue and discussion in education and society. It is about managing the voice in the mind and being mindful about the voice we use to communicate our needs and wants in organisations. The meaning that we, as human beings, give to our voice is framed as much by our values and emotional and intellectual insights as by our communicative abilities. This chapter begins by thinking about the physical voice but concludes that voice also has meaning as a metaphor for being listened to as a person. It reflects on the paths taken on a personal professional journey through four decades of group and institutional work illuminated by psychoanalytic thinking. A series of narratives illustrates the nature of the inner and outer voices that build the psychoanalytic concept—an "institution in the mind".

Developing a professional self

Imagine, if you will, a newly qualified speech and language therapist at the beginning of a professional journey. It is 1961. Trained to assess, diagnose, and treat communication disorders, I work first with older people in hospital and then with children in a Rudolf Steiner community. A seminal paper on language and mind has recently been published (Chomsky, 1957) and the profession is focused on the development of structural linguistics. The application of the study of phonetics is in its infancy. The profession has yet to be influenced by studies of communication in face to face interaction. The disciplined assessment of paralinguistic features such as gesture, gaze, voice quality, and facial expression will not be routine for another ten years (Laver & Hutcheson, 1972). The first stage of my journey coincided with an exciting period of development in our understanding of a holistic model of communication.

My career path led me in 1971 to becoming a lecturer in the newly established Speech Unit of a College of Education (later a University Institute of Education). I worked with practising teachers on the communication difficulties of children with special educational needs. I also worked with students experiencing their own communication problems as they learnt to be teachers. The needs of the students were to focus my attention on what was to become a specialist interest in voice in both its literal and metaphorical sense.

The voice in the mind

Reflecting on my second decade as a qualified speech and language therapist, it seems remarkable that in the 1970s, for the first time, the profession began to think empirically about the relationship between verbal and non-verbal communication. The transitional experience of moving from a health setting to an educational context made me question and broaden my conceptual understanding. The familiar descriptions of speech and language became more nuanced as features of the vocal and non-vocal communication of student teachers were drawn to my attention. I became a student of the analysis of voice quality (Laver, 1972) and of bodily communication (Argyle, 1975).

Laver held seminars on the analysis of voice quality at Edinburgh University, which I found useful for the work I had undertaken with student teachers. His focus was the investigation of a speaker's physical, psychological, and social characteristics and how listeners drew conclusions from various non-verbal aspects of speech. During the seminars, we tested our assumptions about speakers as we listened to audio recordings of their voices. I was particularly interested in the research finding that listeners are inaccurate in the judgements they make about voice quality. In subjective judgements, they operate with stereotypes, and, of the three types of information in voice quality (biological, psychological, and social), it is the biological information that leads to the most accurate conclusions, while psychological and social conclusions are more likely to be erroneous. Voice quality, therefore, is not solely dependent on anatomical potential, but on a more variable strand of the speaker's voice quality, the habitual muscular settings of the larynx and vocal tract which respond to psychological, social, and cultural experience (Laver & Hutcheson, 1972).

As I observed the students' vocal and non-vocal communication, I became particularly interested in the reticent student, the person whose intellectual capabilities in presentations in public were diminished by a lack of authority in voice, gaze, and facial expression. I noted that while the students had the same anatomical potential as their peers to produce resonant, authoritative voices, they habitually adopted muscular settings in the classroom that had the effect of contradicting their authority. Interest in the origins of this non-verbal leakage of their state of mind, often, but not always, due to anxiety in the public sphere, was the next step on my journey to explore the conflictual relationship between the inner and the outer voice.

Losing and finding a voice

The capacity to describe vocal dynamics is important in the analysis of vocal strain and for understanding the physical and psychological experience of losing one's voice. I now felt the need to complement this understanding by exploring the dynamics of the inner voice. I was beginning to ask questions about the soundness of people's inner dialogue as they grappled with life experiences.

In the 1970s, there were many approaches to psychological therapy that offered to make the inner dialogue explicit. I explored Rogerian therapy, Gestalt therapy, transactional analysis, re-evaluation counselling, and personal construct theory, all of which offered to assist in finding one's voice. Eventually, the serendipity that placed me in a Scottish psychotherapeutic context focused my attention on the contribution of Fairbairn, the psychoanalyst who formulated object relations theory.

The analytical group and associated applications

In the early 1970s, the newly established Scottish Institute of Human Relations (SIHR), which was committed to encouraging an understanding of object relations theory, inaugurated a course on analytical groups and associated applications for members of the caring professions. The course provided participants with opportunities to examine some of their personal and professional conflicts within an experiential learning group. The aim was to help members to understand conflicting motives and blind spots in their own relationships in order to become freer to help with these dynamics in others. The application group focused on the way in which these same conflicts might recur in the work setting.

The SIHR programme was the context in which I developed a personal understanding of the psychodynamic/psychoanalytic perspective and its application to communication in face-to-face interaction. The work of the group analyst Bion seemed particularly relevant to the study of voice (Bion, 1970). The way in which he discussed words that can become an "obstructive rigidity" and words that can become a "stumbling block to comprehension" captured the ambivalence that many of the students appeared to feel about their own communication style.

The series of experiential learning groups I was introduced to by SIHR included not only the weekly analytical group experiences over a period of two years, but also different group conferences led by staff members of the Tavistock Institute of Human Relations, among whom was Harold Bridger (Trist & Murray, 1990). If I was learning about self and voice within groups at SIHR, I was learning about self and voice within the context of the organisation with Bridger. He had initiated a task-orientated model of group development concerned with the roles and relationships of participants in organisations. He believed that as well as being purpose-orientated, organisations had also to be learning and self-reviewing organisations. His experiential learning model was designed to make participants aware of both of these aspects, which he called the "double task".

Bridger talked about "understanding the learning to be gained from the music behind the words of the working relationship". He would state that "a growing point" for change existed in most organisational contexts, and that by picking up the weak as well as the strong signals from different sections of the wider, as well as the immediate, environment, it was possible to ensure continuous learning and development of the "growing point". He talked of "creating appropriate institutions or covered bridges of valid kinds where the real underlying work of dealing with anxieties and raising the level of consciousness can go on without blurring issues" (Gold & Klein, 2004, p. 11).

Now more readily referred to as "working below the surface" (Huffington, Armstrong, Halton, Hoyle, & Pooley, 2004), the double task takes account not only of what is being said or done, but of the meaning which underlies thinking and actions. Lawrence, a consultant at many group relations conferences, describes the experiential process of working below the surface as "a living methodology for inspecting the conscious and unconscious realities of groups and institutions and the political relatedness (authority, management and organisation) of individuals in roles within these configurations" (Lawrence, 1979, p. 4).

The institution in the mind

It was during this period of analytical group work that I was first introduced to the metaphor "the institution in the mind". This psychodynamic construct, described by Pierre Turquet in the 1960s and referred to by Lawrence (1979), is a means of illustrating the unstated and often unconscious assumptions that people develop to cope with working in an institution or organisation. The metaphor illuminated my experience of the personal and the professional voice in the institution. Working on my own reticence in the experiential group enabled me to understand the reticent students I was frequently asked to help. I was able to connect my own work on the reticent voice in the mind, with the wider issue of the pressures experienced as I became increasingly aware of the voice of the institution. There was no going back from hearing the music behind the words.

In the narratives that follow, my aim is to capture evidence of my own developing "institution in the mind":

> narrative is the study of how humans make meaning of experience by endlessly telling and re-telling stories about themselves that re-figure the past and create purpose for the future . Deliberately storying and re-storying one's life is therefore a fundamental method of personal and social growth: it is a fundamental quality of education. (Connelly & Clandinin, 1990, p. 3)

The metaphor "institution in the mind" will be developed as if an actual building is to be completed, one which has psychoanalytical foundations, with several storeys or stories, with living spaces for listening to voices.

First storey/story. 1971: self and the institution

I have described the early development of my career from clinical practice in England to lecturing in a Scottish college of education and how, as an inexperienced lecturer, I found support in the application group at SIHR to understand the conscious and unconscious realities of the institutional context in which I found myself.

Later, I would come across the image of the "crawlspace", a symbolic dimension of organisations described by Ingram that allowed me retrospectively to understand the feelings I experienced in the early 1970s as a new member of staff constrained in an unfamiliar institutional role (Ingram, 1986). Ingram describes the visceral experience of being uncomfortable in an institution and of feeling inhibited by the experience of others. If "crawlspace" was occupied by the perceived "underlife" of an organisation, because I was not professionally qualified as a teacher, I felt part of the "underlife" of my institution, the college of education.

As Laing puts it,

> There is nothing for me, outside of here.
> The people are bigger and would push me
>   back into this cave.
> The people, outside, don't want me.
> . . .
> I don't care.
> . . .

> I ache from being stepped on by the people,
> in here, but they don't mean to step on me,
> and it's just a careless mistake that they do,
> I think, I hope.
>
> (Laing, 1965, p. 170)

Whatever I felt about my inadequacy during this period, I grew to believe that the crawlspace was important for the maintenance of the organisation. From what I had learnt from Bion and Bridger, it was a container for ideas whose time had not yet come. From my perspective, I wanted to apply this learning to focus attention on the speech and language development of children and on communication in teacher education. Specifically, I was concerned to share insights on process thinking, which, at that time, were submerged by the content of teacher education programmes. It was time to make process thinking explicit.

I noticed there were other inhabitants of the crawlspace who hoped eventually to be included in designing programmes for innovation and change. I realised that the problem was not one of establishing identity, but, rather, of gaining acceptance as a legitimate member of an educational enterprise. I developed the awareness that being a voice at the edge provided opportunities for making space for development. I joined a staff group, a think-tank, of like-minded colleagues to discuss what constituted an "appropriate education".

As the staff group developed, it was clear that people with different academic histories—educational philosophers, psychologists, sociologists, and teacher educators—had images of the educational process that were in contradiction to one another. The images might be explicitly expressed, but were more often the implicit, unconscious underpinning in discussions, which powerfully influenced behaviour and feelings.

Noting that there was funding available for staff development, I suggested to the assistant principal in charge that, instead of using the funds for individual professional development, we could provide an experiential workshop for our staff group. Its task would be to assist a group of colleagues to gain some understanding of the "institution in the mind". I was given permission to invite a consultant to work with the group to probe the split-off bits of feeling—angry feelings, rejected feelings—that often surrounded thinking and action within the institution.

In the experiential setting, we discussed how the institution, in common with others, while publicly stating its primary purpose, had hidden conceptions about learning, which were not being made explicit. We explored our own different perceptions of the institution and our roles within it. This analysis mobilised the anxiety and, subsequently, the creativity of the members of staff involved. Colleagues gained an understanding of the sense of psychological and emotional containment required by educational organisations and their role as containers for the aspirations of society. Individuals began to feel their own authority as agents for change.

Confident that skilled communication was the key to effective education, I decided to offer an experimental, self-referred, voluntary group experience to enable students to work on their personal communication style with their peers. A psychodynamic approach to the experiential learning of the group was combined with cognitive behavioural strategies focusing on communication skills to manage speech anxiety. This approach shifted the focus from the individual student teachers as transmitters of information to their role as the conductor of classroom dialogue. Reticent students were able to show that listening skills, considerateness, and compassion in communicative relationships might be more effective than performance skills when working with the class as a group. Within the group, the student teachers would find their voice.

Second storey/story. 1980: process building in the institution

In the 1980s, the group work programme I had initiated with student teachers and my work on the oral curriculum in secondary schools came to the attention of the Research and Intelligence Unit in the Scottish Education Department. I was commissioned to co-ordinate a project group to develop the awareness, insight, and skills of Scottish teachers in classroom discussion. The Discussion Development Group (DDG) challenged the assumption that teaching the processes and skills required by the new curriculum could be achieved didactically. A different methodology was required to improve understanding about relationships in the classroom.

An experiential learning programme was designed to meet teachers' needs to develop process thinking in the classroom. The DDG also provided a consultancy support system to enhance discussion projects in schools. At a later stage, a network of teachers and lecturers disseminated the findings of the project to schools throughout Scotland. It was hoped that this exploration of the values, attitudes, and feelings underlying classroom leadership would enable the development of authentic process innovation.

A psychodynamic approach to classroom discussion

It was evident that awareness and insight about the discussion process in the classroom was sparse and the notion that it was possible to learn to discuss was novel. The DDG set out to show that however skilfully the teacher might blend cognitive and behavioural elements of a discussion learning programme, the process would be incomplete without consideration of the psychodynamic elements of the group experience. Levels of feeling, both conscious and unconscious, are significant in discussion. It was this process of lifting feelings into thoughts and then into spoken language, described as the "psychodynamic process", which was regarded as specific to DDG programmes. Key concepts for the project were an understanding of the "open system" and experience of group analysis as applied to learning and teaching. The aim of the open system approach to group relations was, and is, to heighten process thinking. The language used to describe these concepts to teachers was crucial to their acceptance. Lawrence was cited as an advocate of the open system approach: "the open system approach is based on the belief that we can work more effectively and with greater satisfaction if we come to understand in a direct and personal way the dynamics of group and inter-group processes within social systems" (Lawrence, 1979, p. 4). Furthermore "the processes, both manifest and covert, of groups and social systems can best be understood when they are seen in actual operation" (Lawrence, 1979, p. 6).

Concepts from group analysis had been used effectively in higher education settings by Bramley, who had earlier provided consultancy to the staff group. The group analyst, Foulkes, is cited in Bramley (1979) as having likened the group to:

> a hall of mirrors in which parts of ourselves are reflected and counter-reflected; we see facets of ourselves in others and others see themselves in us. We sometimes admire and cherish others and learn from them because they seem to represent our better selves; we distrust and confront or ignore parts of other people which 'mirror' the darker corners of our own personality. It is when group members deny and disown parts of themselves (for example, failing to realise that the attitude adopted by the member next to them, which they are challenging vehemently, is actually an attitude they themselves secretly espouse) that attempts to work become fraught with tension. (p. 88)

This image helped the DDG to find a language with which to discuss the interpersonal distortions teachers observe in class groups that include themselves, allowing them to discuss critical incidents exemplifying psychoanalytic concepts such as transference, displacement, and splitting.

Later, in project work in schools, we made practical use of the split which often occurs between those who contribute to class discussion and those who are silent by explicitly creating listening groups and speaking groups. A student in a video recording about the strategy comments, "I've learnt to listen so she now has a chance to talk."

The discussion of Bramley's work enabled the identification of the "process shapers" in a group that were under the conscious control of a group leader or teacher: these being, physical setting, group composition, and leadership style. These processes were differentiated from unconscious process shapers, such as the different understandings of the boundary system, the resistance/resonance dynamic, and perceptions of personal authority and role that affect the life of the group.

Evaluating the DDG

Commentaries on the work of the DDG have been published in various texts (Francis, 1988, 1990). The following statements from a sample of the eighty-three teachers who participated in the development programme capture the meaning the final report gave to the understanding of classroom discussion in Scotland: (Francis & Davidson, 1986).

> I feel I have developed an awareness of what is going on in a discussion in terms of the underlying factors rather than in terms of what people say.
>
> I had no real notion of how unconscious ideas affected people in a group.
>
> A new perspective for me was concerned with the meaning of "process" – that it should apply to what goes on inside your head, not what you do or say. I suppose until the group I had completely ignored that aspect, for me process was just what people were doing or saying. (p. 28)

The learning experience was evaluated by one teacher:

> I think I've been made aware not so much of my own skills but what's happening in a group of students and what's happening in a group of students that includes myself; and having come to a realisation of what's happening in the group itself, that leads me to feel much more confident to tackle group work and to cope with the problems that come up. (p. 7)

This was different from her initial comments about the more familiar approach to in-service training: "I felt when I came here to begin with that I was going to get a checklist that I was going to go through to make me a better teacher as far as discussion skills were concerned" (p. 12).

However, the learning experience was not without its frustrations. Another teacher commented,

> The whole group thing was the most interesting for me. I knew that it wasn't going to be structured but I had hoped it would be more task orientated and I felt frustrated sometimes that it wasn't and that the group didn't feel task orientated in that way as perhaps I did . . . this was an education for me – how different everyone's perception was of everything . . . I think all the people in our group found this aspect useful that our perceptions of each other were very different from the individuals' perceptions of themselves. (p. 26)

It should be emphasised that this learning took place in an educational context and, therefore, it was dissimilar to the analytical group experienced at SIHR and those described by members of the Tavistock and the Institute of Group Analysis. The DDG advocated applied group analysis using documentary and video resources to complement experiential learning. The boundaries around the task and the psychological levels of the task were configured differently. Teachers who were members of the DDG learnt to understand and respond to the different levels of exploration in group learning and interpersonal learning, distinguishing them from the intrapersonal learning processes of the therapeutic group—an important distinction for school-based work. The teachers brought with them their expectations and assumptions about task, structure, authority, and role, and, by the end of the programme, were beginning to build their own institution in the mind.

The dissemination of the work of the DDG and its application through in-service training in Scottish schools resulted in involvement in movements on self-study, dialogue, and co-operative enquiry, nationally and internationally. In 1989, I was appointed senior lecturer with responsibility for enterprise across the institution.

Third storey/story. 1989–1991: finding the voice of the "intrapreneur"

Voice quality had been the focus of my research and development since 1971 in both a literal and a metaphorical sense. The work on voice in education had developed in stages. At first, it was concerned with voices that are not listened to, that needed support to be heard. Later, it focused on analysing the differences and distortions in the voices heard in classrooms and schools. Perception and interpretation became the focus. Then, the concern was with negotiating language, with consideration for the difficulties inherent in the interpretation of the voices of one group of educationalists by another group.

The dominant voice of the education system of this period was now different. The voice of educational management had become bureaucratic and managerial, characterised by talk of assessment and accountability, of performance indicators and vocational utilitarianism, rather than relationships and communication.

In my role as Senior Lecturer: Enterprise, a series of discussions with groups of colleagues on the language of enterprise in publicly funded institutions was initiated, contrasting perceptions on entrepreneurship with notions of being enterprising in teaching and learning (Francis, 1991, 1992). The concept of "intrapreneurship" was introduced, the art of being enterprising *within* an organisation, connecting it with the work on psychodynamic thinking and the institution in the mind.

The staff groups that participated in the enterprise project reflected on the nature of the interacting discourses which researchers, lecturers, students, and administrators brought to the task of education. Given the financial and business orientation of higher education at the time, they could be described as travelling across linguistic communities, exploring different value systems. Of particular interest was the relationship between three voices in education: technocratic, bureaucratic, and philosophical voices. The technocratic voice spoke of controlling the items and elements of education based on a belief that by structuring and restructuring these components, educational outcomes would be improved. The bureaucratic voice claimed that change could be achieved by a managerial approach to changes in the systems and structures of education. These were instrumental, externalised voices.

It was, however, the intrinsic value of the philosophical voice in education with which the members of the staff groups were most concerned. There were fears that the philosophical voice might be suppressed or drowned out. What were the implications for the education profession if a majority of staff made a strategic decision to lose one of their voices?

1991 was a period of transition. Institutional life had changed. Colleges of education had been, or were in the process of being, integrated into the university system. New colleagues with different institutional histories were working together. The dominant paradigm in education was utilitarian, with a focus on education for employment. There was a mood of financial constraint and restructuring the institution was the primary task of management. It did feel as if the philosophical voice in education had been diminished. There was change, too, at SIHR. In 1991, its mentor, Jock Sutherland, died, and the aims and objectives of the organisation shifted in new directions.

There had also been a shift in my own voice. From a focus on the voice in the mind to an understanding of the institution in the mind, I was now more interested in dialogue with other minds. The work of being creative and learning experientially as a person, then reflective and conceptually thoughtful as a professional, had reached an end-point. I discarded the institutional roles of lecturer, therapist, and researcher and opted for developmental, co-operative roles outside the institution.

Fourth storey/story: voicing the values of the institution in the mind

In 1992 the VECTOR project was established to work on Values, Education, Consultancy, Training and Organisational Research. It was supported by the Gordon Cook Foundation, a charitable trust established by the Scottish philanthropist Victor Cook in memory of his father, to further values in education in the UK. A network of sixty members met in small groups five times a year to discuss values in education and the challenges we observed in the changing philosophy of teaching and learning. This created a forum in which the philosophical and the psychodynamic voice continued to be heard.

The inspiration for VECTOR was the Edinburgh Forum, established by Jock Sutherland, which still meets in Edinburgh. This multidisciplinary forum, founded in the early 1970s, involved different professional voices from across the public, private, and voluntary sectors. It met to discuss values and attitudes relating to public policy in Scotland.

Within the VECTOR network, there were five members with analytical group experience and others who had participated in self-study on group processes. VECTOR was a community of enquiry. We regarded ourselves as partners in dialogue, exploring values' positions and working through current educational issues. One of its members was a head teacher whose school was closed as a result of a local authority rationalisation programme; another was involved with BBC Education and had to cope with the aftermath of the tragedy at Dunblane. The stories of the participants meant that the dialogue was affected by potent issues. Voices that were drowned out in the educational system of the time could be heard in their poignancy.

In 1995, supported once again by the Gordon Cook Foundation, we extended our work across the UK, establishing, with fifteen like-minded organisations, the Values Education Council (VEC UK), with

VECTOR as a founder member. The mission was to form a co-operative community of many voices whose members would work together across the UK to promote the notion of values education. What made this difficult was that the language of values education had such a powerful, pre-existing range of disciplinary associations that its meaning was constantly squeezed. In linguistic terms, we were indulging in lexical borrowing, code mixing, and code switching to form the new language of values education.

Bion captures what was happening as he gives us the image of the container and the contained:

> a word contains a meaning; conversely a meaning can contain a word – which may or may not be discovered. The relationship is established by the nature of the link. The search is for a constant conjunction of elements bound by the attribution to it of a word, a theory or other formulation. (Bion, 1970, p. 106)

Further, "if the formulation survives it can be repeated and if it can be repeated under severe conditions it becomes stronger until it communicates meaning without disintegration" (Bion, 1970, p. 80). Bion urges us to be patient until a pattern evolves. The work is to understand the splits: "if an idea is subjected to splitting it may split again repeatedly, each split growing and having to be split again. Thus one gets not development but division and multiplication – cancerous not qualitative increase" (Bion, 1970, p. 127).

We were not patient enough. VEC spent much of its time engaged in making formulations that seemed to slither and evade containment. Sometimes, the powerful feelings of rivalry and envy caused verbal expression to disintegrate. However, working together did make each organisation more authoritative and enabled productive partnerships. We perceived the range and effectiveness of our individual endeavours and committed ourselves to work alongside, if not to work with, the other. We felt the real meaning of being an organisational network rather than a group.

Fifth storey/story. 1999: creating a communication web

In 1999, Damasio published a compelling neurobiological study of the self. My understanding of the experiences and reflections that are contained in the narratives in this chapter has been enriched by his findings, helping me to make sense of my journey from the neurolinguistic background of the therapist to the psychodynamic thinking significant to the group worker. Damasio's description of the autobiographical self, based on aggregate memory, which stands alongside the conscious core self and the non-conscious proto-self, validates the integrative purpose of this present experience of re-telling these stories. Damasio (1999) describes the autobiographical self thus:

> The autobiographical self is based on autobiographical memory which is constituted by implicit memories of multiple instances of individual experiences of the past and the anticipated future. . . . Autobiographical memory grows continuously with life experience but can be partly remodeled to reflect new experiences. (p. 174)

Damasio goes on to state that "The contents of the autobiographical self can only be known when there is a fresh construction of core self and knowing for each of those contents to be known" (p. 176).

In this fifth narrative, I focus on the semiotic, that is, the signs and symbols, of the communication web which integrates the philosophical, psychological, and political dialogues featured in the previous stories. The unheard voice shifts from psychological and social construct to political construct in this narrative. The psychodynamic insights and psychoanalytic thought that provided early sustenance in the building of the institution in the mind were now being applied to increasingly large groups and networks. As co-ordinator of VECTOR, vice-chair and, later, chair of VEC, it was necessary to continue to connect inner and outer worlds.

The difference between authority and power is a significant psychodynamic concern, and, during this period, VECTOR worked on the values and attributes related to notions of personal and positional power. While I was now outside the institution, I was, nevertheless, still engaged in thinking about relationships between individuals and their organisations.

In the late 1990s, VECTOR was involved in a series of consultations on the voice of civil society and the nature of citizenship. The personal voice of the early narratives was in the process of becoming a political voice. In 1999, we looked for an institution or agency consonant with the values and commitments of VECTOR that could integrate its purpose and be responsive to its analysis of the importance of dialogue in society. The focus on the voice of civil society was timely, as we became involved in the development of the Scottish Civic Assembly and, following the establishment of the Scottish Parliament, a founding member of the Scottish Civic Forum (SCF).

VECTOR contributed to the dialogue on the voice of civil society by joining a working group on the concordat, which defined the relationship between SCF and the Parliament. VECTOR, informed by its previous work on discussion, charted these relationships as a communication web. A poster display and discussion on the proposed communication web was prepared for the plenary meeting at which the SCF was formally constituted. The communication web represented a proposal for "dialogic democracy". Giddens (1994, p. 14) describes democracy as "a vehicle for the representation of interests". He adds: "it is a way of creating a public arena in which controversial issues – in principle – can be resolved, or at least handled, through dialogue rather than through pre-established forms of power" (Giddens, 1994, p. 15).

The vision was that SCF would assist the Parliament by creating a communication web to facilitate discussion, seeking participation from excluded groups and hitherto unheard voices. It would explore the prospects for consensus across civil society, reflecting and recording disagreement or diversity of opinion where it existed. It would not contrive consensus where none could be agreed.

We observed that within the communication system of the Scottish Parliament there were spaces (dialogic space) for different types of communication: a space for the communication of the Executive, a space for large group formal communications within the debating chamber, and spaces for the small group communication of the sixteen committees. The SCF would create groups to shadow the activities of these spaces by investigating and evaluating communication within the spaces and seeking the most effective way to involve civil society in their dialogue. The immediate task would be to observe and analyse the quality of the communication within the web.

Innovative thinking on the role of civil society was needed to commit Members of the Scottish Parliament (MSPs) to a longer-term vision of a participative democracy. MSPs were rightly proud of their new constitutional arrangements, but SCF had to ask if the rhetoric on participation was real. It would suggest that participation as a quantitative concept was insufficient, because SCF aspired to the qualitative notion of dialogic democracy.

This proposal was discussed and implemented explicitly and implicitly over a period of five years until the Parliament decided that it could no longer afford to fund SCF. We concluded that while SCF had developed its own organisational power, it was as nothing when compared with the positional power wielded by a Parliament.

Sixth storey/story. 2005–2010: the unfinished building

Over time, I realised that the building of an institution in the mind would never be finished. As time passed, there would be reconfigurations of the space and the boundaries around the space. In my mind, the relationships achieved through the personal power of the self and the positional power of the roles I had occupied became clearly differentiated. The first enabled healthy attitudes to authority, roles, and systems. In tandem with the second, people could become agents of change. Most important was the mindfulness and compassion aspired to through process thinking and psychodynamic sensitivity. I became aware of the strengths and weaknesses of the different selves—the therapist, the educationalist, the researcher, and the intrapreneur.

In 2005, I found myself in a place described by Craib (1994) as the space occupied by the disappointed self. He elaborates on the notion of integration involved in the disappointed self:

> the form of integration I am talking about here involves both a growth and a limitation of the psyche,and both are, in effect, disappointments. The growth involves the well-recognised process of taking in those parts of oneself that have been denied and projected. (Craib, 1994, p. 175)

When Craib visited a VECTOR meeting, the group explored the idea that we had much in common with Habermas (1971) in perceiving psychoanalysis as an "emancipatory science". We discussed the "false self of modernity" demanded by the functional rationality of the social system and agreed:

> the disappointed self is able to stand back from the desire for narcissistic satisfaction and engage in the processes of thinking that can

> facilitate communicative rationality, the free negotiation and working out of personal relationships that can restrict or counteract the dynamics of the social system. (Craib, 1994, p. 179)

The search for complementarity between the inner and the outer voice continued when the role of chair of SIHR was added to the litany of different selves. SIHR, which might be thought of as a truly Fairbairnian "exciting object" and, as the institution in the mind and of the mind, needed real spaces as well as metaphorical space in which dialogue could take place. In the role of Chair, I became responsible in actuality for keeping a roof on the building. It was both an enlivening time, revisiting the history of SIHR, and a struggle with disappointment, as we tried to maintain the future of the organisation.

Sutherland, one of the founders of SIHR, would talk about "healing the splits" and "fighting the fights you can win", in discussions about suffering and disappointment. These statements contained no false expectation that the splits would be miraculously healed, but emphasised the ongoing work required, in all contexts, on the management of self in action and management in the mind. It is my belief that psychodynamic work enables us to find the powerlessness in power, to be open to the strength in expressions of personal vulnerability, and to find the hopeful voice within the disappointed voice.

Epilogue: the hopeful voice

In 2010, members of the groups represented in these stories came together for a symposium at the Story-telling Centre in Edinburgh to celebrate the hopeful voice (and, perhaps, the disappointed voice) in acceptance of the internal conflicts represented by our stories, and in understanding of the external limitations that had constrained our activities. In a gathering of those who shared intrinsic values, we celebrated individual achievement and community endeavour. The voice was hopeful because of the possibilities of the intellectual and emotional shifts we had encountered. We particularly celebrated the shifts in language and understanding in the past forty years, which made the values contained in these stories progressively explicit. The symposium was a way of completing a process, of reasserting the institution in the mind, of paying tribute to the history and influence of the Scottish Institute of Human Relations. In Charles Taylor's words, "Even as the most independent adult, there are moments when I cannot clarify what I feel until I talk about it with certain special partners who know me, or have wisdom, or with whom I have an affinity" (Taylor, 1989, p. 36).

References

Argyle, M. (1975). *Bodily Communication*. London: Methuen.

Bion, W. R. (1970). *Attention and Interpretation*. London: Tavistock.

Bramley, W. (1979). *Group Tutoring: Concepts and Case Studies*. London: Kogan Page.

Chomsky, N. (1957). *Syntactic Structures*. The Hague/Paris: Mouton.

Connelly, F. M., & Clandinin, D. J. (1990). Stories of experience and narrative inquiry. *Educational Researcher, 19*(5): 2–14.

Craib, I. (1994). *The Importance of Disappointment*. London: Routledge.

Damasio, A. (1999). *The Feeling of What Happens*. London: William Heinemann.

Francis, E. (1988). Group processes. In: J. T. Dillon (Ed.), *Questioning and Discussion: A Multidisciplinary Study* (pp. 259 -279). Norwood, NJ: Ablex.

Francis, E. (1990). Working together on discussion. In: M. Brubacher, R. Payne, & K. Rickett, (Eds.), *Perspectives on Small Group Learning: Theory and Practice* (pp. 301–308). Oakville, Ontario: Rubicon.

Francis, E. (1991). Making the rhetoric real: perceptions of enterprise in educational contexts. *British Journal of Education and Work, 4*: 21–33.

Francis, E. (1992). Change agents, glass ceilings and enterprise awareness in teacher education. *Journal of Assessment and Evaluation in Higher Education, 17*: 139–152.

Francis, E., & Davidson, J. (1986). *Working Together on Discussion: A Study of Process Innovation and Dissemination*. Edinburgh: Scottish Office Education Department.

Giddens, A. (1994). *Beyond Left and Right*. Cambridge: Polity Press.

Gold, S., & Klein, L. (2004). Harold Bridger – conversations and recollections. *Organisational and Social Dynamics, 4*: 1–21.

Habermas, J. (1971). *Knowledge and Human Interests*. Boston, MA: Beacon Press.

Huffington, C., Armstrong, D., Halton, W., Hoyle, L., & Pooley, J. (2004). *Working Below the Surface: The Emotional Life of Contemporary Organisations*. London: Karnac.

Ingram, L. C. (1986). In the crawlspace of the organization. *Human Relations, 39*: 467–486.

Laing, R. D. (1965). *The Divided Self*. Harmondsworth: Penguin.

Laver, J. (1972). Voice quality and indexical information. In: J. Laver & S. Hutcheson (Eds.), *Communication in Face to Face Interaction* (pp. 189–203). Harmondsworth: Penguin.

Laver, J., & Hutcheson, S. (Eds.) (1972). *Communication in Face to Face Interaction*. Harmondsworth: Penguin.

Lawrence, W. G. (1979). Introductory essay: exploring boundaries. In: W. G. Lawrence (Ed.), *Exploring Individual and Oranisational Boundaries* (pp. 1–19). Chichester: John Wiley.

Taylor, C. (1989). *Sources of the Self: The Making of Modern Identity*. Cambridge: Cambridge University Press.

Trist, E., & Murray, H. (Eds.) (1990). *The Social Engagement of Social Science. A Tavistock Anthology. Volume 1: The Socio-Psychological Perspective*. London: Free Association Books.

CHAPTER ELEVEN

Knowing (and not knowing) one's place: organisational ranking and the operation of envy and shame in organisational life*

Marie Kane

Introduction

A significant amount of our time is spent at work; a lot of our energies are devoted to work, yet there is curiously little exploration of our feelings and thoughts about this relationship. There is a substantial body of work that documents the importance of our early years, the travails of adolescence, our relationships with partners, yet our engagement with work, and the factors which influence how we take up our work role, remain relatively uncharted.

The question of how we take up our work role and how we achieve "good enough" internal authority is one of the most recurrent themes emerging from the organisational work that I have been engaged in over the past decades. This work has included a series of three national Scottish Institute of Human Relations "Working Below the Surface Scotland" conferences and a related "Working Below the

* An earlier version of this chapter was presented at the "Working below the Surface Scotland Conference" in Edinburgh, Scottish Institute of Human Relations, 31 October 2010. It was first published in *Organisational and Social Dynamics*, *12*(2): 194–209 (2012) and is reprinted with kind permission of OPUS and Karnac Books.

Surface" seminar series—work which has involved almost 400 participants from a widely eclectic range of professions, and which has taken the psychodynamic, "below surface" understanding of organisational dynamics, promoted by the Scottish Institute, to a wider audience. There has also been the experience of working with managers in long-term work in leadership development on university programmes, and on NHS and other public sector development programmes, as well as more general organisational consultancy work with SIHR and other organisations.

Organisational ranking and the concept of allocated "place" in organisational hierarchy are powerful, yet relatively unexplored, dynamics in organisational life. While the intensity of our awareness of organisational rank will vary individually, we all carry an instinctive sense of our own and others' place in the hierarchical order. There can be strong and punitive reactions, often resulting in envious attacks, to a perceived disturbance in this implicit ranking order, yet there is little overt discussion or exploration of these concerns, which, none the less, play a considerable role in below surface organisational dynamics.

This chapter seeks to explore two main areas in relation to the envious attack: first, our concerns with organisational ranking, making the link between these preoccupations and the prevalence of envious attacks in organisational life: what happens when someone "doesn't know their place". There is also, secondly, an examination of how shame intersects with the manifestation of envy and a delineation of how the envious attack can be understood, not solely as a malign attack on goodness or creativity, but within the psychodynamic framework of an organisational defence against anxiety—in this case, the anxiety of the experience of shame and perceived deficit. The envious attack is conceptualised as an unconscious or conscious defence against unbearable feelings of shame and deficit.

Organisational ranking and hierarchy

Garland's (2006) address to the Organisation for the Promotion of Understanding in Society (OPUS) Conference contained a rare foray into the issues of organisational ranking as she explored this question of hierarchy and "ranking order" in the context of examining the impact of the arrival of a new member into an established analytic psychotherapy group. Introducing her discussion with a reference to her earlier profession as an ethnologist, she noted the intense battles for position amongst primates, linking this to a persisting human consciousness of ranking order. She referred to

> the universal human tendency to *position the self in relation to others along a scale,* usually conceived of as vertical, of relative power, worth, weightiness, significance or importance, judging oneself to be either 'one up' or 'one down'. (Garland, 2006, p. 2, original emphasis)

Garland maintains that our "propensity for dominance and for hierarchical relations derives from the Oedipal situation, into which each of us is born" (p. 2). Each of us is born into a hierarchical configuration, a tiny child born to some variant of adult parental couple. This early configuration establishes a pattern, a lens through which we make sense of the world. Like the primates, we are hugely concerned about our place within the group or organisation. The battle of the chimpanzees/primates, their jockeying for position, the determination of the established members to maintain their perceived "better than" position, is enacted daily in our organisational settings, so common that it is a taken for granted feature of organisational life.

This continual positioning of the self in relation to others is also the subject of de Botton's (2004) book, *Status Anxiety,* where he claims that a concern for status and rank is often the "elephant in the room", a preoccupying concern that is rarely admitted or openly addressed, but, none the less, is pressingly influential in terms our sense of self and interactions with others. He describes status anxiety as "an almost universal anxiety that rarely gets mentioned directly: an anxiety about what others think of us; about whether we're judged a success or a failure, a winner or a loser" and asserts that "High status is thought by many (but freely admitted by few) to be one of the finest of earthly goods" (de Botton, 2004, p. vii).

Where we are in relation to others matters to us all, and wide disparity in position and status harms us all, as has been ably demonstrated in one of the most important books of recent times, *The Spirit Level,* which has demonstrated conclusively that it is relative inequality within societies which results in increased problems of mental ill-health, levels of violence, imprisonment, obesity, etc.: "what [matters] is simply whether you are doing better or worse than other people – where you come in the social pecking order" (Wilkinson & Pickett, 2009, p. 13).

Philosophy of paucity

Part of the anxiety about maintaining rank and pecking order is an underlying worry about availability of resources. There is a sense that, if the other has more visibility, recognition, then, perforce, there is less for oneself. The cake is limited and if someone takes a larger slice, it is felt that the other's success reduces what is available for the rest. Britton (2008), in his exploration of envy, probes the sense of impairment, the feeling that one's own position has been damaged or lessened by someone else's "having". He quotes a Catholic catechism for student priests, which he says "gives as good a clinical description as one could find" of the dynamic of envy: "Envy is the feeling of sadness, uneasiness, or discontent excited by the sight of another's superiority or success: whether in the spiritual or temporal order; and this because we fancy our own merit to be hereby lessened" (Britton, 2008, p. 126).

Britton emphasises the sense of impairment within the manifestation of envy and he goes on to quote Milton's magnificent *Paradise Lost*, where Lucifer "thought himself impaired" and was:

> fraught
> With envy against the Son of God, that day
> Honoured by his great Father, and proclaimed
> Messiah king anointed, could not bear
> Through pride that sight, and thought himself
> Impaired.
>
> (Milton, *Paradise Lost, Book V*, ll. 658–663)

De Botton (2004) illustrates this same dynamic visually (although more bathetically) in two drawings (p. 46). In Figure 11.1, people are of the same height and are untroubled by questions of size. However, we are subject to feelings of unease and envy if one in our group grows even a little taller, even though we ourselves have not diminished in size by even a millimetre (Figure 11.2).

Figure 11.1.

Figure 11.2.

Over-deference to rank order and position

Rank and position matter to us; however, an over-consciousness and deference to hierarchical ranking can have severe consequences, sometimes of a literal life or death magnitude. A chapter in Gladwell's *Outliers* (2008) explores how an over-adherence to organisational ranking has been responsible for many aeroplane crashes worldwide. He describes the concept of "mitigation" which occurs when, for reasons of deference to authority and rank, we sugar-coat or mitigate the impact of what we need to say. The recovered black boxes of many plane crashes reveal that the first officers, subordinate to the captain of the flight, were often acutely aware of the imminent danger, but were unable to be forceful enough in their interventions with someone superior to them in rank order. He quotes from some of these poignant recovered tapes, for example, in the 1982 Air Florida crash outside Washington, DC, the first officer tried three times to tell the captain that there was a dangerous amount of ice on the wings (before take-off) but was unable to make his point forcibly enough:

> The last thing the first officer says to the captain, just before the plane plunges into the Potomac river, is not a hint, or suggestion, or command. It is a simple statement of fact – and this time the captain agrees with him. First Officer: "Larry, we're going down, Larry" Captain: "I know it." (Gladwell, 2008, p. 196)

Gladwell notes that the airline industry has made determined efforts to combat "mitigation" and now trains personnel in a range of techniques of assertive challenge. He remarks that: "Aviation experts will tell you that it is the success of this war on mitigation as much as anything else that accounts for the extraordinary decline in airline accidents in recent years" (p. 197).

Over-deference to hierarchy and rank order is observable in most organisations and has, for instance, been identified as a major factor in cases of malpractice in the health service. A study of 6,500 nurses and nurse managers (Maxfield, Grenny, Lavandero, & Groah, 2011) found that eighty-four per cent of them had observed colleagues/seniors take dangerous shortcuts, yet less than ten per cent felt able to speak up about their concerns.

There are other clear pieces of evidence of the stultifying power of rank order that demonstrate how individuals find it extremely difficult to challenge someone perceived to be in a position of authority over them. The Stanley Milgram obedience and authority experiments carried out in Yale in the 1960s and 1970s showed how most people can be persuaded to administer what they believe are almost fatal electric shocks if instructed to do so by a "scientist" in a white coat (Milgram, 1974). BBC Horizon replicated the Milgram experiment in March 2009 in a programme presented by Michael Portillo (2009), who watched with mounting dismay as nine out of the twelve subjects of the experiment were prepared to administer the near fatal dose, as instructed by the "scientist", in spite of what they believed were screams of pain from the other participant.

Milgram's (1974) work demonstrated how constrained we are by notions of authority and position and how difficult it appears to be to step out of the pecking order, even when required to override basic precepts of humanity. He observed,

> Ordinary people, simply doing their jobs, and without any particular hostility on their part, can become agents in a terrible destructive process. Moreover, even when the destructive effects of their work become patently clear, and they are asked to carry out actions incompatible with fundamental standards of morality, relatively few people have the resources needed to resist authority. (Milgram, 1974, p. 6)

In recent times, Lipman-Blumen (2006) has explored why so many people tolerate what is readily perceived as toxic leadership. Her aim is not to blame the victim, but to more clearly understand what she calls "the web of forces which tempts us to accept leaders who play havoc with our businesses, our governments, our schools, our communities, our societies and possibly, our lives" (p. 24). She delineates clear reasons why people feel unable to challenge hierarchical ranking order, including our need for security and certainty, our need for reassuring authority figures to fill our parents' shoes, our fear of personal powerlessness to challenge a bad leader, and our fear of ostracism and social death.

Fear of envious attack as a consequence of disturbance of hierarchical order

Lipman-Blumen does not include fear of envious attack in her list of reasons why people stay in line and feel unable to take up their full authority to challenge hierarchical order. However, the operation of envy is a feared and powerful dynamic which also serves to disempower individuals. This section of the chapter considers the envious attack in organisational life from the perspective of disturbance of hierarchical or ranking order. In this instance, the envious attack seeks to restore the status quo, extinguishing any creative departure from the implicit or explicit rank order. The envious attack acts here as a leveller, seeking to spoil to ensure and maintain the previous rank position. The envious attack can be a devastating consequence of people stepping "out of line", just as savage as the more physical clashes in the jungle, and is one reason why people might instinctively keep to their allocated organisational place.

Envy is a destructive and another relatively uncharted dynamic in organisational life (with some notable exceptions discussed below). It does not feature on the cultural radar of most leadership/management development work, yet, in terms of loss of key staff, derailment of work, and quenching of creativity, the operation of envy has formidable powers to disrupt organisational functioning. Envy particularly attacks creativity in the workplace.

Case study one

At a charged and painful meeting of an organisational working group which was exploring a sustained internal attack on its externally very successful new venture, a puzzled and bewildered voice asked, "Why is the organisation shooting itself in the foot?" This was indeed the key question. The new venture had had the enthusiastic backing of the organisation's members, who had long called for this kind of engagement with the external world and for this kind of extension of the work of the organisation. The venture had attracted more external interest and participation than any previous event in the organisation's history. It promised to open a rich new area of operation for the organisation, yet it was undermined and eventually rendered inoperable by elements within the organisational leadership. This small group within the organisation's leadership was unable to support a successful initiative that had come from outside their own sphere and control. They had not been closely involved in the development of this initiative and had predicted that it would fail. The subsequent unexpected success of the initiative appeared to pose a threat to their established position, and they moved to suppress it. Because the idea was not conceived by themselves, it was "seen off" and a promising source of funding and organisational development missed, a classic case of "cutting one's nose off to spite one's face", as the proverb brutally puts it. Despite significant and vocal support from many other quarters in the organisation, an envious attack by this small group ensured that the maintenance of their hierarchical position took precedence over the development of the organisation's work. An alternative and significantly more modest competing initiative was supported and, through a combination of denigration and delay, the successful initiative was effectively quenched. The competing initiative subsequently had difficulty with enrolments and did not develop.

Case study two

At an international conference on organisational dynamics, a workshop presenter explored a compelling case about Paul, a Chief Executive from a private sector organisation who had been recruited specifically to revitalise a failing trans-national organisation and who had been patently successful in delivering this goal. After only eighteen months, however, Paul was obliged to leave the organisation, "brought down" by a combination of a few Board members protecting vested interests and the tacitly supported undermining of his authority by an internal rival. These Board members felt threatened by Paul's ability to "be his own man", and to act outside their direct control. His success in turning round the organisation had changed the balance of power on the Board, empowering other Board members who supported him, and thereby disrupting the previous Board hierarchy. The "displaced" Board members sought to regain their powerful position through their active support of an internal rival to Paul, ultimately rendering Paul's position untenable. The restored health of the organisation was as nothing in their insistence on the maintenance of their powerful hierarchical position through their envious attack on Paul's ability and creativity. The integrity of Paul and his competence was not in question; indeed, a measure of Paul's effectiveness and the support he had engendered from others in the organisation was the fact that the employees of the organisation had so respected his leadership that they called for a strike to seek his reinstatement. Following Paul's departure, the organisation again failed and was described by the presenter as "stagnant".

Analysis

This phenomenon of envious spoiling is widespread and a regular feature of individual and organisational consultancy work; it features vividly in the grapevine of organisational life, yet maintains a position in the "shadow side", as there is relatively little open discussion and analysis of envy at work. Because there is no analysis or exploration of the operation of envy in leadership development programmes, or no clear acknowledgment of the prevalence of this dynamic, there is little preparation for the manifestation of envy within organisations. As in the two examples above, successful initiatives which further the corporate interests of the organisation, and which are clearly in the best interests of the overall organisation, are frequently attacked and defeated. Individuals are left marooned, puzzling over the ruins of their endeavours; there is a failure to build up a body of knowledge about the manifestation of envy in organisational life and how it might be dealt with. Bullying and sexual harassment, for example, have now been identified and, to some extent, codified within organisational life, and, while this does not make the problems disappear, it does ensure a common understanding and framework within which unacceptable behaviours can be challenged. However, the envious attack, although prevalent and "depressingly familiar" (as one correspondent phrased it) has no real public acknowledgement; it is as if this phenomenon, as an ingrained feature of the human condition, lies somehow beyond our understanding—we are powerless and unknowing before it.

Envy as an attack on creativity in organisational life

An initial step in terms of developing individual and organisational resilience in the face of envy is to develop more clarity about situations that are likely to stir up envious and destructive feelings. A key underlying feature in these situations is the exercise of creativity. Ambrose (1989), in a discussion about the management of change in organisational life, clearly stated a maxim that should inform leadership development. He wrote, "Creativity nearly always engenders destructiveness in one form or another, and shifting the status quo in an organisation is sure to lead to rivalry and other negative feelings in some quarters" (Ambrose, 1989, p. 150). Someone who takes up their full authority and creativity and conceives and gives birth to an endeavour can stir up strong destructive feelings. It is the actual conceiving of the idea/enterprise in the originator that arouses these envious feelings: s/he is not to be allowed to have or hold on to these good things. For example, a staff member joined a public sector project that had been established some years prior to his arrival by another person. He aspired to leadership of the project, and what became remarkable was his inability or reluctance to acknowledge that the project had been created before his arrival. Prior work was minimised, and any role difference between him and the originator very begrudgingly conceded; it seemed extremely painful to acknowledge that this project had had a prior existence,

A form of envious attack is an obliteration of the origins of an endeavour, a denial of the "maternal/paternal" conception, a turning of the "blind eye". Halton's (2004) observation is acute: "The envy is based on the feeling that the new idea was conceived by someone else . . . and not by oneself. Creativity is uncontrollable, anxiety-making and envy-provoking" (p. 122). Perhaps, in the envy of someone else's creative endeavour, there is also some primitive echo of exclusion from the primal scene.

Creativity entails changing the known order of things; it requires courage and initiative, but it is this very proactivity which arouses envy. Creativity can, of course, be met with a generosity of spirit; however, as Ambrose has indicated, it usually risks stirring up envious and spoiling reactions. Through the creative act, the other person has broken rank, moved outside the corral, and, in our colloquial but telling language, needs to be "cut down to size" or "put in their place". The Australians refer to the "tall poppy syndrome"; the Japanese use a more brutal metaphor: "The nail that sticks out gets hammered down".

This instinctive knowledge of the possible negative consequences of creativity is part of our psyche—and part of popular culture. Our language is full of references to this dynamic: people who are deemed "uppity" (itself an interesting term) or who are seen to have "ideas above their station" are forever being "shown their place". A recent storyline in *The Archers* (the longest running and popular radio serial on BBC Radio 4) introduced a new character, Harry, a handsome and debonair new milkman, who exercised creativity and enthusiasm in his role, suggesting new products and even publishing a blog, activities that were met with ill-concealed fury by the resident milkman, Jazzer, who kept muttering darkly that "Harry needs to be shown his place".

We know that this is so, and the instinctive fear of being "hammered down" can act as a cautionary brake to creativity and potency, depriving organisations, as well as ourselves, of the exercise of our full powers. For example, in one public sector consultancy assignment in the social services sector, all four female team members refused to apply for the post of team leader which had become vacant, all four confessing privately to a fear of the consequences on themselves of such a move, and the resentment/envy which might be stirred up. The result was the appointment of a much less qualified and suitable outsider, and a diminution in the overall impact of the work of the team.

Some reasons for lack of attention to the phenomenon of envy in organisational life

Although the envious attack is depressingly ubiquitous and distressing, and often a salient component of toxicity in organisations, we lack rigorous examination and delineation of this phenomenon; there seems to be a relative dearth of work on the operation of envy in organisational life. In 1994, Obholzer and Roberts noted that

> Although there is a substantial body of work on envy in intra and interpersonal relationships, there is little written about its manifestation in institutions. Yet is it clear that envy in institutional processes is one of the key destructive phenomena, particularly in relation to figures in authority. (Obholzer & Roberts, 1994, p. 44)

This comment was echoed by Stein (2000) six years later in his important study of envy in social systems, where he draws attention to a "fundamental lacuna" in the literature on groups and organisations, noting that "while envy has become a quintessential concept in the literature on individuals, up until recently, it has been virtually absent from the literature on social systems" (p. 195).

There has been, however, more interest in different aspects of the manifestation of envy in organisational life in recent years (Daum, 2002; Kane, 2008, Menon & Thompson, 2010; Stein, 1997, 2000, 2005; Vidaillet, 2008), although it remains a relatively under-researched area in general, with the links between the envious attack and the maintenance of organisational dominance particularly under-explored, as is the concept envy as a defence against hidden shame in organisational life.

We can speculate on the reasons for the relative absence of investigation into the dynamic of envy in organisational life; Stein's thesis is that the focus in the psychoanalytic approach to social systems has been based traditionally on investigating defences against anxiety, a mode of investigation pioneered by Jaques (1955) and Menzies (1960), who shaped a paradigm of enquiry in this area which precluded a study of envy, as the operation of envy does not easily fit this "defences against anxiety" model. Stein conceptualises envy as a form of destructive *attack* rather than a *defence* against anxiety.

The hidden shame behind the envious attack

In seeking to explore the envious attack in organisational life, I have considered above an excessive insistence on maintaining organisational dominance as one of the familiar contexts within which an attack is likely to occur. In this section, I would also like to consider the hidden shame and sense of perceived deficit behind the envious attack. At the heart of all of it are the angry bitter feelings stirred up by another's expression of creativity and personal authority (or good fortune in general) and the need to spoil that "something desirable" for the other person or group. Why should this be so and is it immutably so? Why should the success of the other result in this feeling of "mortification and ill-will occasioned by the contemplation of another's superior advantage" (Onions, 1970).

The Kleinian analysis of envy views our capacity for hate and envy as innate, "though varying individually in strength and interacting from the beginning with external conditions" (Klein, 1957, p. 180). Theorists in the Kleinian tradition accord a central importance to the inherent malignant destructiveness of envy (Spillius, 1993). This tradition views envy as an innate destructive impulse, fundamentally "there" in the human psyche. More recent psychoanalytic work probes and refines this "fundamentally there" view, seeking to expose the precipitating features lying immediately *behind* an envious attack. This work directs a beam of light into the noxious feelings immediately antecedent to the attack, and finds its focus in "the searing, painful experience of shame" (Morrison, 1997, p. x). What is now highlighted is the implicit self-comparison inherent in envy, making more explicit the context within which an envious attack occurs. Through this lens, what is now made prominent is the hidden shame enclosed in an act of comparison: "this comparison must be against a self felt to be inferior, lacking, or in some way defective" (Morrison & Lansky, 2008, p. 181). The argument of this recent work is that *shame* is the neglected affect in our analyses of envy, that behind envy there is always a precedent shame: "the central thesis of this communication is that envy is a comparative and self-conscious emotion lying 'downstream', as it were, from shame" (Morrison & Lansky, 2008, p. 186).

I referred earlier to the relative absence of work on envy in organisational life. Morrison (1997) asserts that shame has suffered similar research neglect:

> We have all felt shame. We have all suffered feelings of inferiority, inadequacy, incompetence; known a sense of defect and flaw, of failure; been scorned by others—such feelings are among the most painful we can experience. We hide them from ourselves and from

> others. Yet, shame has, until very recently, been little explored in psychoanalytic literature. (p. 1)

Broucek (1991) notes that: "secondary shame about shame itself means that shame is apt to be the most unrecognised and unacknowledged of all the affects" (p. 104); and Steiner (2011) acknowledges that "shame and its related feelings have only recently been given prominence by psychoanalysts and tend to be ignored by Kleinian analysts" (p. 3).

This elaboration of the envious attack as a potential defence against unconscious feelings of shame, an attempt to deal with, to expel, these intolerable feelings, provides an additional sharpening of focus of the microscope's lens in the study of the envious attack. The delineation of the antecedent sense of shame enlarges our understanding of the dynamic enacted in these attacks. With its focus on the sense of diminishment and associated shame as a trigger to the envious attack, this recent work makes clearer the precipitating circumstances leading to an attack, shining a searchlight on the terrain behind the attack.

The concept of hidden shame also helps us understand the expression of contempt as another related form of shame defence, where the feelings of shame are kept away from consciousness or denied through an attempt to locate them in the other—a form of projective identification. The expression of extreme contempt for another is often a warning signal of something being repressed or denied. In practice, contempt and envy are closely intertwined, as the expression of contempt enacts the devaluing, spoiling assault which is at the heart of envy: "The object which is devalued need not be envied any more" (Klein, 1957).

Is the envious attack after all a defence against intolerable feelings of shame?

Part of Stein's (2000) thesis is that envy has been relatively neglected within social systems because it does not easily fit into the prevailing "defence against anxiety" paradigm which has influenced our study of organisational dynamics, and he asserts that there is a clear distinction between envy and anxiety:

> envious feelings of ill-will and the desire to see harm done to the other are conceptually quite distinct from the anxieties one may feel about oneself or about the other. . . . Envy is also in this sense diametrically opposed to defences against anxiety: while a defence against anxiety is felt (consciously or unconsciously) to protect the person, the envious attack is inspired by a malevolence which has nothing to do with self-protection. (p. 199)

However, if we recognise the intense feelings of shame and inferiority (conscious or unconscious) as antecedent to the envious attack, then I believe that it *does* become possible to conceptualise the envious attack as a defence against these intolerable feelings. With this shift of the lens, it is then possible to conceptualise the envious attack as a form of defence against anxiety, the anxiety being avoided here being the searing sense of shame occasioned by the recognition of one's own inadequacy or felt inferiority prompted by another's success. The envious attack can be seen as a way of bypassing this anxiety about one's own sensed deficit/inferiority in the impulse to spoil the success of the other.

Conclusion: the envious attack as a weapon to maintain rank order, and the hidden shame behind the envious attack

Envy is a powerful and destructive force in organisational life. The first section of this chapter considered the envious attack in the context of the maintenance of organisational status, utilised as a weapon in the dynamics of dominance and submission. The envious attack can serve to protect and preserve rank order, destroying creative endeavours that are deemed to bypass organisational hierarchy. Envy can paralyse whole social systems and cause pain and suffering in individuals. It behoves us working with organisations to make as much sense as we can of this dynamic—a destructive force feared since the origin of our species. I am not asserting that envy is always present in the dynamic behind an organisational attack; however, the envious attack is frequently used to maintain hierarchical ranking and needs to be understood in that context.

In addition to Stein's rationale for the paucity of work on envy in organisational life (it does not fit our usual paradigm of organisational defences against anxiety), I believe that another reason for the relative absence of exploration of envy in social systems is associated with the great sense of shame, albeit largely unconscious, around the manifestation of envy (both in the envious attacker and in the attacked) and the second part of this chapter explored this sense of individual and group shame and discomfort which serves to keep the issue relatively unexplored. Those who are subject to envious feelings cannot allow themselves to know that they are envious. Envy is so deeply shameful that exposure is profoundly humiliating and the envious person will go to any lengths to deny having these feelings. Indeed, the denial is often so profound that these envious feelings are not allowed to emerge into the conscious thinking of the envious person. Lansky (2008) notes, "being exposed as envious poses, in and of itself, the danger of mortifying shame; often the shame accompanying exposure of the self as envious, is unbearable" (p. 31).

An important development in our understanding of envy has been provided by the recent psychoanalytic work that highlights the hidden shame buried in the envious attack. Building on the perspective provided by this work, I believe that we can conceptualise the envious attack as a defence against the experience of shame and perceived deficit, and that this understanding can enlarge our understanding of the manifestation of envy in organisational life.

References

Ambrose, A. (1989). Key concepts of the transitional approach to managing change. In: L. Klein (Ed.), *Working with Organisations* (pp. 143–160). London: Kestrel.

Britton, R. (2008). He thinks himself impaired: the pathologically envious personality. In: P. Roth & A. Lemma (Eds.), *Envy and Gratitude Revisited* (pp. 124–136). London: Karnac.

Broucek, F. J. (1991). *Shame and the Self.* New York: Guilford

Daum, M. (2002). Dangerous liaisons: projective identification, basic assumption envy and the conflict between love and hate in the relationship between two psychiatric teams, *Organisational and Social Dynamics*, 2: 120–138.

De Botton, A. (2004). *Status Anxiety*. London: Hamish Hamilton, Penguin.

Garland, C. (2006). Some are more equal than others: Oedipus, dominance hierarchies and the establishment: a psychoanalytic point of view.

Unpublished paper presented to the OPUS Conference, London, 18 November 2006.

Gladwell, M. (2008). *Outliers*. London: Allen Lane.

Halton, W. (2004). By what authority? Psychoanalytical reflections on creativity and change in relation to organizational life. In: C. Huffington, D. Armstrong, W. Halton, L. Hoyle, & J. Pooley (Eds.), *Working Below the Surface: The Emotional Life of Contemporary Organizations* (pp. 107–122). London: Karnac.

Jaques, E. (1955). Social systems as a defence against persecutory and depressive anxiety. In M. Klein, P. Heimann, and R. Money-Kyrle (Eds.), *New Directions in Psychoanalysis* (pp. 478–498). London: Tavistock.

Kane, M. (2008). But who can stand before envy? *Organisations & People, 15*(3): 96–103

Klein, M. (1957). *The Writings of Melanie Klein, Vol III, Envy and Gratitude and Other Works* London: Hogarth, 1975.

Lansky, M. (2008). Jealousy and envy in Othello: psychoanalytic reflections on the rivalrous emotions. In: L. Wurmser & H. Jarass (Eds.), *Jealousy and Envy: New Views about Two Powerful Feelings* (pp. 25–47). New York: Analytic Press

Lipman-Blumen, J. (2006). *The Allure of Toxic Leaders: Why We Follow Destructive Bosses and Corrupt Politicians – and How We Can Survive Them.* New York: Oxford University Press.

Maxfield, D., Grenny, J., Lavandero, R., & Groah, L. (2011). *The Silent Treatment: Why Safety Tools and Checklists Aren't Enough To Save Lives.* VitalSmarts, AORN & AACN, www.silenttreatmentstudy.com/silencekills/.

Menon, T., & Thompson, L. (2010). Envy at work. *Harvard Business Review,* April: 2–6.

Menzies, I. (1960). Social systems as a defence against anxiety. *Human Relations, 13*: 95–121.

Milgram, S. (1974). *Obedience to Authority: An Experimental View*. New York: Harper & Row.

Milton, J. (1975). *John Milton: Paradise Lost* (2nd edn), S. Elledge (Ed.). New York: Norton.

Morrison, A. (1997). *Shame: The Underside of Narcissism* (2nd edn). New York: Analytic Press.

Morrison, A., & Lansky, M. (2008). Shame and envy. In: L. Wurmser & H. Jarass (Eds.), *Jealousy and Envy: New Views about Two Powerful Feelings* (pp. 179–187). New York: Analytic Press.

Obholzer, A., & Roberts, V. (1994). *The Unconscious at Work: Individual and Organisational Stress in the Human Services*. London: Routledge.

Onions, C. (Ed.) (1970). *Oxford English Dictionary*. Oxford: Clarendon Press

Portillo, M. (2009). www.bbc.co.uk/programmes/b00kk4bz

Spillius, E. (1993). Varieties of envious experience. *International Journal of Psycho-Analysis, 74*: 1199–1212.

Stein, M. (1997). Envy and leadership. *European Journal of Work and Organizational Psychology, 6*: 453–463.

Stein, M. (2000). After Eden: envy and the defences against anxiety paradigm. *Human Relations, 53*: 193–211.

Stein, M. (2005). The Othello conundrum: the inner contagion of leadership. *Organization Studies, 26*: 1405–1419.

Steiner, J. (2011). *Seeing and Being Seen: Emerging from a Psychic Retreat*. London: Routledge.

Vidaillet, B. (2008). *Workplace Envy*. Basingstoke: Palgrave Macmillan.

Wilkinson, R., & Pickett, A. (2009). *The Spirit Level: Why Equality is Better for Everyone*. London: Allen Lane.

PART IV
MAKING SPACE TO GROW

CHAPTER TWELVE

The heart has its reasons: reflections on working with a relational supervision group

Susan Lendrum

"Le cœur a ses raisons que la raison ne connaît point"
["The heart has its reasons whereof reason knows not"]

(Pascal, 1662, p. 251)

Introduction

In 2007 I was asked to set up a psychodynamic supervision group for clinical psychologists in NHS Fife, who were interested in psychoanalytic ideas. When, nearly four years later, they decided to write an article about our work together and chose this well-known quote from Pascal as the title, I was touched (Pickles, 2012). I reflected, then, that the initially puzzling psychoanalytic ideas must now be sitting more comfortably alongside their years of experience of working in a more cognitive and less relational mode. In this chapter, I formulate some of my own thoughts and theoretical ideas and to try to illustrate these through the group's and my reflections on the supervision of the case study with which they had chosen to illustrate their paper.

The six psychologists who started this group were all very experienced clinicians who were working in either Older Adult Services or Adult Services, although some of the adult patients were very young, still in their late teens. Developmentally speaking, we were talking about a wide range of patients. The psychologists wanted help in working with patients either with whom they felt in some way stuck ("CBT isn't working") or who were constantly being re-referred to the psychological services, or both. They hoped that psychoanalytic ideas about the unconscious, particularly those relating to their relationships with their patients, would help them to understand more about why they might be getting stuck.

We agreed to work once a month for two-and-a-quarter hours, in an open and thoughtful supervisory group where we could share and reflect together, with a possibility of discussing theoretical issues as they might emerge. We further agreed that certain aspects of the patient's world, often unconscious, might well be reflected in the experience of the group members when the patient was presented. In order to allow these deeper processes to emerge and be thought about psychodynamically, about fifty-five to sixty minutes would be allocated to each case, and that, therefore, two presentations per session would be appropriate. I also insisted on strict confidentiality within the group itself and on a commitment to try to explore each person's own feelings as well as their thoughts. Such feelings and thoughts might be evoked by the patient presented, by other group members, or by myself, and I maintained that they were all potentially of informational value.

Having agreed this rather loose contract for working, I think the group was initially somewhat sceptical about my insistence not only on this longer working time than was normal for them, but also on the confidentiality rules and the notion of "feeling exploration". All the group members said they were really interested in the centrality of the patient–therapist relationship, but they seemed somewhat apprehensive about how to use such phenomena as transference and countertransference to enhance their understanding of the patient.

They were also apprehensive about how to work with therapeutic endings, which, initially, often seemed to disappear under the weight of the immediate problem. Many of the patients presented were re-referrals, suggesting that satisfactory endings might not have been achieved. I was interested to see whether learning to work with feelings in the room would lead them to become more confident in their relationships with their patients, with one another, and with myself, and would help them make more satisfactory endings.

My basic aim was to try to understand what was being evoked in group members and in the group process itself by the presentation of the patient and, through this, to understand more about the struggles in the patient–therapist relationship. My very firm boundaries, however odd they initially appeared to the group, are part of the analytic frame and seemed fairly quickly to offer a sense of containment. The informational value of the participants' feelings and perceptions in response to the material presented was gradually able to emerge and be thought about. Soon, a sense of free-floating attention began to develop, alongside a growing focus on the experiences and relationships in the supervision room. This enabled the group to reflect on, and then think about, unconscious processes that might be influencing the patient–therapist relationship. This was very new territory for some group members, who were, understandably, hesitant about the whole business, but, gradually, as insight about their own particular patients began to help them in their work, they recognised the value of their own feelings and perceptions for others' work as well as their own. They really began to engage in the work of the group. I quote here from their recently published article to give a sense of their understanding of emotional responses three years further on:

> Of course, neither person (therapist and patient) can always be fully aware of what factors are influencing emotional responses to each other and the therapist's capacity to form a useful relationship with any given individual. . . . Sometimes, as a result, the therapist might think that they are aware of what their motivation for a particular response has been or that the feelings elicited in them by a patient have been understood, but be mistaken. In all these various ways we may fail to develop the necessary objectivity that is some part of the role we occupy as therapists. . . .
>
> It is for these and other reasons, that all therapies recognise the need for supervision, and that clinical psychologists have emphasised the importance of reflective practice; one point of the latter being to develop both self-awareness and objectivity. (Pickles, 2012, pp. 29–30)

I think I would understand their use of the word "objectivity" to mean not only the capacity to reflect on and think about the experience of being with the patient, but also to be able to think about such phenomena as potential medical conditions or neuropsychological assessment.

It seems to me that there were a number of reasons for the group deciding to write the article. First, they were keen to make this insight more available to other psychologists. Further, given that there has also been an increasing interest within cognitive–behavioural therapy approaches in the nature and quality of the therapeutic relationship and in the notions of reflective practice and self-evaluation, they also wanted to write about something they had actually experienced and which seemed to fit within this more general psychological rubric (Fleming & Steen, 2004).

I shall use the case they chose, together with their reflections, to illustrate how their understanding developed, and I shall quote from their account of their experience of the group supervisory experience.

Theoretical ideas

My theoretical frame for this supervisory work draws heavily on contemporary relational theory which I shall now outline very briefly, before saying something about how it relates to relational supervision and to relational group supervision, sometimes called "case conferencing" (Frawley-O'Dea & Sarnat, 2001).

There are two main strands to the origins of relational supervision: one is the development of psychoanalytic supervision from its inception in Freud's Wednesday night meetings in the Berggasse where Freud lived and practised in Vienna, and the other is the development of relational psychoanalysis, mainly in the USA, but drawing from a loose group of psychoanalysts known as the Independents in the UK, including Fairbairn, a Scottish psychoanalyst. It is here that I would like to begin.

Relational psychoanalysis

Relational psychoanalysis emerged in the 1980s as an attempt to integrate the American interpersonal psychoanalysis's emphasis on the interpersonal interactions in the therapeutic relationship with British object relations theories about the psychological importance of internalised relationships with other people. Like Fairbairn (1943) before them in the Independent tradition, relational theorists, Mitchell (1988), and Aron (1996), supported by the infant research of the past forty years (Stern, 1985; Trevarthen, 1990), see human beings as relationship seeking from birth. Relational analysts generally think that psychotherapy works best when the therapist focuses on both the process of facilitating insight and enabling the therapeutic relationship itself to grow and change and be reflected upon. They hope, thus, to help patients break out of the repetitive destructive patterns of relating to others, internalised from early experiences/relationships, that are at the root of most current psychological problems. Further, they place great emphasis on the mutual construction of meaning in the therapeutic relationship. If both the healthy mind and psychopathological problems are structured by, and mediated through, relationship, then a relational therapy will naturally focus on the vicissitudes of the therapeutic relationship and their meanings. From a postmodern point of view, this relationship is co-constructed and intersubjective, with meanings emerging out of the experience of both participants rather than holding to absolute truths given by an expert. Power and authority are understood to be distributed between two people, one of whom is acknowledged as having greater specialised knowledge and experience, but between whom specific technique, knowledge about the shared experiences in the consulting room together with thoughts about how to apply this knowledge in the therapy with the patient, are mutually derived and negotiated within a relational matrix.

The development of relational supervision

Similarly, supervision has also changed and developed since the Wednesday evening case discussions in the Berggasse. There is an apocryphal tale that Freud, the absolute authority, would tend to insist on his own version of the truth about a certain case. Indeed, the model of psychoanalysis created in Vienna, which developed into the classical psychoanalytic model, particularly in the USA, was a hierarchical one—the senior analyst was the source of knowledge and truth which was to be passed down to the patient. The supervision model that developed in this context was consistent with the classical model in its hierarchical structure and orientation. A supervisee, however bright and creative, was to receive rather than co-construct what emerged into the supervisory work. The supervisor was seen as the natural, objective observer of both the supervisee and the case material. Any discontent or alternative view from the supervisee was regarded in much the same way as resistance in a patient: to be ironed out. The old belief in supervision was that it was a natural outgrowth of career development and that it sufficed to do unto others what was done unto oneself.

One could say that the supervisee was being moulded, however unwittingly, into the shape of both the supervisor and the supervisor's use of authority. This tended to perpetuate the classic hierarchical pattern and might partly explain the cultural lag whereby the development in psychoanalytic supervision still trails some way behind developments in psychoanalysis itself.

Quite early in the history of psychoanalysis, the Hungarian analyst, Ferenczi, who later broke with Freud, presaged a more relational way of thinking about the therapeutic relationship when, in his clinical diary, he wrote about how the patient would, in reality, be very alert to changes in the analyst, however subtle, in response to what the patient actually brought. Ferenczi, here, seems keenly aware of the co-constructed nature of the relationship, but thought of it as symmetric, each being equally and similarly influenced by the other. His interest in the mutuality of interaction did bequeath us another way of thinking about analysis, even though at times it was considered too extreme and monocular to be of much practical therapeutic use (Ferenczi & Rank, 1924).

Ferenczi's thinking about power, authority, and the nature of knowledge or truth did, however, influence his colleague, Michael Balint, whom he supervised in Budapest. Balint, who later came to London, was able to value the idea of mutuality, but was also able to recognise the *asymmetry* in both therapy and supervision, which was to become an important part of contemporary understanding of supervisory effectiveness. His work with groups of doctors in London in the 1960s, described as "teaching about healing in a healing environment", began the tradition of what became known as "Balint Groups" and introduced the notion that the *experience* of learning was part of the learning itself (Balint, 1961).

In the early days of psychoanalytic training, there were two training institutes: Freud and his follower Karl Abraham in Berlin, on the one hand, and Ferenczi and his associates in Budapest, on the other. Berlin's training programme insisted that the analysand's therapist should be a different person from her supervisor because the latter would be part of the assessment of training, whereas the training analyst could offer a safer space to explore any problems arising in the analysand evoked by the training patient. These problems were seen to be due to as yet unanalysed parts of the trainee. Once fully analysed, any countertransference reactions in the trainee would be minimal enough not to get in the way of the therapy. Supervision, then, could be entirely didactic and focus exclusively on the patient and the correct way to interpret the patient's problems, untouched by any experience the trainee might have noticed in herself. In Budapest, on the other hand, it was thought that the analysand's therapist, who knew the trainee best, would be more likely to be helpful in the initial stages of development as a trainee analyst, in that they would be better placed to help her or him understand the impact of their own personal reactions to the patient and to distinguish these feelings from those evoked by the patient's transference.

There was, as one can imagine, much discussion about these different ways of training, but in the end Berlin "won" and, indeed, psychoanalytic training is still largely modelled on that tripartite system of theoretical training, didactic supervision, and personal analysis. The Hungarian training system, although it fell into disrepute on the international psychoanalytic front, nevertheless achieved some recognition again once psychoanalysis began to recognise the value of countertransference more generally.

When the Kleinian psychoanalyst, Heimann, wrote a paper (1950) about the possible value of countertransference in analysis itself, it was part of a clearer recognition that through an exploration, rather than a discounting, of countertransference, underlying internal object relations could be better understood. Given the cultural lag referred to above, it took several more years for the importance of countertransference in supervision to be recognised in the famous paper by Searles (1995), "The informational value of the supervisor's emotional experiences". Searles recounts how he came to understand that material from the patient, unconsciously presented to the therapist and out of the therapist's awareness, might be re-presented or reflected in the supervisory session. A sensitive supervisor might be able to pick up this barely conscious message, partly because of her greater experience and partly because she is not exposed directly to what might be difficult or disturbing material brought into the therapy session. Further, Doehrman (1976) observed that this reflective process not only passed from patient up to supervisor, but also passed back down again if not recognised and explored. When a supervisor can pick up and work with her understanding, then the therapist can bring this awareness to her or his work. If not, then unconscious material can continue to be reflected up and down the supervisory system, causing havoc at all levels. This reflective, or parallel, process, when brought into awareness, can be enormously helpful in understanding the complexities brought to supervision, both group and individual.

These developments helped supervision move from a totally patient-focused activity, initially, to a focus on the development of the supervisee and then towards a reflection on the various processes at work between patient and analyst and between analyst and supervisor. However, questions about authority and truth from the old classical method and questions of mutuality and (a)symmetry in supervision still remained.

Current relational supervision: authority, mutuality, asymmetry and ethics.

Postmodern approaches to supervision include descriptions of it as relational, intersubjective, or contemporary, and these stances are thought to offer an alternative to more traditional approaches.

The supervisor's authority now has to be earned or constituted not so much by what she knows (although that is also important), but by how she works with the processes experienced and understood in the supervisory relationship. The focus is no longer exclusively on the specific nature of the patient's troubles "out there", it is now also enriched by how these troubles influence the various processes in the room. It is also focused on how the resources of all three members of the supervisory triad can be garnered towards really understanding the patient and helping her or him, and perhaps also the therapist and even the supervisor, to change.

This style of working requires that supervisors consider how they view their authority from a postmodern perspective. Postmodernism is more of a trend than a separate orientation. It has relevance for how therapy is developed, practised, and evaluated, reflecting the way people nowadays understand knowledge or truth, including knowledge about psychological health and therapy. It emphasises the importance of pluralism and diversity along with the need for dialogue in both therapy and supervision.

Within analysis itself, therapists are faced with the difficult task of attempting to become an expert on the patient's mind when that mind is viewed as ambiguous and amenable to multiple interpretations rather than "prefigured and distinct" (Mitchell, 1997). Therapist and patient may jointly arrive at an interpretation of what is going on, but this is by no means the final, or necessarily the best, interpretation. If it holds true that the authority of the therapist and, therefore, by implication, the supervisor can no longer rest on their role as expert on the patient's mind, how is the supervisor to work skilfully in negotiating possible meanings as well as holding on to her or his own ultimate legitimate authority?

Nowadays, working in a postmodern paradigm like this, the therapist finds herself in a world of multiple meanings rather than absolute truths, no longer able to assert what is true or how things should be done without considering alternatives introduced by the patient. Similarly, the supervisor needs to be aware of alternative meanings brought by both supervisee and patient. The supervisee is then confronted by a position of having to negotiate with both patient and supervisor about how she, herself, will work with the patient. This concept of negotiation is a central factor in the supervisory relationship, and each person will have some, although not necessarily equal, authority in deciding what is true and what is best practice for this patient at this time.

There are, indeed, limits to what can or should be open to negotiation. Any negotiation needs to take into account the differing interests of all parties (patient, supervisee, and supervisor), and sometimes these processes are not reconcilable. Every supervisor has core beliefs, which she must be willing to uphold, using her authority creatively, or else she sacrifices her integrity.

The supervisor has to take account of the stage of development of the supervisee in relation to the use of negotiation and the use of her authority. She also has to know when to stay with a sense of not knowing in order to allow a deeper understanding to be achieved in the end. The supervisor's ability to tolerate ambiguity and to work with the supervisee's point of view when different from the supervisor's assists a transformation of the power dynamic within the relationship that can lead to a more creative space for psychological thinking. Here, the supervisor has chosen to encourage the empowerment of the supervisee rather than using her own power to impress, intimidate, coerce, or instruct the supervisee.

Yet, within this relational view of the supervisory relationship, there is clearly a tension between the areas of mutuality and asymmetry. Just as with parent and child mutuality, the supervisory mutuality contains important differences in the degree and nature of influence which one participant exerts upon the other, as well as important differences in their roles, functions, and responsibilities. The supervisor clearly carries the responsibility for a number of areas: the supervisory frame, defining and maintaining boundaries, ethical considerations, and the psychodynamic focus of the work. She also takes responsibility for assessing the learning needs of her supervisee and adjusting her approach towards meeting these. Further, she also stands up for her own values and beliefs, while also taking responsibility for negotiating these when the dyad is in conflict and is prepared for the possibility that some disagreements are not resolvable. She must acknowledge, both to herself and to her supervisee, the power they each hold in relation to teaching and evaluation. Lack of acknowledgement of the power differential between them can result in serious consequences, as the supervisee might find it almost impossible to feel free enough to address these important differentials.

Supervisors are constantly faced with the challenge of finding ways to use their power and authority so that they are experienced by the supervisee as empowering, effective, and liberating, rather than unproductive, oppressive, and demotivating.

Group supervision

A further strand in this thinking is the use of relational supervision in groups. The triangular nature of supervision with individuals, with its three connected poles of patient, therapist, and supervisor, is similar to the triangular structures within group supervision, although the number of supervisees is clearly greater and there may be many more patients metaphorically in the room. Yet, there are also significant differences for members as well as for the group supervisor. She has the potential to harness the supervisory capacities within the group members, to create a learning atmosphere in which all the richness of the multiplicity of responses, images, and thoughts of the different supervisees can be brought into a free-flowing associative process to understand deeper levels of the therapy presented. Above all, she can enable the group to stay focused on task and become a more functional "work-group" (Bion, 1961). She may use her group knowledge and experience to help the group to work through the more destructive states of mind, into which groups can fall, which oppose and disrupt the more constructive, creative, reflective, and thoughtful processes.

She might also notice when processes unconsciously presented and experienced in the group could be reflecting aspects of the case which might have been difficult for the therapist to perceive or recognise when presenting, but which, when understood by the group, can be harnessed for learning in the group. Further, she should be in a position to engender a process of negotiation through which the group struggles to construct a more or less single understanding from the myriad of perceptions expressed in response to the case.

Although the supervisor might be more clinically experienced than group members, there is, nevertheless, a mutuality of the actual experience of the patient presented in the room. In the old days of didactic supervision, with the focus entirely on the patient's problems, or psychopathology, the authority would have rested with the group supervisor and there might be little awareness of group processes or the way they reflected the patient's inner world. In our postmodern times, however, with authority more equally shared, different aspects of the "truth" may be held by different members. This experiential method in a group allows a holding and valuing of different "truths" in which meanings can emerge, a more thoughtful truth be negotiated, and this understanding used to create interpretations more in tune with the patient's inner world.

The case

From the theoretical material above, it will be clear that my expectation of a group who had worked this way for some time would be that they would feel contained enough to focus on affective states and would use the group not only to reflect on their feelings in order to help their colleague in her work, but also to develop professionally themselves from the experience.

Case presentation

The presenting supervisee described in detail someone we might call a "heart sink" patient. This fifty-nine-year-old, rather unkempt academic had recently retired to look after his wife, who had serious health problems. But, however hard the therapist tried to engage him in reflections on himself or his childhood, she described how he constantly deflected her with tales of the inadequacy of the various services offered and of the dramatic events provoked by his wife's illness. Although he was apparently able to talk of fears that something would happen to his wife, she could get no sense of the relationship between them. She reflected then that there were probably significant gains for him from being his wife's carer, such as that he would not need now to socialise, to travel far from home, or to think too much about himself. She also described how he told her of graphs he was making of his wife's illness patterns and of the various approaches he had been offered. She went on to say that she had brought him to the group partly because of her "heart sink" reaction, but also with a hope that a different approach might just *not* repeat the relatively ineffectual previous interventions. She was clearly reflecting on her own experience of him and hoping to make sense of it in terms of some, as yet, hidden story.

In the following section, I describe my understanding of the group responses to the patient as presented. As they reflected further, they began to draw some tentative hypotheses about the patient's hidden struggles and possible therapeutic needs.

Responses, reflections, and progress

I remember being struck at the time by the lack of affect in this experienced therapist's initial presentation and the sense of pervasive anxiety that this case appeared to evoke in her. Normally, it would be my intention to direct my focus on to the group's reaction to the patient presented, but here I was struck by my own sense of disconnection from the patient and, indeed, exclusion from the group. I was, therefore, not at all surprised to observe that the group initially struggled to feel anything at all in relation to the patient. We all tried to stay with this feelinglessness for a while in order to understand it, uncomfortable as it was. Gradually, some members began to express irritation with the patient's apparently defensive manoeuvre of talking only about his wife and her complaints against the NHS. Then, very quietly, one of the women members tentatively expressed a sense of sadness. This seemed to change the dynamic in the group, and another woman then wondered about fear and loneliness. The men, however, continued their disconnected irritability. I wondered with the group about this interesting phenomenon that the men seemed stuck with their irritability while the women *seemed* to be discovering gentleness. This was not a usual pattern for this group, so it seemed significant, but I feared that the group might foreclose on their thinking at this point and encouraged them to try to stay open to exploration. The group then became more thoughtful and began to wonder whether this might indeed reflect a pattern in the patient's early life. Whether or not this turned out to be the case for this patient, it did bring the question of early connections into the room and the group was then able to think about the patient's huge defences (the graphs, the refusal to speak about himself, the attack on the services provided). We could then begin to see the possibility that unconscious terror of recognising an inner sadness or vulnerability might well have made intimacy terrifying to him. His defensive behaviour in the sessions became understandable. The image of the patient in the room had moved from a cardboard cut-out figure to a human who had suffered loss and, we thought, probably deep humiliation and shame. The presenter, who had been fairly quiet during the male–female discussion, came in with relief, saying she felt much more engaged and said that she had the hunch that he might well have been humiliated and she wanted help with a formulation to try to re-engage with her patient.

Once the group could begin to think psychologically about this man, there was no stopping the members and the ideas flowed thick and fast! It felt like a full-blown psychological feast and, at this point, as I remember it, the group was tempted into wide ranging theoretical ruminations, analysing the patient. Yet, my anxiety was mounting. The time was moving on in the session and it seemed to me that this man could only take in very small and clear psychological bites. I thought that the therapist might need help in formulating some very basic, digestible morsel of interpretation that her patient would be able to take in and use in order to engage. I felt like the bad fairy at the feast, but it seemed really important to me to be very firm with the group in stopping the free-floating ideas about the patient and focusing on the very essence of the underlying fears about relationship, the possible origin of these fears, and the ways he had necessarily protected himself, which were no longer useful to him. We might then be able to come up with a proposal for a therapeutic engagement, which he would be free to engage with or not. I had to engage with an energetic authority to keep the group to task. This patient had managed to get himself consistently abandoned by psychological services, thus, presumably, repeating some rejection, as yet unexplored, from his early experiences. It seemed to me that there was an ethical imperative to use the full skills of the group to help the therapist really engage with this man, but it was difficult. I feared the group members were in danger of going off on their own psychological cleverness, perhaps defending themselves against the cold isolation of the patient, perhaps, in turn, repeating some kind of intellectual defence against the pain of abandonment. However, there was no further time to await the development of process here. Therefore, I chose to use my authority to suggest to the group that they stop the intellectual discussion of the patient and focus very firmly on the therapist's needs for something concrete to take to her relationship with the patient. I needed to be very clear and focused in guiding the group's thinking but, in the event, the therapist was able to go away with a much clearer idea of how she might be with her patient, less frightened by his fear and more engaged and engaging with his underlying vulnerability. She seemed to know what she might say to him.

When she saw him again, she did indeed manage to hold on to the work of the group and had offered him her formulation of underlying pain, together with the option of actually working in therapy. He responded well to this and she then gave us a moving account of the narrative story of his life, which he had begun to reveal: his lost parents, lost family, and the emotional tenor of his family home, which constituted the emotional background to his isolated, dry, intellectual, mathematical career. The group members were touched by the emotional impact she had been able to achieve and wanted to reflect upon this experience in relation to some of their own patients.

Thinking about the processes in the group

This kind of reflecting in the group had clearly enabled the participants to think about the informational value of the initial impact of the case description on their own feelings. Subsequently, having noticed the different gender responses, they were able to make a tentative hypothesis about the patient's early years, which, whether or not it reflected his actual experience or was a random phenomenon, led them into thinking about early experiences of longing and loss which, unconsciously presented in the first therapeutic encounter and firmly defended against, had rendered a therapeutic connection with the therapist extremely difficult. The therapist then unconsciously transferred this disconnection into the supervision group. Once the group was able to bear the discomfort of the patient's defensive disconnection, the members were then able to connect up themselves and become sensitive to the hidden vulnerabilities of the patient. We could then think about a possible formulation in terms of relationship.

However, when the group went into their wide ranging theoretical ruminations, analysing the patient, I had an important task; to nudge the group towards formulating and reformulating insights about the patient–therapist relationship in clear and simple words which could be offered by the therapist before the end of the session and understood by the patient. The participants began to see the need to offer something of a very basic psychological nature in order to make sense to this apparently non-psychologically minded person and to cut through, or work round, his intellectual defences. The therapist, too, had to feel confident about the formulation and its use, so there was quite a bit of co-constructing and negotiation in the group until she felt comfortable enough with the ideas and their communication. They had to be brought back to the *therapy relationship itself.*

In the event, the therapist seems to have brought a calm, confident clarity and purpose to the therapy session after the supervision session, which enabled the patient, after initial hesitation, to engage with her and to commit to a much clearer and contracted therapeutic endeavour. Once the initial resistance to engaging had been overcome, she seems to have enabled a deeper and more functional relationship to develop between them. From her account, the patient was very touched by this deeper understanding and seems to have been able to attach more securely to her and, thus, begin to grieve earlier losses, strengthening him, one hopes, against the feared losses ahead. It has also, apparently, enabled the married couple to be more open with one another, thus helping them face the future in a more genuinely co-operative and collaborative way.

This particular patient had demonstrated very clearly in his presentation how difficult it was for him to begin to relate in a more open way to another person. He had effectively shut his therapist out. The group, in the end, enabled the therapeutic couple to become "unstuck" in their relationship and create a more genuine *beginning* to a potentially authentic therapy. Returning to this case in another group session also gave the group, I think, a sense of having been involved in a useful, collaborative venture.

Conclusion

Group learning

It is almost uncanny how often there is an extraordinary pull towards the patient in supervision. The group, or, indeed, the individual supervisory dyad, can get caught up in clever, intellectual analysing of the patient, rather than reflecting on the relational processes in the room, which can throw light on the deeper relational processes affecting the therapy. As illustrated in the case study reflections, the group seemed pulled towards a kind of analysing of the patient, which, intellectually fascinating as it might have been to pursue, was taking us away from the therapeutic relationship. What the supervision seemed to be replaying was the very avoidance of relational elements in the room through the intellectual expositions, just like the patient and the therapist. This intellectual play was very seductive, for me, as it had been for the therapist, and I had to summon considerable energy to pull the focus back, at this point, to what was happening in the room. Once the group could see the powerful effect of this parallel process, they were able to make space to reflect with the therapist on what had been happening in the therapeutic encounter and see what the patient's needs were in reality, and how they were being firmly denied. In such a case, it is often the uncomfortable countertransference feelings evoked in the group that are avoided, or it might be the countertransference experiences in the supervisor which are defended against. Other difficult group processes may also be avoided through the seductive lure of analysing the patient. But, of course, the patient is the very reason we are there and we need to return to the patient at many stages in the process of supervision. The fascinating irony is, however, that by moving from the patient's problem to the actual experiences within the supervisory relationships, we can often discover useful therapeutic information about the patient's inner world, which he will be seeking to defend against.

As this group's initial scepticism and apprehension about the boundaried psychoanalytic method gradually gave way to trust in me and in the group experiences, they grew in understanding and perception of the way in which affective experience is at the heart of the work. They can now work with the "relationships in the room" and recognise the triangular nature of supervision as well as the interpenetration of unconscious processes in both sets of relationships. They continue to get caught up with, and then become able to reflect on, the information provided by their experiences with all the patients they present. Thus, their initial hope that they would come, through a greater appreciation of the unconscious, to understand more about their relationships with their patients and the ways in which loss and bereavement can affect those relationships in myriad ways, seems to have been fulfilled.

In the introduction, I mentioned the group's early difficulties in achieving satisfactory therapeutic endings, resulting in the many re-referrals within the service. It seemed as if the painful experiences of loss in both patient and therapist had to be hidden and driven underground. The therapists were certainly being touched by this pain, but were thinking either that they should not be touched, or they were able to recognise the feeling being evoked, but were deeply unsure what to do with it.

As the work developed, they became more trusting and respectful of their own feelings in their experiences with their patients, and so the denial of loss in the patients became more real for them. There was a growing sense that these feelings, so wondrously expressed in music and poetry, were also part of their very own human experience and entirely normal for human beings. It often happens that the non-presenting members of the group are able to pick up extremely painful feelings of loss and despair which were, perhaps, too painful for the presenting therapist to bear on his or her own. Having been able to reflect on this in the group, it has then been possible to explore ever more painful areas in the therapy, leading eventually to stronger relationships and more effective therapeutic endings. Recognising, articulating, and having a humane empathy for the painful experiences of others is surely an important part of the therapeutic endeavour. The psychoanalytic supervision group became a place to explore and understand this endeavour. I have been most moved by the courage of this group in moving into these difficult places. Their training, in general, had taught them to give less weight to feelings and to deliver the therapy within the boundaries set by the scientific evidence that supports it. The pressure from within the system to think concretely and to seek immediate, measurable results has influenced their work, and their learning, therefore, has tended to be less concerned with feelings and relationships and more about the patient as an object of treatment. Their own feelings were regarded as a hindrance and as vulnerabilities rather than tools of interpretation. Resisting this pressure and making space both in supervision and in therapy has been hugely challenging. They have come a long way.

My learning

My experience of reading what the group had written about their learning experience in the group gave me food for thought. I was surprised at how much psychoanalytic thinking they appeared to have intellectually internalised and wondered whether my surprise represents the enormous difficulty of translating theory into practice, particularly when faced by the emotional despair of the patient presented so graphically in the room. The theory is known. It is often extraordinarily difficult to articulate it in practice. I need to remember this, again and again, in supervision. It was abundantly clear from their writing that they had learnt and experienced an enormous amount about the possible unconscious processes which were affecting their work. They had really taken on board not just the theory of parallel process, but could usually notice and work with the phenomena when they appeared and started to influence the processes in the group. They understood much more of how their reactions to patients could be thought about and reflected upon in the context of the therapeutic relationship as presented to the group. This could then be used, not just for insight, but also to enable changes in their relationships with patients. They do, indeed, seem to have got what they came for.

My supervisory position is privileged in two senses: on the one hand, as group supervisor, I am focused on the group and its process rather than on the replayed feelings from the therapeutic encounter (although I am not immune to those, as illustrated in the case presented) and, on the other hand, I have experienced many hours of supervisory and therapeutic practice which renders these experiences somehow "known" in a way that is still quite new for many in this group. This long experience enabled me to create a clear frame and confident contract which, in turn, enabled strong feelings from the therapy to be safely experienced and processed in the supervisory group so that the relational elements could be reflected upon and usefully used in the therapeutic encounter. In the supervisory space, the feelinglessness in the group's initial response was clearly a reflection of the patient's inner state, paralleling the process of his relational self, and the later over-intellectualisation in the group seemed, too, to parallel the defence of the patient against the threatening inner world of his feelings.

After review, the group decided they wanted to try to create for themselves a holding environment, to hold on to the feeling focus of the work, to be vigilant about reflecting on, rather than reacting to, experiences, and to be aware of the prevalence of the sad, angry, and painful feelings which so often go "underground". These are the very things, which a psychoanalytic approach can offer. It will be very interesting to see how this develops as the psychodynamic work is increasingly internalised.

References

Aron, L. (1996). *A Meeting of Minds*. Hillsdale, NJ: Analytic Press.

Balint, M. (1961). *The Doctor, his Patient and the Illness*. London: Pitman Medical.

Bion, W. R. (1961). *Experiences in Groups*. London: Tavistock.

Doehrman, M. (1976). Parallel processes in supervision and psychotherapy. *Bulletin of the Menninger Clinic, 40*: 9–104.

Fairbairn, W. R. D. (1943). The repression and return of bad objects. In: *Psychoanalytic Studies of the Personality* (pp. 59–81). London: Tavistock/Routledge.

Ferenczi, S., & Rank, O. (1924). *Die Entwicklungsziele der Psychoanalyse*. Wien: Internationaler Psychoanalytischer.

Fleming, I., & Steen, L. (2004). *Supervision and Clinical Psychology: Theory, Practice and Perspectives*. New York: Brunner-Routledge.

Frawley-O'Dea, M. G., & Sarnat, J. E. (2001). *The Supervisory Relationship: A Contemporary Psychodynamic Approach*. New York: Guilford Press.

Heimann, P. (1950). On countertransference. *International Journal of Psycho-Analysis, 31*: 81–84.

Mitchell, S. A. (1988). *Relational Concepts in Psychoanalysis: An Integration*. Cambridge MA: Harvard University Press.

Mitchell, S. A. (1997). *Influence and Autonomy in Psychoanalysis*. Hillsdale, NJ: Analytic Press.

Pascal, B. (1662). *Pensées*. Fragment 397, M. Le Guern Edition (1997). Paris: Gallimard, Folio Classique.

Pickles, C. (2012). What therapists feel: using subjective responses in group supervision to understand the therapeutic relationship in a presented case. *Clinical Psychology Forum, 229*: 29–34.

Searles, H. S. (1995). The informational value of the supervisor's emotional experiences. In: *Collected Papers on Schizophrenia and Related Subjects* (pp. 157–176). London: Hogarth Press.

Stern, D. (1985). *The Interpersonal World of the Infant*. New York: Basic Books.

Trevarthen, C. (1990). *Brain Circuits and Functions of the Mind*. Cambridge: Cambridge University Press.

CHAPTER THIRTEEN

Thinking under fire: the experience of staff at the front line of mental health services

Grant Wilkie

Introduction

I am a psychiatrist working in the NHS in the second decade of the twenty-first century. My official title is "Consultant Psychiatrist in Psychotherapy", a rather awkwardly constructed title, but perhaps an apt term to describe the awkward position of someone whose training leads him to sit on the cusp between psychoanalysis and psychiatry. As part of my work, I supervise trainee doctors who are new to psychiatry. I am interested in transitional processes, and how these can either lead to the development of the self, with growth and increasing maturity, or become stuck, leading to a regression or restriction of the self's full potential. I am particularly interested in the way that the environment can either support or hinder this period of internal growth.

It has always seemed to me that much of the work of a psychiatrist and other mental health workers is to do with transition. Clinically, our patients present at points in their life where they are struggling to make a particular life transition. Examples might include the late adolescent trying to establish an identity; the mother who presents with postnatal depression, for whatever reason unable to make the transition to parenthood, stuck in a sort of no-man's land, reluctant to move forwards, but unable to return to the previous life; the career-driven woman, or the self-made man, who might have achieved great narcissistic rewards through the work sphere, but who collapse or might even have what might be called a nervous breakdown when their official working life comes to an end; or the couple whose relationship splinters and fragments in the face of a reality that perhaps nobody should have to face—the death of a child.

Psychiatrists need to understand the ways in which transitional processes affect people in the process of change, as in the examples above. They need to understand the transitional impact on their patients when they move from one form of care to another, say, for example, from the community to an in-patient setting. They also need to understand and be able to manage the impact of transition on themselves and other team members, when established ways of working are challenged and replaced with new organisational procedures and structures.

In educational terms, most would agree that a professional training involves more than the simple acquisition of knowledge and skills. It should go further, assisting the development of a professional maturity, enabling the individual practitioner to grow into their new professional skin. In a previous paper, my colleague, Derek Raffaelli, and I focused on the transition that senior trainees in psychiatry make when they take on the consultant role (Wilkie & Raffaelli, 2005). We argued that young consultants' sense of themselves at work, their identity-in-role, is determined in part by the way they are defined or allowed to be by their organisation, in part by the way their role is shaped often at an unconscious level by the teams they work in, and, of course, crucially, by what they bring of themselves to the role.

In the process of making this transition, we argued that there would be an inevitable period of unease, enhanced vulnerability, and, at times, a defensive rigidity with a measure of identity confusion. Organisational knowledge, often implicit in the clinical teams and management structures, can assist this process, as can the passage of time. However, we felt that for these new consultants, the opportunity to talk about their experience in a peer group (the Transition Group), and the opportunity to learn from each other's experience, was crucial in helping them to develop a robust professional identity.

In this chapter, I examine another period of transition that occurs at the start of training when young psychiatrists are moving from being general medical doctors to becoming psychiatrists. I am particularly interested in understanding how they develop the new ways of thinking about clinical matters that they need in order to take on this role, and in a particular education structure—the Balint group—which is built into their training in order to help them do this. I show how psychoanalytic thinking and practice can contribute to this process and also explore its relevance to understanding the organisational contexts of mental health services more generally.

First of all, however, I want to say something about the sort of patients and the problems they present to the trainee psychiatrists who are in the throes of the transitional processes previously described. Therefore, I begin by presenting a fairly detailed example from my own clinical work to demonstrate the way in which mental illness can fragment self-experience, and, through projective processes, locate (as it were) unwanted aspects of the self in the minds of other people. In this example, it is the minds of other family members that become caught up in the projective processes, but, as the chapter develops, I look at the impact of these projections on the minds of psychiatric trainees and the way that reflective groups, such as the Balint group described, can help mental health staff to reflect on and process their experience. Finally, I use these doctors' experiences to think more broadly about the impact of caring for the mentally unwell, and, in particular, the ways that psychotic thinking can impinge on the collective organisational mind of the mental health services, whose task it is to contain and understand these disturbed states of mind.

The patients

Patients often present to psychiatrists at a point when their ability to think has been overwhelmed. They have literally "lost their mind", or, at least, one could say that the part of their mind that can make links and contain extreme emotion has been short-circuited. In place of a mind that can think things through, they resort to more primitive devices so that experience becomes fragmented, unwanted mental contents are evacuated into other minds, and mental events (feelings, beliefs, desires) are converted into physical objects or somatic events, as in the example below.

Vignette 1: electric shock treatment

A patient of mine, a young man in his early twenties, who came from a large family, first presented to psychiatric services in late adolescence with an acute psychotic breakdown. This followed a period when his father had been seriously ill. His psychosis took the form of voices "catching him" unawares and accusing him of being gay. The patient, whom I will call "M", responded well to medication. He subsequently left home and went abroad to study languages. He remained free from psychotic symptoms and managed to pass his degree, although he remained socially isolated with few friends, and, it seemed, no drive or passion for life.

Unable to find a job, he returned home with his "tail between his legs". Fairly quickly, things fell apart again, and, following an incident in which he attacked his father, he was re-referred to the psychiatric services. This time, there was some doubt in the psychiatrist's mind as to whether this was a further episode of psychosis or whether his behaviour was a reaction to being back home, and without a job. I was asked to see the family as a unit, and I also saw M on his own.

M is a tall, lanky, young man whose body language and diction conveyed a sense of awkward restlessness. His clothes sense struck me as stylish, bordering on the bizarre. Initially, he blamed his aggressive outbursts on his parents, who, he claimed, were "never off his back" and left him "no space to breathe". He also complained of what he called "electric shocks", down one side of his body. He had been referred to a neurologist and a CAT scan of his brain was reported as normal.

It emerged, in the course of the sessions with his family, that his shocks only came on when his mother was in the same room as him and, further, he accused her of laughing about him in a contemptuous way. He also accused his father of behaving like a woman. The apparent confusion about sexuality and closeness seemed to connect to the time when he had first become acutely unwell as a teenager. At that time, and in a confused and terrified state of mind, his mother told me he could only get to sleep if he shared her bed. M was extremely embarrassed when his mother talked about this and felt that she was deliberately trying to humiliate him.

When seen on his own, M's thinking seemed to clear and he described feeling less "fuzzy". In the presence of his family he seemed quite different—isolated and often appearing to be quite out of touch with what was being discussed. He would laugh inappropriately, as if at some private joke, or would suddenly come out with a comment that appeared totally unrelated to what was being discussed. To my mind, it was as if the family's thinking mind had been attacked and M's "thought disorder" was being played out in the context of his family.

The fact that this young man's first episode of psychosis occurred at the very time when he might have been separating from his family and finding his own identity is, I think, relevant. One can see the way in which painful emotional states of mind, including uncertainties about sexuality, ambivalence about closeness and separateness, and experiences of shame and humiliation, are displaced and then enacted in the network of family relationships. This example illustrates how psychosis can fragment the self, leaving bits of the patient's mind located in other family members. I think it also demonstrates how a relational problem, for example, his relationship with women in general and his mother in particular, can, under the influence of psychotic processing, be turned into a somatic event, in this case the electric shocks. In place of a relational problem that can be thought about there is a dislocated sensory experience.

Whatever the *cause* of this dysfunction (and this chapter is not about aetiology), I would argue that a primary goal for those trying to help is to provide a "container" in the form of a containing mind, which can assist the patients in recovering for themselves a mind that can learn to think again.

The doctors and the Balint group

Doctors new to psychiatry are involved in a steep learning curve, a developmental pathway, which involves the acquisition of knowledge and technical skills, but they are also involved in a transition and, in this process, need to establish a new professional identity. They will, of course, come to psychiatry with ideas about what it means to be a psychiatrist and they will meet other people, staff and patients, who will have ideas about what psychiatry is and is not. In the end, however, they need to sort this out for themselves if their identity at work is to be authentic and true to themselves. They need, for example, to make up their minds about what is and what is not mental illness, to decide what treatment involves and how they will be involved in this, and to learn to think on their feet. Crucially, I would argue that, in order to manage the patients and manage themselves, they need to learn, through experience, to recognise, trust, and make use of their own subjective experience in a way that their medical training might not have prepared them for. To a degree, this different way of professional thinking flies in the face of a scientific approach which champions objective knowledge only.

Perhaps in recognition of this, The Royal College of Psychiatrists (2004) has made it mandatory that all trainees new to psychiatry should participate in weekly groups where the focus is on the doctor–patient relationship, run along lines similar to the groups for general practitioners that Balint described in the 1960s (Balint, 1964; Salinsky, 2009). The focus of these groups is not so much on the "facts" of diagnosis and treatment, but on the interpersonal *relationship* between the doctor and his or her patient. In a group setting, trainees take it in turn to present a clinical encounter that has left them feeling uneasy, confused, disturbed, or stuck. Usually, what they bring is something about their experience of being on-call.

Being on call is perhaps one of the most stressful experiences that trainees new to psychiatry have to face. When everyone else has gone home, the on-call doctor inhabits the shadowy borderland that lies between community and hospital. Without doubt, the role of the on-call doctor in a psychiatric setting is a crucial one. Patients and their relatives are often presenting to mental health services for the first time and their interaction with the psychiatrist at the point of crisis plays a critical role in shaping the evolving narrative of what the problem is. At this point of crisis, patients and their relatives implicitly (and often literally) demand that something must be done. Yet, there is an equally powerful imperative, real or imagined, from senior colleagues, often lurking in the back of the trainee's mind, to avoid admission and at the same time keep the patient safe. Although a consultant is always available "on the end of a phone", in the dead of night, the trainee doctor is essentially alone in their decision making and without the support of technology (there is, as yet, no blood test for madness). In the end, they have to fall back on their own resources. Their task is to remain sane and to make sane decisions in the face of madness, "thinking under fire", as Bion (1982, p. 289) puts it.

The Balint group helps trainees to process their experience and the discussion usually moves from the "facts" of the encounter to a much broader narrative, which might include a discussion of the patient's early life experience, their personality, the role of other staff involved, the doctor's feelings about the various characters presented and, crucially, how the doctors feel they are being "used" in the evolving clinical drama. As the group discussion develops, other members come in, perhaps reflecting on similar experiences or speaking about their own emotional response to the material presented. If things are going well, then it is as if the group breathes life into a problem, which at first sight seemed stuck, hopeless, or incomprehensible. Trainees gradually learn to value their own subjectivity and they also learn from the responses of other trainees that there are different ways of thinking about what is going on.

Of course, it is not always that straightforward for those presenting, since it is not just about objective facts that are "out there", but instead about what is going on inside. Each time they present, the doctor is taking an emotional risk. In a sense, they are presenting themselves—their vulnerability, prejudices, and even their hatred—and in these acts they are opening themselves up to the gaze of others, with the possibility of narcissistic injury and the paralysing shame that can follow in its wake.

Vignette 2: the dispensing machine

A doctor, who had initially trained in anaesthetics, but was now doing an attachment in psychiatry as part of her training to become a GP, spoke about a patient whom she had felt forced to admit against her better judgement. The case consisted of a young man who had been brought to Accident and Emergency by the police following a suicide attempt. The patient, who lived alone and was unemployed, was well known to the local addiction services. There had been numerous attempts to deal with his multiple addictions to alcohol and drugs. He was known to have had a very chaotic childhood and had been brought up in a series of children's homes, with several failed attempts at fostering and adoption.

At interview, the patient claimed he was deeply depressed, that nobody was doing anything for him, that he needed to be in hospital and given powerful drugs to take his depression away. If something was not done, he would "do it properly next time" and kill himself. However, in his account of what had happened, there were a number of inconsistencies and he made frequent use of psychiatric jargon. Although he claimed to be hearing voices, objectively there was no evidence that this was the case.

The doctor, normally a highly conscientious and empathic trainee, said that she felt utterly manipulated and struggled to establish any sort of relationship with her patient. Unable to make a decision, she finally managed to track down the patient's consultant, who, I think, she wanted to make the decision for her. In talking about it in the Balint Group, the doctor said that she felt the consultant was annoyed at being contacted and that the decision had been left with her. Eventually, given the repeated statement about suicidal intent, she felt pushed into an admission. Although nothing was said, she felt that the nurses on the in-patient unit (who knew the patient from previous admissions) disagreed with her decision. She said that she felt utterly de-skilled and stupid.

In the discussion that followed, the doctor said that the effect of this case had stayed with her for days afterwards. It felt, she said, as if her brain had been "numbed". She had great difficulty getting interested in any of her patients and found it difficult to make decisions about their care. Other trainees came in, describing similar experiences. This seemed to help and allowed the doctor to go further, saying that she felt she was being treated "like a robot", "a sort of dispensing machine" whose only function was to hand out pills or prescribe admission, rather than a doctor who was trying to establish a therapeutic relationship with her patient. Her isolated, rather hopeless and mindless position, seemed to mirror that of her patient and his impoverished bleak existence where only "things", alcohol or drugs, could bring some temporary relief.

The group went further, speculating that the patient's impoverished chaotic childhood with, presumably, multiple attachment failures, had led him to give up on relationships. Perhaps his only way of relating to others (including the doctor) was through a sort of robotic relationship in which he felt himself to be a machine that could only be "fixed" by another machine. This seemed to go some way to explaining the doctor's feeling of being "numbed". It felt as though what had been projected into the doctor's mind was a sort of negative state, a powerful attack on her ability to think and feel. She, too, had withdrawn (luckily temporarily) from normal emotional engagement with others.

Thinking about her problem in this way seemed to be helpful to the doctor, who ended up saying that the reason she had decided to get out of anaesthetics was because of organisational changes, which meant that she had lost much of the contact with patients, which she valued, and it was as if she had become "simply a cog" in a large organisation machine.

Vignette 3: a repetition and an enactment

Another doctor presented the following case for discussion in the Balint group.

A woman in her late forties had been diagnosed with a particularly aggressive form of pre-senile dementia. Within the space of months, the progressive destruction of her brain had brought her to a point where, most of the time, she no longer knew who or where she was. Her family became involved and initially managed to keep her at home, with fairly minimal support. However, the situation came to a head when the patient, in a confused state of mind, wandered on to a motorway in the middle of the night. The police were involved and the patient was admitted to hospital where she was detained under the Mental Health Act.

A few days later, the out-of-hours junior psychiatrist was called to the ward by nursing staff. The patient's eldest son, a trainee social worker, had turned up unexpectedly, insisting that he could manage and that he was going to take his mother home. The doctor said he had found himself close to losing his temper with the son, whom he felt was being totally unrealistic about the severity of his mother's condition. It transpired that the son was particularly angry when the doctor used the term "detention". He said this made his mother sound like a prisoner when, in fact, she was just ill.

The other doctors in the group, as is often the case, began to ask for more details, inviting the presenting doctor to elaborate on the clinical narrative. What emerged was that the patient's husband had been a violent alcoholic and her children had been brought up in an atmosphere of threat and intimidation. The patient, seemingly unable to leave "the man she had married", had been kept captive, trapped in a travesty of a relationship.

The group became interested in the idea that the whole family was struggling to deal with the loss of the mother, and that the son's anger, focused on the doctors, together with his inability to face up to reality of the situation, was a reflection of the family's struggle to come to terms with what was happening. Some members of the group admitted that they also did not like the legalistic language used in the Mental Health Act and how this did not sit easily with the rest of the work they tried to do as doctors. However, the group also wondered why the son was so violently opposed to the doctors and, in particular, the use of the word detention, with its links to prison and criminality. Perhaps his training as a social worker was relevant here, but there was also the thought that the whole of the family's previous experience of being kept a "virtual prisoner" by the father was relevant. Perhaps what was being replayed was an old story with the doctors being drawn into the position of the imprisoning father with whom the family were at war.

As a postscript, in the Balint group a few weeks later, the doctor who had initially presented this case said that things had moved on and he felt that he was now working alongside, rather than against, the family. What seemed to have been "therapeutic", as he put it, was that the family had contested the section and taken it to a mental health tribunal where, having heard both sides, the decision was made by the tribunal to uphold the section, a decision the family accepted. It seemed to me that a harsh paternal superego, located in the psychiatrist and originating in the family's early life experience, had been replaced by a more benign form of authority, located in the tribunal, which had allowed the family to begin the process of grief.

Associative thinking and potential space

I want to use these examples to illustrate how, in order to engage in a meaningful way with those suffering from mental disorder, psychiatrists need to utilise two very different ways of thinking. The first, which might be called "scientific thinking", underpins much of their medical training and seeks to objectify illness. The second, which I call "associative thinking", does not come so easily and requires a different stance, which has to be learnt, *through experience,* in the process of making the transition from trainee to psychiatric practitioner. It is important to emphasise that both ways of thinking about mental disorder are necessary and that both objective and subjective knowledge are required to come to a true formulation of the patient's problems.

At the risk of gross simplification, it is possible to delineate these two modes of thinking as shown in Table 13.1.

Associative thinking comes into existence through a process, akin to Keats' (1899, p. 277) description of "negative capability": "when a man is capable of being in uncertainty, mysteries, doubts without any irritating reaching after fact or reason". It has similarities with Bion's (1967, p. 279) notion of reverie, in which he suggested that therapists should approach each session "without memory, desire or understanding".

It is important to emphasise that this "unknowing" state of mind is anything but passive; rather, it is the cultivation of an *actively* receptive mind through which enhanced understanding of the other can be achieved. This state of mind does not seek to categorise consciously or to name experience, but, rather, awaits the arrival of an emergent *gestalt*. It involves a sort of uncoupling, defocusing process, which,

Table 13.1. Scientific and associative thinking.

Scientific	Associative
Values objective reality	Values subjective reality
Makes use of convergent thinking	Uses divergent thinking
Involves "focusing in"	Involves "standing back from"
Seeks to understand the other's experience in order to make a diagnosis	Seeks to understand the other's experience in order to understand relational patterns and build an authentic narrative
Mainly concerned with conscious thought	Includes unconscious modes of thinking
Seeks logical/linear connections	Accepts circular/isomorphic connections
Aims at certainty	Values "unknowing" states of mind

paradoxically, involves becoming more emotionally involved while standing slightly back from the clinical phenomenon concerned.

Associative thinking occurs in an area of experience for which Winnicott (1971) used the term potential space. Ogden (1985, p. 139), building on Winnicott's ideas, describes the way in which potential space opens up through a dialectical process between two opposing concepts, for example, "me" and "not me":

> Winnicott's concept of potential space might be understood as a state of mind based upon a series of dialectical relationships between fantasy and reality. Me and not me, symbol and symbolised, etc., each pole of the dialectic creating, informing and negating the other.

Ogden (1985, p. 138) draws a distinction between *empathy*, where the individual is free to play—"one plays with the idea of being the other while knowing that one is not"—and *projective identification*, which occurs outside the domain of potential space:

> Interpersonally, projective identification is the negative of playing; it is the coercive enlistment of another to perform a role in the projectors unconscious fantasy. The effect of this process on the recipient is to threaten his subjective state as psychic reality. Instead his perceptions are experienced as "reality" as opposed to a personal construction.

Projective identification emanates from a part of the mind—the psychotic part in Bion's (1957) terms—which attacks linking of mental events and, in this process, negates subjective reality so that experience becomes concretised and stripped of meaning. The psychotic part of the mind can only communicate (with other minds) through a sort of violent evacuation, a malignant form of projective identification. Bion (1962) used the term "alpha function" to describe how another mind, a functioning mind (the recipient), can potentially process these inchoate chunks of experience, which he called "beta elements", giving them meaning through the symbolic function of language. In this way, the unthinkable can be thought about, and, in the process, managed and contained. To quote Ogden (1985, p. 138) again,

> The "processing" of projective identification . . . can be understood as a therapist's act of re-establishing a psychological dialectic process in which the induced feeling state can be experienced, thought about and understood by an interpreting subject.

In line with this thinking, I am proposing that trainee psychiatrists, on call, and at the front line of psychiatry, are repeatedly exposed to the malignant projective processes of madness. In the Balint group, by opening up of pockets of potential space, trainees learn to make use of associative modes of thinking and engage in "serious play" (Trist, 1987, p. xxii), which allows them to metabolise their experience, to put it into words, and find different ways of thinking the problem. In time, the alpha function (Bion, 1962) of the group is internalised, enabling members to think in a quite different way about their work.

The organisation of mental health services

Although this discussion has, up to this point, focused on a particular group of staff—doctors training to be psychiatrists—I think it has relevance to other front-line staff involved in managing those who present with mental illness, and, indeed, for the overall organisation whose purpose is to contain and process madness.

I have suggested that psychotic processes exist to attack the links between mental events and the linkage of normal interpersonal relatedness, as originally described by Bion (1959). Through mechanisms such as splitting, fragmentation, ossification, concretisation, isolation, and alienation, the psychotic part of the mind seeks to disavow psychic reality. Lively thought and normal curiosity become impossible and the potential space, within which symbolic creative activity can occur, is lost.

Under these circumstances, the normal cohesion of the self falls apart as the linkage between different aspects of experience is lost. This is manifest in a variety of ways: thought without affect; affect without thought; thought that lacks any sense of personal agency but can only find expression through alien "voices" or intrusive thoughts ("thought insertion" in the jargon of psychiatric practice); thoughts that seem to be "stolen" from the mind ("thought withdrawal"); language which has lost all connection with a coherent narrative process ("loosening of association", "thought disorder", "word salad"). The disconnection of body from mind ("depersonalisation"), the splitting of self from environment ("derealisation"), the dislocation of the self from the social (alienation): these are all parts of the disjointed and disconnected experience of those who live through mental illness.

The most devastating effect of severe mental illness is not the "active" symptoms—hallucinations, delusions, etc.—but what psychiatrists call the "defect state". Relatives often complain that the patient is simply "not there". What is described is a gradual disintegration of the personality, characterised by apathy, deadness, and emotional blunting, leaving a mind incapable of making emotional links, alienated and cut off emotionally from themselves and other people.

It seems likely that when the minds of these patients meet the minds of the staff whose job it is to engage with the madness, there will be an element of contagion. In a sort of viral process, unwanted fragments of the patient's mind will, if unmodified, infect the unconscious organisational mind, so that whatever has been evacuated might then be enacted, between staff and patients, between staff and staff, and between staff and the organisation.

This might lead, at times, to feelings of omnipotent grandiosity, but, more commonly, staff are left in a confused and impotent state of mind, accompanied by a deadening concretisation of thinking. If left unmodified, these attacks on thinking can, in themselves, traumatise the collective mind of the team and, indeed, the whole organisation, progressively wearing the organisation down and leaving it in a fragmented and de-energised state. A sort of organisational "defect state" ensues.

If organisational structures mirror psychotic ways of thinking, for example, through un-joined-up thinking, lack of space to reflect, and professional isolation, then it is more likely that the psychosis will take hold. Under these circumstances, the organisation might find it impossible to hold back a negative spiral of demoralisation leading to alienated and "robotic" states of mind with a defensive disengagement from the task, accompanied by deep cynicism, low morale, and staff burn-out.

For example, an overwhelmed and essentially leaderless community team for which I worked as part of my psychiatric training held a weekly ward round every Tuesday afternoon. The "Cardex", which contained the patient's notes, was ritually wheeled out, and every single patient on the team's case-load was "discussed". However, there was no real discussion because there simply was not time. As far as I remember, very few decisions were made and only rarely was a patient discharged from the books. Yet, it seemed as though the very act of touching the patient's notes and saying the patient's name was felt, in some sort of magical way, to help the staff team feel that each patient had been considered and all would somehow be kept safe.

Another example is the use of risk assessment questionnaires by which patient's risk of harm "to self or others" can apparently be quantified: you get a score at the end of it! I have no doubt that questionnaires (and something similar could be said for integrated care pathways and other protocols) have *a place* in the overall assessment and management of psychiatric patients. Yet, as Main (1990) points out, good ideas can, over time, become used in quite different ways from what was initially intended. "Ideas" become "procedures" with the promise of certainty where, in fact, no certainty exists. Thinking becomes ossified, and the capacity for normal curiosity is lost. Similarly, "evidence-based practice", if not tempered by the reality of clinical engagement, and the sort of associative thinking previously described, can become reified to the point of "non-sense", which fails both patients and staff struggling to make sense of chaotic ways of thinking.

Garland (1998), in her work on psychic trauma, describes the way in which the ability to think creatively is dependent on the internalisation of an object, originally the mother's mind, which can contain extreme emotion and allow thinking to take place. She suggests that severe or cumulative trauma attacks this containing function, leaving a mind increasingly concretised and incapable of symbolic thought.

> Babies with mothers who can take the panic out of their anxieties, eventually take into themselves some version of a mother who can manage – who can get hold of something important emotionally without being knocked off balance by it. . . . And this internalised version of the mother forms the basis of the child's eventual ability to manage and eventually to think about its own anxieties . . . *about* them, rather than just going on being caught up in them. This job is done intuitively by most mothers, with help from a *supporting environment*. (Garland, 1998, p. 109, my emphasis)

In an analogous way, those who work in the front line of mental health services need to be supported in, and protected from, the cumulative trauma which arises out of the experience of repeatedly having to deal with psychotic modes of relating. Just as a mature, creative, maternal mind can help the infant develop the ability to deal with extreme emotional states, so the organisational "mind" that supports individual practitioners in mental health needs to function in a way that recognises the particular pressures and anxieties that dealing with madness places on their staff.

An organisation which deals with mental illness and the management structures set up to lead staff need to understand and absorb some of this anxiety, *but not be overwhelmed by it* to the point of mindless activity in the sort of "numb" or "robotic" ways of functioning described in the earlier clinical examples. Staff working in mental health need to feel that they are working from a secure base (Bowlby, 1988), which means (concretely) a building, and a building that is fit for purpose. They also need to feel *grounded*, part of a real, as opposed to a "virtual", team where they have ongoing, real contact with other members of their team. Working in isolation should be kept to a minimum. Crucially, however, in order to avoid the toxic impact of mental illness, staff need the opportunity to reflect on their work experience in what Hinshelwood (2001) calls "a culture of enquiry": "Institutions engaging with patients who short circuit their own thinking and reflecting on their experience need to establish specific means for developing the capacity to reflect, as a function of the institution" (p. 102).

Opportunities to reflect on work experience, "the periodic suspension of business", as Bridger (1989, p. 222) puts it, for example, through groups such as the Balint group previously described, enable staff to talk about their clinical experience and the emotional impact of this work, or to explore the functioning of a team, or organisation. This can help to keep alive the staff's ability to think clearly in the face of an experience that seeks to nullify thought.

Conclusion

This chapter is about something that is, in a way, fairly obvious and self-evident, that is, the ways in which psychotic thinking can disrupt and disorganise the minds of those who attempt, as part of their job, to make sense of seemingly mindless disturbance. I have argued that in order to carry out this task, the staff who get involved need to feel part of an organisation that implicitly understands and supports them in this work. I have also suggested something which seems fairly straightforward and ordinary: that psychiatrists and other front-line staff need time and space, built into their working day, to reflect on and process the madness which is all around them at work. It can be a difficult job.

References

Balint, M. (1964). *The Doctor, his Patient and the Illness*. London: Pitman.

Bion, W. R. (1957). Differentiation of the psychotic from the non-psychotic personalities. *International Journal of Psycho-Analysis, 38*: 266–275.

Bion, W. R. (1959). Attacks on linking. *International Journal of Psycho-Analysis, 40*: 308–315.

Bion, W. R. (1962). A theory of thinking. *International Journal of Psycho-Analysis, 43*: 306–310.

Bion, W. R. (1967). Notes on memory and desire. *Psychoanalytic Forum, 2*: 271–280.

Bion, W. R. (1982). *The Long Weekend: 1897–1919 (Part of a Life)*. Oxford: Fleetwood Press.

Bowlby, J. (1988). *A Secure Base: Clinical Applications of Attachment Theory*. London: Routledge.

Bridger, H. (1989). Courses and working conferences as transitional learning institutions. In: E. Trist & H. Murray (Eds.), *The Social Engagement of Social Science: A Tavistock Anthology* (pp. 221–245). Pennsylvania, PA: University of Pennsylvania Press.

Garland, C. (1998). *Understanding Trauma. A Psychoanalytic Approach*. London: Duckworth.

Hinshelwood, R. D. (2001). *Thinking about Institutions: Milieux and Madness*. London: Jessica Kingsley.

Keats, J. (1899). *The Complete Poetical Works of John Keats*. Cambridge: Houghton, Mifflin.

Main, T. (1990). Knowledge, learning and freedom from thought. *Psychoanalytic Psychotherapy, 5*: 59–78.

Ogden, T. H. (1985). On potential space. *International Journal of Psycho-Analysis, 66*: 129–141.

Salinsky, J. (2009). A very short introduction to Balint groups. http://balint.co.uk/about/introduction/. Accessed 20 September 2012.

The Royal College of Psychiatrists (2004). *Requirements for Psychotherapy Training as part of Basic Specialist Training*. London: Royal College of Psychiatrists.

Trist, T. (1987). Prologue. In: G. Amado & A. Ambrose (Eds.), *The Transitional Approach to Change* (p. xxii). London: Karnac.
Wilkie, G., & Raffaelli, D. (2005). In at the deep end: making the transition from SpR to consultant. *Advances in Psychiatric Practice, 11*: 107–114.
Winnicott, D. W. (1971). *Playing and Reality*. New York: Basic Books.

CHAPTER FOURTEEN

Ministers ministering to ministers: psychoanalytic reflections

Murray Leishman

Introduction

The invitation to contribute to this book prompted me to reflect on my involvement in the creation and early activities of the Scottish Institute of Human Relations (SIHR). I had trained as a minister and worked for some time as a parish minister before, in the 1960s, taking up the post of Chaplain at a psychiatric hospital, the Royal Edinburgh Hospital. In this chapter, I begin by reflecting on those times and then turn more specifically to the coming together of ministry and psychoanalysis under the auspices of the SIHR. Drawing on examples, I illustrate how we made space for psychoanalytic thinking and practice at that interface.

By the end of the 1960s, there was a useful crisis in the politics of the unconscious in Scotland. Dr Ronald Fairbairn was dead. Dr Winifred Rushforth, who had set up the Davidson Clinic, bringing low-cost psychotherapy to the community, was in her mid eighties. Scotland had had its share of brilliant soloists, but links between them and with psychoanalytic communities elsewhere, were tenuous. There was no professional body to carry forward the work begun, or to offer training. For that, they had to go to London. Dr Rushforth did what she could. She instituted a summer school, which offered a forum for discussion of psychoanalytic and psychotherapeutic ideas. She invited speakers from across the psychotherapy spectrum to come to Edinburgh to help develop awareness of the value of psychoanalytic thinking and psychotherapy. Her own training had been at the Tavistock Clinic in London, and she saw herself as a Freudian at root, although she was essentially eclectic and interested in a number of different approaches and ideas.

Despite her Freudian roots, one of her great interests was in the area of spirituality, and she brought together a group of ministers from the Church of Scotland in a joint venture of psychotherapy and church. This might seem surprising in that Freud is typically remembered for his antipathy towards religion and as an avowed atheist (Gay, 1989). The psychoanalysis he invented is sometimes thought of as made possible by, as well as contributing to, the retreat of religion in Western Europe (Black, 2006). Freud described psychoanalysis as "secular pastoral care", positioning it as a successor to religious forms of care and healing. Since then, psychoanalysis and the varieties of psychotherapy it has spawned have often been referred to as secular forms of confession.

Freud's infamous split with Jung did not encourage his followers to challenge his negative views of religion. However, not all were silenced. For example, the Swiss pastor, Oskar Pfister, and the French scholar and student of Eastern mysticism, Romain Rolland, both corresponded with Freud over many years, contesting his views of religious faith (Freud, 1936a; Meng & Freud, 1963). There were others, too, including several whose Scottish heritage had strong religious foundations, such as Hugh Crichton-Miller, who founded the Tavistock Clinic in London, and his colleague Ian Suttie, whose book *The Origins of Love and Hate* included a psychoanalytic defence of religious beliefs (Suttie, 1935).

While Scottish religious thinking may have made its way into psychoanalysis via the ideas and writings of psychoanalysts from the 1920s onwards, psychoanalytic ideas took longer to filter into the Scottish ministry. An interest in psychoanalytic thinking existed within the churches, as was shown in the life of the Scottish Pastoral Association, founded in 1959. Its interdisciplinary journal, *Contact*, first published in 1960, brought together people from medicine, social work, counselling, psychology, and the churches. However, making psychotherapy more accessible to individuals who happened to include some members of the clergy did not foster psychodynamic thinking about the diverse range of issues lay and ordained ministers faced within their parishes.

It was then our great good fortune that the Director of the Tavistock Clinic in London, Dr John Dearg (Jock) Sutherland chose, on his retirement from the Tavistock in 1968, to return to his native land to pull together the different strands of psychodynamic thinking and practice here. After his arrival in Edinburgh, he spent two or three strenuous years making contact with social work agencies and field workers, psychiatrists in training, sociologists, university departments, and representatives of the churches. Some people thought he was putting the cart before the horse by attending to the environment before establishing a psychodynamically based organisation. Many of us hoped he would move quickly towards setting up a psychoanalytic training. However, he believed that you had first to create an interest among the constituents and demonstrate the usefulness of psychodynamic ideas. Without a sense of the importance of unconscious processes in all our relationships, who was going to be interested in training? In addition, of course, Scots are canny. They give their returning offspring a mixed reception. Contained in questions such as "What kept you so long?" from the enthusiasts and, from the sceptics, "Are you bringing us a lot of fancy ideas from the south?", the ambivalence was scarcely concealed.

To illustrate the development of his ideas about the application of psychodynamic thinking beyond the confines of the consulting room, Jock described some of his joint work with seminal figures in London. For example, Dr Michael Balint had invited him to join discussions on the theme of *The Doctor, His Patient and the Illness*, as Balint's 1957 book was titled.

Then again, Jock had deeply appreciated working with Dr Wilfred Bion in the early years of the Second World War when they joined with an army team in rebuilding the British Forces after Dunkirk. He was particularly impressed by Bion's use of the "leaderless group", initially in the selection procedures of the War Office Selection Board and, later, at the Tavistock Clinic (Bion, 1968). This offered a living example of personal relationships in a situation where the conflict between self-interest and concern for others was an active reality.

Here was a tailor-made method for learning about self in relation to others. When Jock floated the idea of an organisation for Scotland, and it was agreed that the time was right, the Scottish Institute of Human Relations was formed. The provision of "analytic groups" was central to it, forming a conduit for psychoanalytic ideas to spread in the surrounding professional community. For Jock, the dissemination of psychodynamic knowledge was essential. His vision was for a society informed by what he saw as a new understanding of persons in relation. From 1976 to 1996, some ninety professionals—psychiatrists, social workers, nurses, clergy, marriage guidance counsellors, and others—grew in this understanding through the experience of the analytic groups run by the Institute. Some of the members of these early groups continued this initiative by forming groups within their own professions, to encourage thinking about the unconscious processes involved in their work. These were "application groups" rather than analytic groups, but they were informed by the understanding passed on and developed through the analytic groups. One of these was the clergy group-work project.

The clergy group-work project

In the early 1970s, while I was training in psychotherapy at the Scottish Institute and a full-time chaplain in a psychiatric hospital, my chaplain colleagues and I developed a forum for members of the clergy to meet together with other members of the professional staff. The purpose was to develop a more effective ministry by the churches to people who were psychologically distressed, and, more generally, past, present, or potential patients of the hospital. It was open to members of the clergy from all of the churches in the hospital's catchment area, some 170 people in all.

To launch the clergy group-work project, we joined forces with consultants who specialised in community psychiatry. We were joined intermittently by several other consultants and their trainees as well as by senior nursing staff, social workers, and occupational therapists. Attendance at our monthly meetings ranged from two to twenty-two clergy, and between one and five members of the hospital staff. Regular meetings continued for twelve years, at which point I left the chaplaincy to go into private practice as a psychoanalytic psychotherapist.

The initial focus of these meetings was on the hospital visits made by members of the clergy to their parishioners. Never easy in a general hospital, this issue can be fraught with difficulty and anxiety in the psychiatric hospital, not only for the visiting minister and the clinical staff, but also for the patient. Yet, ministers' visits can be supportive to the staff and therapeutic for the patient, both during hospital admission and on return home, possibly for years afterwards. Since the church group might represent the only tolerant and friendly support system available to some patients in their home setting, we felt it was important to give thought, effort, and NHS and church time to exploit these visits and to maximise their benefit to the patient in hospital and afterwards. This included helping to rehabilitate "the visit" from being seen as a daunting chore by the minister, or as an unwelcome intrusion into medical mysteries by some clinicians.

Since most patients with mental health problems feel bad and useless inside themselves, the doctors and nurses who care for them can very easily pick up these same feelings about the work they do on the patient's behalf. An easy way of failing to deal adequately with these feelings is to attribute them to others in the patient's world, such as their family. Clergy are usually associated with family feeling, and individual clergy, by their temperament and the culture of their church, might be too quick to accept the attribution of uselessness to themselves, as if that represents a true state of affairs, rather than the projection into them of the patient's feelings. Klein described this process of "splitting off parts of the self and projecting them on to (or rather into) another person" (Klein, 1955, p. 143) as "projective identification", a common occurrence in the consulting room, but equally likely to occur in any setting in which people are struggling with strong persecutory anxieties. As Bion further emphasised,

> in many cases the person doing the projecting acts in such a way as to get the analyst (or other recipient of the projection) to have the feelings appropriate to the projector's phantasy, and sometimes the recipient finds himself feeling pressure to act on the feelings. (Spillius, 1988, p. 83)

As we also quickly discovered in the group, wherever there is care there is also rivalry. Because this inevitably carries echoes of his or her own early life, the patient both suffers from this rivalry and will try to exploit it in order to control it. The best that the professional carers can do is to be aware of their rivalry and try to manage it better. Good minister/bad doctor, or the reverse, is a destructive split with a family root.

We soon realised that if we were to harness psychodynamic knowledge for pastoral work, it was essential to devise a setting where hitherto unrecognised factors might not only be talked about but, from time to time, experienced, and then identified in a way that would be helpful to the participants in the group. Until there is that element of shared experience, in general and in detail, little progress is made beyond bookish and half-sceptical preoccupation with Freudian talk. The role of the psychodynamically trained person in the group was to point to the unconscious patterns emerging that frequently reflected those occurring in the work that was being described.

To mitigate the anxiety that participants would feel about entering an unfamiliar situation, it was important for the setting to feel reliable, with meetings taking place on the same day, at the same time, and in the same place, which was free of interruptions. The reliability of the setting could be experienced only gradually over time. The size of the group was also a significant factor. We found that with fifteen or more people, the quality of contribution went down markedly. Therefore, we decided to divide into four groups corresponding to the divisions of the hospital catchment area. People seemed to feel less anxious in the smaller groups and it was easier to establish mutual trust.

Those of us who were training in psychoanalytic psychotherapy sought to avoid presenting ourselves as experts who would tell our fellow ministers what they ought to do. We saw the groups as opportunities for mutual learning and the relationship we tried to establish was that of colleagues, with each person in the group having their own area of expertise which could be pooled in order to better understanding the work-related difficulties being presented. There were those who criticised what we were doing, of course, on the grounds that "a little knowledge is a dangerous thing", and we were none of us experts in this new way of understanding human distress, but we were fortunate that there were also medical personnel who recognised that not to use this understanding was the greater danger.

Group meetings moved through different phases as participation built up and patterns were established, only to change again as new leaders and contributors emerged. For example, there was what we called the "Tell me, Doctor" phase, much in evidence at the outset of the project and recurring from time to time. Characteristically, some ministers would try to push the psychiatrist out of the role of colleague into that of lecturer. There might be a call to "say something about schizophrenia", or to comment on a newspaper article on alcoholism. A psychiatrist might duly oblige and describe the incidence of the syndrome, symptoms, diagnosis, treatment programmes, and outlook. There the process tended to stick. An authoritative expert had been found who relieved group members of the need to reveal their uncertainties. Ironically, hard on the heels of the "Tell me, Doctor" phase, and part of what I took to be the same dependency, would often come angry and aggressive attacks on psychiatrists in general. Psychiatrists were hauled over the coals for "undermining people's faith" or "advocating free love as therapy". Incidents were recounted where ministers had felt excluded or humiliated in their hospital work. However, if, instead of taking up the role of expert, the psychiatrist responded in a different manner, perhaps questioning the questioner about his experience of dealing with a schizophrenic parishioner or his efforts to help a heavy drinker, then something different happened. A living person emerged rather than an abstract illness and the minister's authority was confirmed out of his own work experience. The psychiatrist could select his medical lore more appropriately to fit the profile. The rest of the group often reported on the usefulness of such exchanges about the particularities of a case and might go on to offer parallel or contrasting experiences. As confidence grew, people were prepared to be more open about asking the group for help with work rather than to propose an abstract topic for discussion. We decided to widen the scope of the group to include any pastoral work outside the hospital. In what follows, I offer some disguised examples from the work of these groups.

Example 1: learning from group experience

A priest described the family he had visited at home that day. The son of the house, a young man in his twenties, in a promising professional career, without warning to his family, had thrown himself out of a window and killed himself. The group entered into a long discussion about the ethics of suicide and the Christian view. As it went on, people seemed to become more and more dejected. The priest dropped out of the discussion at an early stage and appeared quite preoccupied.

When this state of affairs was pointed out, the priest revived and said that he had been thinking about his struggle to get through to the young man's mother. She was a highly educated *grande dame* who alarmed everyone by talking about what had happened, but showing no signs of grief and seeming indifferent to her son's self-destruction. The group began tentatively to talk about their emotional responses to his account and to elicit more information about his experience. Towards the end of the meeting, the priest reflected on the parallels between the group's initial response and that of his parishioner. There had been an intellectual discussion, which seemed to be covering up people's feelings of shock and despair. He realised that he needed to find a way of avoiding getting caught up in the mother's intellectualising in order to be able to reach her grief.

The unconscious is a potent dimension in every aspect of life, but it is often overlooked. When the unconscious patterns can be identified, then psychodynamic knowledge can be harnessed and applied to pastoral work. The shared experience of this group gave the priest a way of articulating his own struggle in working with this family. Through a "parallel process", as Searles (1955) described it, in relation to supervision, the presenter's predicament is communicated to the group in such a way that it is experienced within the room and can be thought about as a "live" issue.

Example 2: thinking under fire

A priest opened a meeting by saying, angrily, that he wished someone would give him a book about baby battering. One or two suggestions were made by a psychiatrist and a rather guilty and uneasy general discussion took place about the evils of child abuse. The priest was then asked if he had something specific in mind. At this, he launched into an attack on the local social work department, accusing them of monstrous bungling and described how they allowed a three-year-old child to be fostered by no fewer than five people. He had tried to speak to the senior social workers about the case, but had been given the brush-off.

Several ministers in the group worked hard to draw out their colleague by sympathetic questioning, especially about his feelings of humiliation and rage in the face of officialdom. Apparently, he knew the parents well and they hoped he would get their child back from care. Someone said that "it must be awful for him to realise he was about to fail them". It was then pointed out that there must have been some reason for the child being taken into care, and it emerged that there had been allegations of bullying.

In talking over this experience, it began to dawn on everybody in the room that the priest had been made to feel the sense of failure and fear of the authorities that belonged to the parents. He, being a kindly and receptive person, took it on board and was now actively taking their part in an uncritical manner. The ministers in the group identified with their colleague because they had been in similar situations, but, because they were not in the same impasse at that time, they were free to point out some features to which he had been blinded.

In this case, the feelings of the parishioners were projected into the minister and when he started to have feelings that did not belong to him, we could say he identified with the projection. "Projective identification", as we saw in Example 1, seems to work in this way: when faced with unbearable things about themselves, guilt at their own violence to their child, the parents split themselves and projected their bad selves into the nearest sympathetic person, while remaining the good and outraged innocents. Recognising these processes helped us be aware of the need not to get caught up in them. The upshot was that the minister returned to the social work office and attended a review meeting, ensuring that he was there to declare his continued interest in the family. He continued his pastoral care of the family, but this time in collaboration with the social workers.

The great psychotherapist and thinker, Dr Wilfred Bion, is reputed to have said that you do not have to be super-intelligent to do this kind of work, but you do need to know how to use the intelligence you have when you are "under fire". When conditions of trust in a group develop, the members experience the pleasure of being listened to and responded to by their fellow professionals. They are enabled to think more freely, and to take account of their emotional responses, so that they can use their intelligence more effectively when under fire. These features are apparent in the next example.

Example 3: sustaining compassion in the face of unconscious attack

A minister described how he had, for some months now, given many hours of ministering to a particularly tragic person who, after being chronically ill all his life with a rare disease, had now been told he was terminally ill. He sought help and support from his minister which at first was rewarding, as he was a seriously religious person, widely read, intelligent, and likeable. Now he was calling or phoning nearly every day and the minister was feeling increasingly uneasy. He came to the group visibly shaken. He had made enquires and discovered that there was not a shred of truth in the man's account of his situation. When confronted with incontrovertible evidence, the man denied having said these things and was angry with the minister for believing ill of him and accusing him of making it up.

Everybody in the room had had similar experiences with "impossible people" who were variously described by psychiatrists as "psychopaths" and by the ministers as "congenital liars". It was pointed out that such a person could be thought of as a terrified infant, ransacking the world for genuine care, to the extent of lying to achieve it. When he *did* achieve it, as in the case of the minister's sympathetic attention, he became insatiably greedy, and then became alarmed and anxious at his own unacceptable greed. Klein wrote extensively on greed, describing it as

> an impetuous and insatiable craving, exceeding what the subject needs and what the object is able and willing to give. At the unconscious level, greed aims primarily at completely scooping out, sucking dry, and devouring the breast. (Klein, 1957, p. 181)

This was indeed the minister's experience. Without claiming that this was the only way to make sense of the parishioner in question, it had the merit of giving the minister a new perspective on an overwhelming situation. He reported later that he could deal with this man much better if he thought of him as being rather like a toddler. What he held on to when the going was rough was the notion of pastoral work as re-parenting of a lost child. With the help of the group, a pastoral situation which had become impossible was changed into one which was just plain difficult.

Some members of the group began to feel the need of theoretical study and a number turned to the work of the Congregationalist minister and psychotherapist, Dr Harry Guntrip, to find a working theory which does not de-humanise, but does some justice to the depth and complexity of human beings in their relationships (Guntrip, 1961, 1971). Getting the drift of Guntrip's object relations theory helps us to see the panicky child in the adult, and to keep in touch with the adult and child both in ourselves and in the other.

One of the toughest problems in the pastoral care of disturbed people, as in therapy, is that interest, sympathy, and concern can provoke an unconscious attack of a sadistic kind. If the minister, or the therapist, becomes immersed in guilt about failing to find the "right" response, he fails to see the conflicted nature of the individual's desires, as the following example illustrates.

Example 4: winning and losing

A minister described his struggle over the past twenty-five years to help one of his parishioners. He gave a detailed account of the man's unhappy childhood and youth, when he had been bullied by a sadistic father. He had two unsuccessful marriages, a number of children, and a number of unsuccessful professional appointments. He had attempted to kill himself several times and always came back to the minister with endless requests for help, guidance, support, and "salvation". The minister described himself now "as being quite beaten" in human terms, but, of course, the Gospel might yet transform this man.

He was asked if the man could do anything at all. To our astonishment, the reply came back that he was extraordinarily gifted with those less able or younger than himself. He was in periodic demand among young people, especially in organising successful concerts and summer camps, but then, when everybody went away, he seemed to fade again and go off to live in seedy rooms, and could be met endlessly walking the pavements.

It was put to the minister that he could tell the man just what he had told the group: that he, the minister, was "beaten, humanly speaking, in his efforts to help him". For twenty-five years, the minister had "witnessed to the inexhaustible riches of the Gospel and stuck at it with marvellous tenacity". "But", said a colleague, "would it really be true that the Gospel would be less rich if he were to admit that he was beaten and *he* needed help? Had he not become identified with the Gospel rather than being a witness to it?" Or, to see it from the man's point of view, could we say that here was a frightened boy permanently needing to defend himself against his attacking Father by "beating" Father?

The man's problem was that he *had* to beat the minister and bring his heroic efforts to nought, while the minister's problem was that he felt that he, as "the bearer of the Gospel" *had* to win. The result was stalemate. We might think of this in terms of Winnicott's argument that a key task of adolescence is to triumph over others through "the death of rivals or the establishment of dominance" (Winnicott, 1971, p. 144), while the parental task is not to compete or retaliate, but "to survive intact" (Winnicott, 1971, p. 145). As the minister unravelled some of the elements of aggression in the relationship, which had rather dominated and preoccupied him, he felt sufficiently free to withdraw from the battle that had caused the impasse, surviving the attacks rather than competing for dominance.

There are people who need to make us feel over and over again that we are failing them, that we are unsatisfactory and not giving them what they need, because that is what they experienced with their parents in their early lives. When that happens, we urgently need the help of colleagues to shift the centre of gravity from our guilt to the individual's conflict. We, in the ministry, have a personal and professional weakness for clinging to the omnipotent fantasy that life can be wholly gratifying and conflict-free.

Example 5: thinking systemically; relocating responsibility

Sometimes, the group had the effect of helping people to act more spontaneously as themselves. A minister reported that a man had asked him urgently to intervene. Some friends of his had been shocked and stunned by the behaviour of their teenage son. He had been caught stealing girls' underwear from a neighbour's clothes line. The police were called. The parents were quite overwhelmed, unable to speak very coherently, but were beginning to say that they felt they would have to leave the town. The minister told the group he was, with great foreboding, on his way to see the couple, after the meeting. As he recounted their story, he remembered his own childhood and told the group about his own theft of a fishing rod, remarking that "all kids steal something sometime" and that he could remember the thrill of it still. The group urged him to go and tell the boy's parents that same story.

He did this, and, in a slow and painful discussion, the parents began to face the fact that they had brought into the world a child who was sexual, curious, and aggressive, in the way that Winnicott (1958) described as normal and healthy. They began to see that the boy's behaviour had more to do with his own frustrated curiosity about his sexual identity than with "wickedness" or "perversion". They were eventually able to acknowledge something of their own marital conflict, take responsibility for their own private, sexual lives, and to seek further professional help in marriage guidance. With that, the son's compulsion to steal underclothes subsided.

Conclusion

The clergy groups brought home to us a number of significant facts. The need for personal help seemed to be growing at such a rate that any psychiatrist, clergyman, or person who worked to support people in distress, and who had the necessary "ear", capacity, and sense of commitment to people to offer, would have his or her time and resources stretched to, and beyond, the limit. Further, those who worked for months and years giving help at a personal level to struggling people needed to give close attention to their own learning and development, and abandon any notion of having "arrived". Pastoral care was and remains the art of the possible. Friends and colleagues provide the vital service of assisting us to abandon some of the grandiosity, which is liable to persuade us that we are capable of working miracles. Centrally important, the personal development and continuing learning that is crucial if we are not going to raise human hopes and dash them again by our own panicky withdrawal, consists largely of the development of "negative capability", described by John Keats in his letter to his brothers:

> I had not a dispute but a disquisition with Rilke upon various subjects; several things dovetailed in my mind and at once it struck me what quality went to form a Man of Achievement especially in Literature, and which Shakespeare possessed so enormously – I mean Negative Capability, that is, when a man is capable of being in uncertainties, mysteries, doubts without any irritable reaching after fact and reason. (Keats, 1899, p. 277)

Our practice in the cure of souls needs a better, deeper, and more comprehensive theory of the person in his inner world and social relationships than theology alone can provide. As I have illustrated, psychoanalytic ideas can be immensely helpful. As with any other body of knowledge, psychoanalysis can be used to mystify others, but it can also be made to earn its bread. As a result of my experiences with colleagues, in the clinics and in the churches, I would suggest that we can indeed look in this direction for help to light up some of the dark places in our work and to develop a new language of the person in relationship which we can share with others.

References

Balint, M. (1957). *The Doctor, His Patient and the Illness.* London: Pitman.

Bion, W. R. (1968). *Experiences in Groups and Other Papers.* London: Tavistock.

Black, D. (2006). Introduction. In: D. Black (Ed.), *Psychoanalysis and Religion in the 21st Century* (pp. 1–20). London: Routledge.

Freud, S. (1936a). A disturbance of memory in the Acropolis. *S.E., 22*: 239. London: Hogarth.

Gay, P. (1989). *A Godless Jew.* New Haven, CT: Yale University Press.

Guntrip, H. J. S. (1961). *Personality Structure and Human Interaction: The Developing Synthesis of Psychodynamic Theory.* London: Hogarth.

Guntrip, H. J. S. (1971). *Psychoanalytic Theory, Therapy and the Self.* London: Hogarth.

Keats, J. (1899). *The Complete Poetical Works and Letters of John Keats, Cambridge Edition.* Boston MA: Houghton Mifflin.

Klein, M. (1955). On identification. In: *Envy and Gratitude and Other Works, 1946–1963* (pp. 141–175). London: Virago Press, 1988.

Klein, M. (1957). Envy and gratitude. In: *Envy and Gratitude and Other Works, 1946–1963* (pp. 176–235). London: Virago, 1988.

Meng, H., & Freud, E. L. (Eds.) (1963). *Psychoanalysis and Faith. The Letters of Sigmund Freud and Oskar Pfister.* New York: Basic Books.

Searles, H. (1955). The informational value of the supervisor's emotional experiences. In: *Collected Papers on Schizophrenia and Related Subjects* (pp. 157–176). New York: International Universities Press, 1965.

Spillius, E. (1988). Part Two: Introduction. In: *Melanie Klein Today: Volume 1: Mainly Theory* (pp. 81–86). London: Routledge.

Suttie, I. D. (1935). *The Origins of Love and Hate.* London: Kegan Paul, Trench, Trubner.

Winnicott, D. W. (1958). Aggression in relation to emotional development. In: *Collected Papers: Through Paediatrics to Psychoanalysis* (pp. 204–218). London: Tavistock.

Winnicott, D. W. (1971). Contemporary concepts of adolescent development and their implications for higher education. In: *Playing and Reality* (pp. 138–150). London: Routledge.

CHAPTER FIFTEEN

A plea to "see into the life of things": thinking psychoanalytically about later life

Susan Maciver and Tom C. Russ

Introduction

Freud (1905a) famously wrote that analysing older adults—people over fifty—was not advisable and, until the past decade or so, with the notable exceptions of Erikson (1963) and King (1974), later life has continued to be relatively neglected by psychoanalytic thinkers. More recently, mercifully, this has begun to change and there have been a number of publications reflecting psychodynamic approaches to thinking about and working with older people (Davenhill, 2007; Evans & Garner, 2004; Quinodoz, 2009; Russ, 2011; Waddell, 2002). The article by Russ (2011) describes the first of two study days on working with older people provided by the Working with Older People Interest Group at the Scottish Institute of Human Relations (SIHR). Because psychoanalytic work with older people has been marginalised for so long, we have found the opportunity for interaction with others interested in such work invaluable. In this chapter, we contribute to the growing literature in this field by illustrating both the potential of working with older people individually and taking psychoanalytic thinking into institutional settings such as care homes.

We aim to explore the stresses associated with ageing. These stresses are many and varied, and could include, for example, the loss of career and status, of health and faculties, of partners and friends through illness or death, together with other unwanted changes in personal circumstances. We illustrate the impact of these stresses as they present in individuals, and systemically at an organisational level. Since relatively little clinical material has been written in this area, we draw a number of our illustrations from literature, especially Shakespeare's *King Lear*. We move from thinking about case studies of fictionalised, composite, or anonymised clients and their relatives to thinking about the impact on staff of working with older people whose functioning and capacity to communicate might be seriously impaired. Throughout the chapter, we refer to Bion's ideas on containment, and Bowlby's on attachment, which we consider crucial in understanding and responding to older people. In the final section, we draw together thoughts about projective processes, highlighting the use of projective identification as an unconscious means of communication and Menzies Lyth's work in examining the defences against anxiety inevitably and unconsciously adopted by workers in contact with vulnerable people, particularly the residents of care homes.

King Lear—age without maturity: "Ripeness is all"

Shakespeare's *King Lear* (2005) confronts the reader with the terror of growing old without maturing or becoming "wise". Lear, a powerful, virile king for most of his long life, decides to divide his kingdom between his three daughters in exchange for their protestations of love and promises of care for him and his retainers. Cordelia, his youngest and favourite daughter, wants no part in this, explaining that her devotion should belong to the man she marries, while her sisters, Goneril and Regan, go along with Lear's plan. Lear then banishes Cordelia, the only daughter who has his real interests—as opposed to his narcissistic needs—at heart, and he is left to the untender mercies of the other two. Before long, he falls out with them, outraged at the restrictions they try to impose on him: in a fury he ricochets from one to the other, until he finds himself an outcast, homeless and virtually alone, his mind teetering on the edge of madness. As the fool points out to him, Lear is like an omnipotent baby, used all his life to imperiously controlling his family, court, and environment. This means that he has very little understanding of the needs of others and a poor understanding of what it is to love. He does not have the internal resources—in psychodynamic terms, "good enough" relationships with internal objects—to survive the losses.

The term "object" has the unfortunate connotation of something inanimate when the opposite is the intended meaning: it refers to the relationships with significant people (usually mother and father) in the external world that have been internalised in the inner world of the psyche. These internal relationships are important in sustaining the personality throughout life, particularly under adversity. Lear's outrage and distress cannot be contained inside his own mind and neither is there anyone or anything at hand to provide that containment: metaphorically, as well as literally, he has been turned out of house and home. The concept of containment was defined by Bion (1967a) as the capacity of one person mentally to take in the sometimes primitive and bodily expressed emotions of another, and hand them back in a changed form. Similarly, the mother receives her baby's terrifying feelings of helplessness and disintegration and is able to process these feelings and bring comfort and reassurance. Bion called this process "maternal reverie".

As Lear—uncontained—rants on the blasted heath, calling down heaven's vengeance on his daughters and the entire uncontrollable universe, the fool laconically comments, "Thou shouldst not have been old till thou hadst been wise" (2005, I, v, l. 49). Meanwhile, Edgar also expresses the importance of achieving maturity in age when he says,

> Men must endure
> Their going hence, even as their coming hither: Ripeness is all.
> (V, ii, ll. 9–11)

This is poignantly taken up by Edgar's father, Gloucester, Lear's contemporary, friend, and loyal retainer, who also endures cruelty at the hands of an adult child (Edmund), so that his experience parallels Lear's. His son Edmund's co-conspirator blinds him as punishment for his loyalty to Lear. In his anguished regret at having disowned his loving child, Edgar, Gloucester begins, as Lear does, to develop empathy for the lonely and dispossessed, and can say simply, "I stumbled when I saw" (IV, i, l. 18).

These words bring to mind Bion's (1962) emphasis on the importance of "learning from experience", which can be understood as the deep conscious and unconscious reflection that leads to maturity and integration of aspects of the self, a capacity which Wordsworth described in his poem, *Tintern Abbey* as "see[ing] into the life of things" (l. 49). By the end of the play, both Gloucester and Lear have repudiated the earthly riches, status, and concern for rank that once defined them and are ready to take their leave of the world, believing that they will live on in the hearts and minds of their loving children; tragically, as Cordelia is killed, in Lear's case this is a delusion.

The emotional impact of the play derives considerably from the experience of watching two elderly men who are forced to dispense with the trappings of wealth and with the intrapsychic defences that served them ill or well through most of their lives. Both are thoroughly shaken, and struggling to live with a greater sense of what really matters and to find meaning in what is happening to them. For the onlookers, characters within the play and audience or readers alike, it is a profoundly moving and deeply painful experience. At the end of the play, Albany talks for all of us when he says we must "Speak what we feel, not what we ought to say" (V, iii, l. 326).

The idea of *ripeness* in contrast with *rottenness* appears in Waddell's (2002) chapter, "The last years". She, too, quotes from Shakespeare, this time from *As You Like It* (1988):

> And so from hour to hour, we ripe and ripe,
> And then from hour to hour, we rot and rot;
> And thereby hangs a tale.
>
> (II, vii, ll. 26–28, in Waddell, 2002)

She goes on to elaborate:

> the extent to which we "ripe and ripe" only to "rot and rot" is dependent on the indissoluble relationship between physiological/neurological and psychological factors—between the body/brain and mind. As a person physically deteriorates, early problematic psychological constellations, if unresolved, are likely to be replayed; infantile defences, if underlying anxieties remain unmodified, are re-erected; childlike needs, if unmet, resurface. (pp. 238–239)

The extreme example of Lear resonates with the unhappy experience of some older people who are ill-equipped to be reconciled with loss and change and achieve a more mature dependency. Their anger at growing older, at inevitable losses including—very significantly—loss of status, can lead to a rather embittered older age where there is a constant harkening back to past glories, or a rather obdurate hanging on to what they see as prestigious titles and positions. For many, the increasing tangibility of death is a further challenge. Waddell observes that the developmental task posed by "the prospect of death is the ultimate test . . . to come to terms with loss and to undergo the pain of experience . . . rather than to evade it by defensive measures of conduct or of character" (Waddell, 2002, p. 218).

Jane: a latter-day Lear

Jane was in her late sixties when she reluctantly sought psychodynamic counselling. She had been divorced for many years and had two grown-up sons whom she saw from time to time. Her relationship with them and their partners was poor, mostly because of their failure to meet her rather exacting demands. She was also upset that retirement from her academic career had brought a leisure that she could not seem to enjoy. In session after session she wept and raged at past disappointments in her personal life. The defence of keeping herself extremely mentally active, busy, and well regarded in the academic realm no longer sufficed to protect her vulnerable self that felt neglected and useless. This feeling was frequently projected into the counsellor, who struggled with the impression that they were getting nowhere, that she was not capable of helping Jane, and most certainly was not her intellectual equal. The counsellor had to contain and process this very difficult countertransference so that she could, in time, talk with Jane about feelings of abandonment and sadness beneath the rage. With this came an almost overwhelming regret on Jane's part at the roads not taken and at the extent to which she felt she had sacrificed her relationships with her ex-husband and her children to her academic ambition. In time, Jane also understood that her extreme fear of intimate relationships had been engendered by her early emotional experience of a remote, successful father and a rather depressed and nervous mother, compounded by years in boarding school where an ability to excel scholastically won the approval of her teachers. Jane's therapeutic experience confirms Waddell's belief that such a relationship can lead to "personality development continuing, or even beginning, in an emotionally containing environment, however late in life" (Waddell, 2002, p. 229).

James and Dora: thinking about attachment

It has been widely acknowledged for some time that the degree of "ripening" or "rotting" is inextricably linked with the early attachment experiences of infancy and early childhood, thanks largely to the work of John Bowlby and other attachment researchers. Bowlby (1969, p. 194) described attachment as "the lasting psychological connectedness between human beings", and later wrote of the need for a secure base from which to explore the world and to which one can retreat when anxious or troubled (Bowlby, 1988). Although this is an internal experience that derives from an external one (proximity to the mother and the knowledge that she can reliably be found), in later years it is often located in the outside world. One thinks of the distress of elderly people when moved from their familiar surroundings, of how disorientated and lost they can be. In some, even in those who enjoyed travel when younger, there is a growing reluctance to leave home, as though the physical "secure base" is needed when the internal sense of one recedes.

This was very evident in the case of James, a retired GP who, in his seventies and following some health problems, was only confident about going anywhere when in the company of his wife, Joan. This apparent change of character puzzled and irritated Joan, and interfered with her interests and friendships since he was also reluctant to stay in the house by himself. His early attachment experiences threw some light on what was happening. James was adopted aged two and a half years, having previously been in foster care since he was a week old. His mother had been young and unmarried and the stigma attached to illegitimacy at that time meant that she probably was given no choice by her family but to give him up. His adoptive mother was an anxious, busy woman who went on to have a son and daughter of her own. It would have been difficult for him to feel she had space in her mind for him.

Significantly, James married Joan when he was a student and, supported emotionally by her, lived quite a successful life. He insisted she worked part time and put pressure on her to retire very early while he continued to work. The sense of her waiting for him at home was obviously very important for his functioning. He could leave her, but she was not allowed to leave him. This unspoken contract became much more apparent in his seventies, with him shouting out and interrupting all her phone calls on one pretext or another, so that she had to choose times when he was absorbed in television before she could contact her friends. Loss of his profession and his status in the community through retirement, together with health worries, conspired to make James treat Joan not as a partner, but, projectively, as if she were his mother, always on the brink of abandoning him, so that he became ever more querulous and demanding.

Bowlby (1988) described this inner, unconscious template of ways of relating to significant others as "the internal working model", and went on to classify attachment behaviour as secure or insecure: within the insecure category were subsets of anxious, ambivalent, and disorganised attachments. In older age, there is frequently a tendency for patterns of attachment to become more pronounced as the individual, like James, is faced with the stresses, both psychological and physical, of ageing.

Dora's story offers an interesting comparator. Dora also had an early separation from her mother, in her case because her mother died when she and her twin brother were two weeks old, leaving behind, not only the twins, but four other children. The family lived in a remote part of South Africa in the early years of the twentieth century, and after their mother's death the twins were wet-nursed by Zulu women. At age three, they were separated from their Zulu carers when the family returned to Scotland to live on a farm in the Highlands, where they were cared for by their father and a rather stern maiden aunt. A characteristic of Dora's was her love of the sun and her daughter reports a memory of her mother in older years, holding her face up to the pale spring Scottish sun with her eyes shut in blissful communication with the light. The warmth perhaps kept her in touch with her African infancy, so that she felt held by its heat.

Widowed at a comparatively young age, Dora found a "good enough" parental couple in her daughter and son-in-law and was able to live alone, though in frequent contact with them, and enjoy her friendships and garden. She did, however, become increasingly dependent on the cigarettes that resulted in her death, aged seventy. The smoking perhaps represented not only her regression to satisfying an infant need, but also ambivalence towards facing the last stage in life. In her last five years, she repeatedly insisted to her daughter that she thought of the physical privations of old age with a shudder of dread and had no wish to endure them. She, too, would quote *As You Like It*, saying she had no wish to be, "Sans teeth, sans eyes, sans taste, sans everything" (1988, II, vii, l. 166). She was deaf to the idea that it could be otherwise, and, indeed, had no role model, having had a mother who died aged twenty-seven and a father who, like her, died at seventy. In later life, Dora fared rather better than James. In wondering why, one has to return to their earliest experiences. Although Dora's affectional bond with her Zulu nurse ended abruptly when she left Africa, she had had the experience of being securely attached to her care-giver. The presence of her twin, with whom she had a lifelong, loving relationship, was also a protective influence. Together, these factors meant that she could respond to supportive relationships in her old age in a relatively mature way compared with James, who, fearing a repetition of early abandonment, regressed to quite infantile behaviour.

Bowlby's observations about the significance of early attachment relationships and their powerful capacity to be repeated in later relationships (Bowlby, 1969) is especially meaningful when considering the loss of "significant others" in older age. This becomes especially important when we consider the increasing dependence older people perforce must experience in relating to new carers. These new dependent relationships become the vehicles for powerful, often misunderstood, and destructive projective processes.

Caring for older people

Neglect and abuse of older people is all too common. Indeed, in health and social care environments, older adults are extremely vulnerable. Mandelstam (2011) even goes so far as to claim that neglect and abuse are "a systemic, rather than sporadic and opportunistic, affliction within our health services" (p. 34). How is this possible? How is it that altruistic health and social care workers neglect and abuse the very people they join their professions to help? The majority of institutional responses to malpractice take one of two forms: (i) increased regulation to identify "bad apples" and (ii) increased training. Increased professional regulation, revalidation, and background checks are all laudable and are likely to be helpful. However, one suspects that a number of perpetrators of abuse of older adults might have had excellent appraisal files. On the other hand, increased training in response to episodes of neglect frequently receives media attention, satisfying the desire that something should be done. In the main, this training seems to centre around either improving communication or provoking compassion—a word which is in danger of becoming a piece of jargon.

If we examine the flip-side of compassion, we discover more difficult emotions. Being exposed to frail, sick, and dying people, let alone having to care for them, is demanding, stirring up anxieties and even hatred (Winnicott, 1949). These emotions can make the carer feel even worse; they thought that they were a "good person" and should not feel this about people who are dependent on them. Such challenges associated with the caring role have been recognised for a long time.

Menzies Lyth (1988[1959]) published a study of nursing staff of a London teaching hospital which, though extremely well-known, has not had as much influence on the health service as could have been hoped. While not explicitly about the care of older people, since two thirds of patients in an average hospital are over sixty-five, there is much of relevance to later life in her observations. It is also important to remember that, while she wrote about nursing staff, there is no group or discipline, including doctors, who are uniquely protected against these pressures. During the course of their study, the investigators'

> attention was repeatedly drawn to the high levels of tension, distress and anxiety among the nurses. [They] found it hard to understand how nurses could tolerate so much anxiety and, indeed, [they] found much evidence that they could not. (Menzies Lyth, 1988, p. 45)

A number of unconscious defences against this anxiety were identified: dropping out of training, frequent changes of job, seeking postgraduate training, and sick-leave, particularly for minor ailments, which necessitated only short-term absence from work.

Considering this anxiety in more detail, Menzies Lyth highlighted particularly exposure to suffering and death, duties which include unpleasant tasks, and intimate physical contact with another person, arousing feelings that are difficult to control. All this was worsened by having to encounter psychological stress in colleagues, patients, and their relatives and to accept their projected emotions. She drew parallels between these anxieties and the conflict between an infant's primitive (life-giving) libidinal and (death-dealing) aggressive, unconscious phantasies:

> Because of the operation of aggressive forces, the inner world contains many damaged, injured, or dead objects. The atmosphere is charged with death and destruction. This gives rise to great anxiety . . . [The infant] fears that his libidinal impulses and those of other people cannot control the aggressive impulses sufficiently to prevent utter chaos and destruction. (Menzies Lyth, 1988, p. 47)

Segal (1957) wrote about the difference between "symbolisation", where something *represents* something else—for example, saying that a hospital ward is like a battlefield—and "symbolic equation", where something is felt to *be* something else. The former can reduce anxiety, when elements of phantasy situations are seen in objective reality (i.e., the hospital ward), but the situation on the ward is mastered, giving reassurance about mastering the phantasy situation and the associated anxiety. A similar process is described by Hamilton (1935) in his novel *The Plains of Cement*, when Ella, the barmaid of "The Midnight Bell", wakes up in a painful psychological state:

> After breakfast, however, Ella's introspections, as usual, imperceptibly vanished as she busied herself in the bar. By demonstrating her brisk command over one inanimate object after another, she set up a symbolic process which put her soul in countenance, and by ten o'clock she was the despotic marshal of a fiercely trained army of tumblers, and her vital self. (Hamilton, 1935, p. 386)

However, when the metaphoric dimension is lost, medical staff's primitive anxieties, stirred up by the work, dictate actions that are often highly inappropriate to the real situation. For example, the demanding, incontinent man becomes a being whose sole *raison d'être* is to attack the ward staff. Thus, the full extent of primitive infantile anxieties, stirred up by the work on the ward, is experienced in consciousness.

In order to avoid being flooded by this intense and unmanageable anxiety, in Menzies Lyth's study the nursing service itself had evolved a number of unconscious, but effective, defensive techniques against this anxiety. Nevertheless, we must not forget that, even though they were not observed in this particular study, doctors, in addition to all other disciplines, also defend against anxiety in a number of ways, including, in Menzies Lyth's study, splitting up the nurse–patient relationship, adopting an attitude of detachment and denial of feelings, attempting to eliminate decisions by ritual task performance, reducing the weight of responsibility in decision making by checks and counter-checks, collusive social redistribution of responsibility and irresponsibility, purposeful obscurity in the formal distribution of responsibility, reducing the impact of responsibility by delegation to superiors, and avoidance of change. Menzies Lyth's study remains fresh decades after it was written, but the fact that it is still relevant is also frustrating. It feels as if little progress has been achieved in acknowledging the difficulties and challenges of caring for others, in any professional discipline, and "compassionate care" does not seem to incorporate these insights into its training. One can only wonder if Mandelstam (2011) would have had as much material had Menzies Lyth's study of 1959 been more influential.

Perhaps, however, we should not be too surprised at our failure to apply these ideas. The anxieties these processes defend against are considerable, and the demands of continually facing up to them in the real world of the hospital or care home might simply be too much. It is very painful to be reminded of the likelihood of ill health and the inevitability of ageing and death, and few, if any, are capable of functioning without some form of denial. However, if space can be made for a little reflection and understanding it might help, even in a small way, towards preventing the worst cases of abuse and neglect. Staff discussion groups would seem to be the ideal forum in which to attempt to foster this attitude.

Containing projective processes in a staff discussion group

It is rare to find discussion groups along the lines of Balint groups, familiar from general practice and psychiatric contexts (Balint, 1957), for nurses or general hospital doctors, and almost unheard of for care assistants. Balint groups offer an opportunity for staff to discuss individual cases that have got "under their skin" to seek to understand why this is so, and what it was about the interaction that might have stirred up emotion in the member of staff. Without such a forum to discuss the countertransference and to process emotions, these feelings become more likely to be dealt with by absence from work, or even by neglect or abuse of patients. Encouragingly, a recent article highlighted the importance of staff from all hospital disciplines feeling supported,

> if they are to continuously provide high quality compassionate care to patients. One way of supporting staff, of showing them their health and wellbeing matter, is to offer them opportunities for compassionate dialogue about their experiences of delivering care – its rewards, frustrations and challenges – and their resulting thoughts and feelings. (Cornwell & Goodrich, 2010, p. 10)

The pilot project described in this article does not mention Balint, but the discussion groups sound similar, starting with a discussion of a particular case. However, an important difference seems to be that the discussion, rather than focusing on the specific relationship between clinician and patient, as in a Balint group, moves on to a general discussion of work: "participants ask questions, share experiences and reflect on the challenges of delivering care both in this and analogous situations" (Cornwell & Goodrich, 2010, p. 11).

More than half a century ago, Menzies Lyth showed that a psychoanalytic perspective is extremely helpful in understanding the experiences of those in hospital, but these insights into specific, individual relationships between people still seem to get lost in generalities. In order to discuss these issues further, we now explore two specific relationships in a fictionalised care home, where we will focus our attention on the care assistants, who often have most contact with the residents. Indeed, with the changes in the nursing profession in recent decades, it is now care assistants, both in hospitals and care homes, who carry out many of the duties formerly undertaken by hospital nurses in the 1950s.

Case study: care workers in a nursing home

A large proportion of residents in care homes have dementia, and this home is no exception. A number of its residents are in the advanced stages of dementia, suffering from impairment of most or all cognitive domains, frailty, and significant functional decline. However, it is also home to a number of individuals with more moderate levels of dementia. The building is old and not particularly suitable for its purpose. Attempts have been made to make it "dementia-friendly", with signs on the doors (pictures and large text), but they have only been partially successful. A few mobile individuals spend much of their day wandering round, but a number are bed-bound and totally dependent.

Violet is one of the younger residents, in her mid-seventies. She has moderate dementia, but is able to move around the home by herself and her memory problems do not cause her many day-to-day problems in this supportive environment. After she had been living here for a few weeks, she developed a physical health problem that required the visiting doctor to see her most days. Each time the young male doctor came to see her, she flirted unashamedly, which rather embarrassed him. On one occasion, while he was kneeling by the side of her chair in order to take blood from her, she began to stroke his hair. Since it was difficult to find the cause of her medical problem, she had to have frequent blood tests. However, she did not see these as a hardship, but greeted them, and him, with a wink and the comment, "It gives you an excuse to come back and see me." It took the embarrassed young doctor some time to make sense of Violet's flirtatiousness. After some reflection, and later discussion at a Balint group, he began to understand that, in the middle of the anxiety of her uncertain prognosis, she might have been terrified of being forgotten, and one way of guaranteeing that she was not forgotten was by being flirtatious. Had he understood this at the time, his practice with her might have been different, and he could have attempted to contain some of her anxiety by reassuring her that she remained in his mind and acknowledging his appreciation that the uncertainty of the diagnosis was worrying for her. This process of attempting to understand the emotional state of the patient is essential to providing good care, but a supportive environment is also required in order to reflect on one's experience.

Violet's case also exemplifies the fact that many people working with older adults are substantially younger than their patients or clients. This "young–old dyad" can result in complex transference and countertransference phenomena. The younger clinician or carer might start to think of their own grandparents and their relationship with them, or, alternatively, might see the patient one-dimensionally as a sweet old lady or a grumpy old man. Conversely, the patient might feel that the clinician is too young to have any experience or that the carer will have nothing in common with them, and, thus, will not be able to help them. They might even envy the younger person's youth and health. Acknowledging these feelings and allowing patients to express them can begin to help a working relationship and provide a context for caring.

Communicating emotional states: Rachel

Rachel is ninety years old and has advanced dementia. She has lived in this care home for the last two years and is confined to her bed for the majority of time. She is not able to do anything for herself and the care assistants have to help her to eat, drink, wash, and use the toilet. There are often two staff looking after her when a particular task has to be done. The younger care staff often ignore Rachel and chat to each other while they work, gossiping about what they did at the weekend.

Menzies Lyth (1959) would see this as a defence against the anxiety stirred up in them by caring for such a frail, vulnerable human being, and for whom they have to perform intimate tasks. In a care setting, important new attachments can be formed with care staff even by very frail individuals. When patients need someone else to wash them, dress them, and feed them, the bond that is formed can be very strong. For patients like Rachel in the advanced stages of dementia, the importance of touch in the relationship must not be underestimated. In settings where there are relatively few staff changes and where staff are in a position to reflect on their experience and the patient's inner world, these bonds can be literally vital. However, when patients on long stay units are moved, as, for example, when a continuing care ward is closed, the breaking of these bonds is hard for staff and patients alike; anecdotal observations are that less than a third of the vulnerable patients who are moved survive for longer than six months, much to the grief of the staff who previously cared for them.

Rachel does not have any family living nearby—her husband died twenty years ago, her two children moved away and have families of their own, and all her friends are dead. Her children visit infrequently and, in between, she has no visitors. Her only regular contact is with the staff of the home. However, even though Rachel has lost the ability to speak, this does not mean that she cannot communicate.

The perceptive carer

As is noted above, one powerful means of communicating emotional states to another person is via projection. Projective identification describes that process whereby the person into whom the emotions are projected experiences these emotions and starts to behave as if they were their own (Klein, 1946).

For example, one day, one of the care staff felt differently when she was feeding Rachel. It was not a nice feeling and when she began to think about it, rather strangely, she felt alone and ignored. She wondered if Rachel might be feeling that way, too, and began to speak to her. Although she was not able to reply in words, Rachel made eye contact with the care worker and appeared to brighten up during the course of the conversation.

The perceptive care worker was able to reflect on her feelings and think about them in the context of her relationship with Rachel. Not every member of health and social care staff is as sensitive and able to reflect on their feelings in this way. In the absence of a reflective space to understand and process such emotions and think about their origin, a care assistant's ability to work with and adequately care for the person can become impaired.

This situation of someone, unable to communicate verbally, projecting difficult emotional states into someone else in order to manage them parallels the mother–infant relationship and the process of maternal reverie mentioned above. The mother's capacity to contain and detoxify her infant's intolerable projected emotions enables a fundamental learning process. Bion (1967b) even hypothesised this was the way in which we learn to think. An unsupported care assistant, who is unable to process projected emotional communications and feed them back helpfully to the individual, adds to the isolation the person with dementia already experiences.

Conclusion

Over sixty years ago, in *Childhood and Society*, Erikson (1963) described the "nuclear conflict" of old age as "ego integrity v. despair". He acknowledged that he lacked a clear definition for this life stage, but attempted to convey its meaning by pointing to aspects of the state of mind associated with that conflict, seeing "the acceptance of one's one and only life cycle as something that had to be and that, by necessity, permitted of no substitutions" (p. 241) as central. His implication is that it is this acceptance that makes it possible to let go of life with grace when the time comes. In this chapter, we have acknowledged that the present, as well as the past, context in which older people find themselves powerfully influences their inner world. We believe that the despair that Erikson juxtaposes with ego integrity is a lived response to intolerable living conditions which then becomes, or reinforces, an internal state of mind.

In the examples we have given, we have highlighted the urgent need for containment felt by us all when we are filled with primitive anxieties and how desperate it is, for those requiring help and helpers alike, to be left alone with these feelings. We have discussed what happens when containment is absent, when the partner, family member, or professional cannot receive or process projections, so that the struggling person is left "all at sea", as an elderly client once described herself and her situation. We have suggested that this situation is unlikely to change until containment in the form of a listening, reflective presence—be it supervisor, therapist, colleague, or friend—is there for the carer or relative.

As writers of this chapter, we wish to acknowledge our own container and secure base. SIHR's own special interest group has provided us, and other SIHR members from a variety of professional backgrounds, the opportunity to share and develop our understanding of psychodynamic perspectives on older age. The group's work confirms that feeling adrift is not, of course, confined to elderly people, and it is a state of mind and being with which psychodynamic thinking has always been concerned. It does seem, however, that the additional stresses associated with ageing, whether their origins are internal, external, or both, can exacerbate difficulties or rock a relatively stable personality. Transition to each major stage of life presents a sometimes formidable task of dealing with loss and change. Reflecting and thinking at deep, and sometimes unconscious, levels about the "roads not taken", and coming to terms with the choices one has made, including the choices one does not even remember making, is soulful work which puts to the test the quality of internal object relations. This is particularly acute for older people who have to confront the anxieties of powerlessness and loss and the fears of being abandoned.

In his beautiful poem "Moraturi Salutamus", Longfellow reminds us that although a few go on to achieve great things in old age, this is the exception rather than the rule, and he comments,

> they show
> How far the gulf-stream of our youth may flow
> Into the arctic regions of our lives
> (Longfellow, 1875, ll. 250–252)

He goes on to capture the perspective that older age can give that is unique to that stage and precious in a particularly bitter-sweet way:

> And as the evening twilight fades away,
> The sky is filled with stars, invisible by day. (ll. 284–285)

Psychodynamic approaches can support all of us, professionals and older people alike, in coming to know and value the "ego integrity" so movingly described and help the helpers provide safety, respect, and dignity, so that older people, well or ill, can have moments at least of seeing the stars that are "invisible by day".

Acknowledgements

We would like to thank Murray Leishman for introducing Longfellow's poem to us.

References

Balint, M. (1957). *The Doctor, his Patient and the Illness*. London: Tavistock.

Bion, W. R. (1962). *Learning from Experience*. London: Heinemann.

Bion, W. R. (1967a). *Second Thoughts*. London: Heinemann.

Bion, W. R. (1967b). A theory of thinking. In: *Second Thoughts*. London: Heinemann.

Bowlby, J. (1969). *Attachment and Loss.* London: Hogarth Press and The Institute of Psycho-Analysis.

Bowlby, J. (1988). *A Secure Base*. London: Routledge.

Cornwell, J., & Goodrich, J. (2010). Supporting staff to deliver compassionate care using Schwartz Center rounds – a UK pilot. *Nursing Times, 106*: 10–12.

Davenhill, R. (Ed.) (2007). *Looking into Later Life: A Psychoanalytic Approach to Depression and Dementia in Old Age*. London: Karnac.

Erikson, E. H. (1963). Eight ages of man. In: *Childhood and Society* (2nd edn). New York: Norton.

Evans, S., & Garner, J. (Eds.) (2004). *Talking Over the Years: A Handbook of Dynamic Psychotherapy with Older Adults*. London: Routledge.

Freud, S. (1905a). On psychotherapy. *S.E., 7*: 256–268. London: Hogarth.

Hamilton, P. (1935). *The Plains of Cement*. In: *Twenty Thousand Streets Under the Sky*. London: Constable.

King, P. H. M. (1974). Notes on the psychoanalysis of older patients: reappraisal of the potentialities for change during the second half of life. *Journal of Analytical Psychology, 19*: 22–37.

Klein, M. (1946). Notes on some schizoid mechanisms. *International Journal of Psycho-Analysis, 27*: 99–110.

Longfellow, H. (1875). Morituri Salutamus: Poem for the Fiftieth Anniversary of the Class of 1825 in Bowdoin College. In: *Selected Poems*. Harmondsworth: Penguin.

Mandelstam, M. (2011). *How We Treat the Sick: Neglect and Abuse in Our Health Services*. London: Jessica Kingsley.

Menzies, I. E. P. (1959). The functioning of social systems as a defence against anxiety: a report on a study of the nursing service of a general hospital. *Human Relations, 13*: 95–121. [Reprinted in Menzies Lyth, *Containing Anxieties in Institutions. Selected Essays, Volume 1* (pp. 43–99). London: Free Association Books, 1988].

Quinodoz, D. (2009). *Growing Old: A Journey of Self-discovery*. London: Routledge.

Russ, T. C. (2011). Inside story: thinking about human relations in older age. *British Journal of Psychotherapy, 27*: 211–213.

Segal, H. (1957). Notes on symbol formation. *International Journal of Psycho-Analysis, 38*: 391–397.

Shakespeare, W. (1988). As You Like It. In: *The Arden Shakespeare*. London: Routledge.

Shakespeare, W. (2005). *King Lear*. Harmondsworth: Penguin.

Waddell, M. (2002). *Inside Lives: Psychoanalysis and the Growth of the Personality*. London: Karnac.

Winnicott, D. W. (1949). Hate in the counter-transference. *International Journal of Psycho-Analysis, 30*: 69–74.

Wordsworth, W. (1798). Lines written a few miles above Tintern Abbey. In: W. Wordsworth & S. T. Coleridge, *Lyrical Ballads*. Harmondsworth: Penguin.

INDEX